Makers of the Modern Thoroughbred

By the same author

An Introduction to the Thoroughbred
The Classic Racehorse

In the multi-billion pound world of thoroughbred racing, the breeder plays a vital role in the racehorse's career. Ever since the foundation of the Derby in 1780 – an event which signalled a dramatic change of course in the thoroughbred's evolution – perhaps the most exciting aspect of the whole racing business has been the mixing and matching of blood lines to achieve the fleetest of the fleet.

Makers of the Modern Thoroughbred examines the techniques and philosophy of some of the greatest breeders of this century. Each one of this elite, internationally renowned band has made a unique contribution to the development of the modern racehorse: these are the Aga Khan, Marcel Boussac, Elisabeth Couturié, the Earl of Derby, Bull Hancock, Jack and Jim Joel, the Duke of Norfolk, Captain Tim Rogers and Federico Tesio.

Peter Willett, one of the world's leading authorities on breeding, identifies the different methods and theories adopted by each of these outstanding individuals in their endeavours to produce the perfect racehorse.

Peter Willett, one of the world's leading experts, has been writing about the thoroughbred for more than thirty years. He has also played an important part in the development of the pattern race system which now sets the standard of the best racing in all the principal racing countries of the world. In 1981 his special position in his own field was endorsed by his election for a five-year term as President of the British Thoroughbred Breeders Association. He is a member of the Jockey Club, and of their Flat Race Pattern Committee, as well as of the National Stud Stallion Advisory Panel.

Makers of the Modern Thoroughbred

Peter Willett

Stanley Paul
London Melbourne Sydney Auckland Johannesburg

Stanley Paul & Co. Ltd

An imprint of the Hutchinson Publishing Group

17–21 Conway Street, London W1P 6JD

Hutchinson Publishing Group (Australia) Pty Ltd
PO Box 496, 16–22 Church Street, Hawthorne, Melbourne, Victoria 3122

Hutchinson Group (NZ) Ltd
32–34 View Road, PO Box 40–086, Glenfield, Auckland 10

Hutchinson Group (SIA) Pty Ltd
PO Box 337, Bergvlei 2012, South Africa

First published 1984
© Peter Willett 1984

Set in Linotron Bembo by Input Typesetting Limited, London

Printed and bound in Great Britain by Anchor Brendan Ltd,
Tiptree, Essex

British Library Cataloguing in Publication Data
Willett, Peter
  Thoroughbred breeders of the world.
  1. Racehorse breeders—Biography
  I. Title
  636.1′2′0922   SF336.A2

  ISBN 0–09–158400–0

Contents

Acknowledgements

Copyright photographs are acknowledged as follows:
R. Anscomb, *British Racehorse*, Rex Coleman, F. Jarry,
J. Noye, Popperfoto, Press Association, Recoupé,
Sport and General Press Agency, Fiona Vigors

Introduction

The evolution of the thoroughbred has depended on the continuous interplay between the types of racehorse being produced by breeders and the types of races available to run them in. Breeders try to produce horses capable of winning the races which bear most value or confer most prestige; and those responsible for race programmes try to devise race conditions to attract the most talented performers. External pressures, whether economic, promotional or merely fashion and whim, cause intermittent shifts in aim and emphasis by one party or the other, and the consequent resolution of forces projects the thoroughbred into a new phase of evolution.

The most revolutionary happening in this age-old process was the foundation of the Derby in 1780 and its rapid elevation as the principal criterion of racing merit so that, sixty years later, it could be described fairly by Lord George Bentinck, one of racing's former dictators, as the 'Blue Riband of the Turf'. The race owed its genesis to a dinner-table conversation between Sir Charles Bunbury, the first dictator of the Turf, and the twelfth Earl of Derby, one of the leading owners and breeders of the time. The event could be interpreted as the supreme example of an initiative by the racing authorities that changed the course of Thoroughbred evolution. An initiative taken by men of the towering prestige of Bunbury and Derby must have had a deep impact on the minds of the majority of breeders. But this interpretation must be qualified by the reflection that Bunbury and Derby would not have thought that a race for three-year-olds in the late spring – the first four runnings were over a mile in contrast to the distance of 1½ miles which has been the rule ever since, and the regular date of the first Wednesday in June

9

was not settled until the twentieth century – was a worthwhile innovation unless horses with the speed and precocity to race effectively over limited distances at that stage of their lives were already in production. Indeed, the foundation of the St Leger, albeit run in the early autumn and initially over 2 miles, had preceded the Derby by four years and indicated that the change from tests of endurance for horses maturing at five years of age or older to tests of speed for more quickly maturing horses was gathering momentum. There were two sides to the Derby equation.

Bunbury himself owned and bred the first Derby winner, Diomed, and Diomed, though a failure at stud in England, had a dynamic effect on the evolution of the thoroughbred in North America after he was exported to Virginia at the age of twenty-one. Derby owned and bred the eighth Derby winner, Sir Peter Teazle, but was so intoxicated by his success that he rushed impetuously into a blind alley of excessive inbreeding and ruined his stud. The earldom had to pass through five generations before it was held by a man with the will, the wisdom and the luck not only to restore the fortunes of the family on the Turf fully but to raise them to unprecedented heights of worldwide fame and influence.

One breeder above all others bridged the gap between the old-fashioned, slow-maturing type of horse and the faster, more precocious type that was to take over the racecourse entirely during the nineteenth century – the third Duke of Grafton. The successor to Lord Chatham as Prime Minister in 1767, Grafton was strangely irresolute and indecisive in affairs of state for a holder of the highest political office; and for a statesman he was often wanting in foresight and even common sense, as when he proposed to plant an avenue of trees stretching 18 miles from his home at Euston Hall to Newmarket so that he could drive all the way to the races over the grass, but was forced to abandon the project 6 miles short of the objective because he had failed to realize that he would have to cross another owner's land. But there was nothing indecisive or haphazard in his breeding operations, for he latched firmly on to the fact that there was a potent blood affinity between the two great late-eighteenth-century stallions, Eclipse and Herod, and exploited it to become the first of the great Classic breeders in the new age.

Eclipse and Herod had raced in the days of races run in 2- and 4- mile heats, and it is the surest proof of their extraordinary adaptability that their progeny were able to excel in the new era of speed and precocity. When their influence was united, the produce often were irresistible. Grafton's first Derby winner, Tyrant in 1802, was by Eclipse's son Pot-8-0s out of a mare by Herod's son Woodpecker. However, the keystone of his success was his faith in Waxy, whom he first patronized as a stallion and later purchased for his own stud. Waxy, the winner of the Derby in 1793, was by Pot-8-0s out of Maria by Herod. According to the nineteenth-century writer, 'The Druid', Waxy was a very handsome rich bay, with a white stocking on his off-hind and especially beautiful quarters. He had the idiosyncrasy of being uneasy unless he had the company of a rabbit in his paddock. Of more practical importance, he was such a prepotent sire that 'The Druid' called him 'the modern ace of trumps in the stud book'. Grafton's pre-eminence as a breeder, and the pre-eminence of his son, the fourth Duke, after his death in 1811, sprang from his decision to mate Waxy repeatedly with his mare Prunella, by Herod's best son Highflyer, and with her daughter Penelope. These matings produced the Derby winners Pope, Whalebone and Whisker, besides Web, the dam of another Derby winner, Middleton.

The story of the Dukes of Grafton and the Eclipse–Herod cross is an indication of the way an individual breeder can stamp his influence on the whole course of thoroughbred evolution, and of the way individual stallions and mares can have a similar effect – or could in the days when breeding was based on annual foal crops numbering no more than a few hundreds. The influence individual breeders are able to exert has diminished inevitably as the thoroughbred population has increased, and in the late twentieth century, with the world annual foal crop exceeding 100,000, no man could dominate Classic breeding or channel the course of evolution to the same degree as the Graftons. Nevertheless, in the twentieth century certain breeders have influenced the breed to an extent totally out of proportion to the numerical strength of their operations. The seventeenth Earl of Derby, by breeding Swynford, Phalaris and Hyperion, and Federico Tesio, by breeding Donatello II, Nearco and Ribot, have provided the sinews of top-class pedigrees in every country in which the thoroughbred is produced.

Breeders like Derby and Tesio can be regarded as veritable 'makers of the modern thoroughbred'. They do not stand alone. Others have made significant contributions to the progress of the breed, and in

11

the choice of certain of them for study in this book attention has been paid to the manner in which the interaction of different, and in some cases diametrically opposed, mental attitudes, has woven a tapestry of thought enriching the whole story of the thoroughbred. The romantic attachment of a breeder like Elisabeth Couturié to the idea of the thoroughbred as a noble creation has balanced the commercial flair of breeders like Bull Hancock.

A century and a half ago the search for makers of the thoroughbred could have been justly confined to Britain. In the twentieth century the British thoroughbred has become a horse of the world, and the nine breeders featured in this book include three from Britain, two from France and one each from Italy, the United States, Ireland and India. The choice reflects the fact that racing and breeding have achieved an international dimension. It does not pretend accurately to reflect the relative importance, in thoroughbred terms, of the countries represented. It is one of the fascinations of the subject that the impact of an individual breeder is not ineluctably related to the size, or even the overall quality, of the national thoroughbred population within which he is operating. The aim has been to choose breeders whose thinking and practice have contributed to the evolution of the modern thoroughbred, irrespective of their nationality.

The intervention of Bunbury and Derby in the evolutionary process through their joint promotion of the race which became the prinicpal criterion of selection is the clue leading to the realization that it is not breeders alone who have shaped or directed that process. Admiral Rous, who has been called alternatively the third dictator of the Turf [following Bunbury and Bentinck] and a kind of 'perpetual president' of the Jockey Club for much of the second half of the nineteenth century, is the most striking example of a man who exerted a strong influence on the development of the Thoroughbred without ever achieving prominence as an owner or breeder. His 'Standard Weights for Age', published in his book *Laws and Practice of Horse Racing* in 1850, was the basis, with periodic revisions, for fair competition between horses of different ages over the full range of racing distances, and so enabled the important races involving members of various age groups to become valid criteria of selection supplementing the Derby and other Classic races for three-year-olds only. His vigorous and decisive opposition to campaigns, instigated not only by influential members of the Jockey Club but by powerful sections of the press, to impose severe restrictions on two-year-old racing ensured the progressive development of precocious speed as an intrinsic aptitude of the thoroughbred; and foreshadowed the attitude of the Aga Khan to the same issue threequarters of a century later. And his stand on the 'reciprocity' issue of the 1870s, when some leading British owners wished to ban French horses from important British races unless the important French races were thrown open to British competition, guaranteed the survival of international racing and secured the base for its later expansion as another key to the problems of selection.

International racing found its apotheosis in the European Pattern system and the spread of the concept of Pattern or Graded Stakes races throughout the racing world in the second half of the twentieth century. That concept sprang from the doctrine enunciated by the sixteenth Duke of Norfolk in the report of his Committee on the Pattern of Racing in 1965. Pattern and Graded Stakes racing transcends national divisions of the total thoroughbred population and provides universal standards of performance for the selection of breeding stock. In Britain the Pattern idea led logically to the creation of a race planning department, with a standing supervisory committee chaired by a Steward of the Jockey Club, responsible for ensuring that the races available matched the needs of the thoroughbred population

Bernard Duke of Norfolk was much more prominent as an owner and breeder than Admiral Rous, though he could not be designated a maker of the modern thoroughbred on the strength of his activities as a breeder alone. It was his authorship of the Pattern race system which placed him in the mainstream of the tradition of Rous, Bunbury and the twelfth Earl of Derby as a man who helped to shape the destiny of the thoroughbred by external influence. Norfolk was a man of distinction outside the narrow precincts of the Turf; his masterly handling of state occasions in his capacity of hereditary Earl Marshal made him a national figure, and his disinterested dedication to public service set him apart as the last true English aristocrat. His broad appeal to the affections of his fellow-countrymen on and off the Turf qualified him as a suitable case for study among the makers of the modern thoroughbred.

13

1

Bernard, Sixteenth Duke of Norfolk 1908–75

When the sixteenth Duke of Norfolk died on 31 January, 1975 he had twenty-six horses, all but three of them home-bred, at the Castle Stables, Arundel, in training for the approaching flat-racing season. His collection of nineteen broodmares at the Angmering Park Stud 3 miles down the Worthing Road, though slightly reduced from the total of a few years earlier, was still sufficient to make him in a numerical sense one of the leading owner-breeders in Britain; and the previous year he had achieved his most cherished ambition as an owner by winning the Ascot Gold Cup, Ascot's greatest race since 1807, with his home-bred Ragstone.

Nevertheless, it is not simply, or even primarily, as a breeder that he made his most striking or his most enduring contribution to the progress of the thoroughbred. He deserves to be remembered first and foremost as an administrator and an innovator whose influence extended far beyond the confines of Britain and the jurisdiction of the Jockey Club. There was a lengthy period when no committee appointed by the Turf authorities with far-reaching terms of reference seemed complete without his participation, usually as chairman. The 1961 Jockey Club Committee on the Doping of Racehorses, of which he was chairman, made recommendations which, on being implemented, were decisive in controlling this abuse which posed a grave threat to public confidence in the integrity of racing. However, it was through the Duke of Norfolk's Committee on the Pattern of Racing four years later that he was able to shape the evolution of the thoroughbred in a degree equalled by few, if any, individual breeders. For the report of this committee proclaimed a new philosophy, that the Turf authorities must ensure that a series

14

of races, over the right distances and at the right time of the year, are available to test the best horses of all ages. This philosophy, translated into the British Pattern race system by the Jockey Club with the financial support of the Levy Board, expanded into the European Pattern, sophisticated and refined into groups and grades, spread throughout the racing world to inspire new means of identifying, testing and promoting high-class performance in the thoroughbred. Pattern races, or Group races or Graded races as they are variously called, have become universal criteria of excellence, and consequently of the selection of breeding stock.

For twenty-seven years (1945–72) he was the sovereign's representative at Ascot under King George VI and Queen Elizabeth II, a post which gave him overall control of racing there and abundant scope for the showmanship and organizing ability which served him so well in another capacity, that of hereditary Earl Marshal. His regime saw the substantial expansion of the Ascot programme that made the course one of the busiest in Britain; the realignment of the straight mile; the installation of a modern drainage system; the introduction of National Hunt racing; and the rebuilding of the stands. But expansion was achieved without cost to the Ascot tradition of staging the best in racing. He put into practice the philosophy of his own Pattern committee so assiduously that when he retired from Ascot twenty-four Pattern races, nearly a quarter of all British Pattern races, were run there. Fifteen Pattern races were run at the royal meeting alone, but quality was encouraged over the whole range of the Ascot programme by the due allocation of prize money and the careful planning of race conditions.

Bernard Norfolk's policy at Ascot was a perfect reflection of the Pattern race philosophy of which he had been the principal author. Theory and practice thus were matched as the two sides of the same coin, emphasizing his benign and potent influence for quality in the modern and in the future thoroughbred. The personal characteristics which supplied the motive force for this notable contribution to racing and the racehorse were an intense public spirit, great powers of application and an idealism which rejected anything shoddy or second-rate. His vision of the thoroughbred was aristocratic, just as his vision of his own place in society involved an aristocratic balance of privilege and responsibility.

That vision had its origins in his family background and

upbringing and had gained sharper definition from the circumstances of his own life.

The Howards of Norfolk have been one of the great families of England since the fifteenth century. John Howard was created Duke of Norfolk by Richard III in 1483, and died fighting for his king on Bosworth Field. In succeeding centuries the ducal line has suffered more vicissitudes than normal for great families under different systems of government and sovereigns of different religious persuasions, for most of the Howards have been Catholics. The line has produced warriors, statesmen, eccentrics, philanthropists and even a saint – St. Philip Howard, who died for his faith in the Tower in 1595 and was canonized nearly four centuries later. At the same time the Dukes of Norfolk accumulated enormous landed wealth and, in later times, valuable urban properties. Honours and titles have accumulated as freely as wealth.

The fifteenth Duke was one of the most admirable in the line. Devout and unassuming, he directed most of his considerable energy to good works within and without the Catholic Church. As the lay leader of the Catholic community in England he worked tirelessly for his co-religionists, and was largely instrumental in securing a cardinal's hat for John Henry Newman. He held the post of Postmaster General in the government of Lord Salisbury in the 1890s and resigned in order to serve in the Boer War, though he was already well into middle age. As Earl Marshal he successfully challenged the Lord Chamberlain for the right to make the arrangements for the funeral of Queen Victoria, but the College of Heralds was so ill-equipped for the task that a visitor to the office on the eve of the funeral found it in a state of 'absolute chaos'. However, the experience enabled the Duke to get his eye in for later state occasions, which included the coronations of Edward VII and George V.

The fifteenth Duke's first wife died in 1887 and his son Philip, the only child of that marriage, was a chronic invalid and died unmarried at the age of twenty-two. Two years later the Duke married Gwendolen Constable-Maxwell, Baroness Herries in her own right. On 30 May 1908, when he was sixty years old, she presented him with a son and heir.

The birth of the boy who was to become the sixteenth Duke

caused great excitement in the family and among the people of Sussex. An old carter who drove into Arundel that day found the High Street empty and the shops deserted. Suddenly a terrific cheer sounded from the top of the hill and as he drove round the corner he found hundreds of people crowding round a notice pinned to the castle gates. A moment later the bells of St Philip Neri pealed out, and the guns boomed from the castle. Years later the carter told a *Morning Post* reporter: 'There was little sleep in Arundel that night. Some of us were dancing by lantern light until the small hours. Others went to prepare a bonfire on the Downs so that the whole district should learn the news.'

The *Sussex Daily News* reported that nearly every house and cottage on the Duke's vast estates put out flags in honour of the baby Earl of Arundel and Surrey, and carried this report of the christening:

The baptism took place in the private chapel of Arundel Castle, and it was a general holiday for miles around . . . When the ceremony was over the tenantry crowded round the Duke in the Great Hall, and Lady Rachel [his sister, not quite three years old] cut the christening cake, the bells rang out throughout the town and, on the word of the oldest tenant, everyone drank 'Long Life to the Earl of Arundel'.

The paper also recorded that the baby Earl never stopped crying during the church service; thereby, no doubt, letting out a whole legion of devils.

Unhappily the fifteenth Duke was not to see his second and sole surviving son rise to manhood, nor was Bernard to have the benefit of paternal guidance during some of the most important formative years of his boyhood. The fifteenth Duke died in February 1917, so at the age of eight his heir succeeded to the sonorous style and titles of Bernard Marmaduke Fitz Alan Howard, Duke of Norfolk, Earl of Arundel, Surrey and Norfolk, Baron Fitz Alan, Clun, Oswaldestre and Maltravers, Earl Marshal and Hereditary Marshal and Chief Butler of England. He was Premier Duke and Earl of England, and twenty-eight years later, on the death of his mother, acceded to the title of Baron Herries of Terregles in the peerage of Scotland.

Bernard Norfolk was no natural scholar, and the spasmodic and uncoordinated education which he received as a result of his mother's whims did not help him to overcome his limitations. He did not attend a prep school. For the winter of 1919–20 his mother rented a villa at Biarritz in south west France, and Bernard was dispatched to school there every morning in beret basque and a fiacre. He did not prove an apt pupil in French, but he acquired a fondness for the beret and wore it for playing golf in later years.

He had to depend on a tutor for the rest of his elementary education until he was sent to the Oratory, the Catholic school founded at Edgbaston by Cardinal Newman, in May 1920 when he was just short of his twelfth birthday. Even then his schooling lacked continuity. He was taken away from the Oratory in 1921 on account of ill health, returning a year later when the school had moved to Caversham near Reading. After that he was a regular boarder until May 1925, when his mother again gave illness as the reason for his failure to appear at the beginning of term; nor was he seen at the Oratory again.

Bernard Norfolk was retiring and inconspicuous as a schoolboy. Father Philip Lynch, who taught him at Edgbaston and Caversham, remembered him more than half a century later as a boy who was 'quite pleasant' and 'gave no trouble'. Father Philip found little evidence of academic ability in him, but added that the interruptions, which he attributed to excessive maternal anxiety over his health, gave Bernard no chance of cultivating such talents as he did possess.

It was on the cricket field that Bernard Norfolk made his only real mark on school life. He played for the Oratory Second XI in the summer term of 1924 and, although he achieved a batting average of only 3.28 with a highest score of 12 not out, he was the regular wicket-keeper with an excellent record of stumpings, a sure sign of a good eye and quick reactions. His love of cricket, whether as player or administrator, remained constant throughout his life. He was intensely proud of his beautiful ground at Arundel Castle, surrounded by fifty-six different varieties of trees and boasting a playing surface so true that first-class teams from abroad regularly opened their English tours there with a match against a team of the Duke's own choosing. He was president of the M.C.C. in 1957–58, and did a long stint as chairman of the Sussex County Cricket Club. He twice took teams of first-class English players on private tours of the Caribbean and, to the surprise of most people inside and outside the world of cricket, was appointed manager of the M.C.C.

team which toured Australia and New Zealand in the winter of 1962–63, with Alec Bedser as assistant manager and Ted Dexter as captain. Although the Australian part of the tour ended in a disappointing stalemate with Australia retaining the Ashes, Bernard Norfolk emerged with a good deal of credit. As Colin Cowdrey, one of England's most talented batsmen who became a close friend of the family, summed it up: 'No manager could have gone to more trouble to care for the team . . . and the Australians came to love and respect him.'

Those distinctions in cricket lay far ahead when he left the Oratory. He had hoped to go up to Christ Church, Oxford, but failed the entrance examination. However, he spent an academic year at a crammer's in Oxford which enabled him to take part in many aspects of university life and ride in some of the University point-to-points. Although neither of his parents had shown any interest in the Turf, Bernard, like many an undergraduate before and since, found that life in Oxford gave the leisure to cultivate an incipient love of horse racing. After the 1927 Derby he wrote to his sister Rachel from his rooms in Woodstock Road:

What a race it must have been, I do wish I had been there. But I went to the Union Club and heard it on the wireless. The man kept saying 'It is a race between Call Boy and Hot Night and Hot Night is going best.' I left the place all of a quiver and could hardly drive the car.

In fact Call Boy beat Hot Night by 2 lengths. Bernard lamented that his double had gone, but did not name the horses he had backed. In any case he was never a big better. A few years later he complained to Rachel that he had left a Newmarket meeting the poorer by 4s 10d on balance. Betting odds, mathematical calculations, indeed money matters in general, tended to be outside his interest and beyond his comprehension.

If there were echoes of the feudal past in the circumstances of Bernard Norfolk's birth and christening, there were still clearer undertones of traditional pomp and splendour in his coming-of-age celebrations. Arundel, the main country seat of the Dukes of Norfolk for centuries and the centre of the family's Sussex estates

19

which then extended to 16,000 acres, provides a perfect setting for extravagant pageantry. Approached from the south, Arundel is one of the most enchanting sights in the whole of England. Beyond the River Arun, which enfolds them in a semicircle, the massive grey walls of the castle loom above the compact little town, whose high street rises steep and broad from the central square. To the west the Cathedral Church of Our Lady and St Philip Howard stands silhouetted above the skyline. Behind castle and cathedral the ground slopes upwards more gently through the woods and green open spaces of Arundel Park to the summit of the South Downs, giving, in reverse, sweeping views of the lower reaches of the Arun and the town of Littlehampton to the south, and the coastal plain to the south east and south west. These striking advantages contrived by man and nature were exploited to give a quasi-royal air to the three days of celebrations at the end of May 1929.

The programme began on Thursday, when Bernard Norfolk, accompanied by his mother, attended a solemn mass and Te Deum in the cathedral. There was a family dinner party in the evening, and after dinner Bernard drove three miles to Bury Hill, one of the highest points of the Downs, to light a giant bonfire built by workers from the estate. The fire, fed with barrels of tar through the night, could be seen not only in most of Sussex and the neighbouring counties of Surrey and Hampshire, but by passing ships far out in the English Channel.

On Friday Bernard drove with his mother in an open carriage drawn by two magnificent bay horses to Littlehampton. There, after a twenty-one gun salute, he was presented with a portrait of himself by the local artist Frank Beresford, while an aeroplane circled over-head trailing streamers with the message 'Long Life and Happiness'. Back in Arundel, where the streets were decorated with flags and bunting, he attended a ceremony in the crowded town square, and mounted a platform to receive from the hands of the mayor a gold cigarette box to which 700 of the inhabitants had subscribed. In his speech of thanks he said that he was happy to have been able to fulfil his father's chief wish, which was that he should be brought up to love and understand Arundel.

The climax of the celebrations was reached that evening with a banquet in the Baron's Hall of the castle. Two hundred guests dined at long tables decorated with flowers in the Norfolk colours of red and white. The dinner was served on the family gold plate and comprised seven courses.

The features of the third and final day of the coming-of-age programme were a luncheon for the tenant farmers, followed by a fête in the castle grounds to which the contributors to the gifts from Arundel and Littlehampton, together with all the people living on the estate, were invited. The guests totalled 6000, including 1500 children from fourteen different schools. Bernard played his part in the entertainment by taking some of the children for rides in a trap drawn by a Shetland pony. The festivites concluded with a firework display in Arundel Park.

Every aspect of the celebrations was given extensive coverage in the national as well as the local press. The *Leeds Mercury* expressed the consensus in the statement that the three days had recreated 'the pomp and glory of the Middle Ages'.

In photographs taken about the time of his coming-of-age he appears boyish, shy almost to the point of being gauche. In many of them he wears black-rimmed glasses – in later life he wore glasses only for reading – which give him an owlish rather than a studious look. Nevertheless, the circumstances of the celebrations, with all their implications, must have affected his conception of his place in the structure of society, encouraging notions of a natural and indefeasible superiority to the ordinary run of men. Such notions could have generated a dangerous and self-indulgent conceit. He was indeed confirmed in an assumption that he was entitled to respect, even to deference in some matters. But he was mercifully freed from the worst manifestations of social pride not only by the simplicity of his own character but also by an overriding sense of his obligations. He was unswerving in his conviction that the respect due to his rank and position was balanced by a corresponding duty to serve with absolute self-dedication in every capacity, national or local, sporting or charitable, that fell to his lot.

The coming-of-age clearly shored up his self-esteem. The source of his unbreakable sense of duty is less obvious. His father had undoubtedly possessed a similar and well-developed sense. However, the fifteenth Duke died too early for either his example or his precept to influence Bernard's social conscience decisively.

After his father's death his guardian, Baron Fitz Alan of Derwent, Uncle Edmond, played an important part in shaping his character and encouraging the faith and regular religious observance that sustained him all his life. His mother was another consistent and enduring influence in his family circle. A woman of dominant, sometimes domineering, character, she never failed to instil into Bernard, as well as his three sisters, an awareness of their social obligations. She had a passion for lavish hospitality, both at Arundel and at the family's London house, Norfolk House in St James's Square. The staff were transported from Arundel for her grander London luncheon parties, which enabled the youthful Bernard to meet many of the leading figures in public and political life.

Neither his father nor his mother had any interest in horse racing, but his mother's love of entertaining and idea of the primacy of Arundel Castle in the social life of Sussex induced her to invite large house parties for the annual four-day race meetings at Goodwood at the end of July which marked the end of the London season. One of the regular guests was Henry (later Sir Henry) Abel-Smith, whose friend Jim Carruthers was a serious student of form and used to send them tips which Bernard Norfolk followed at Goodwood and elsewhere. Abel-Smith helped to kindle Bernard's interest in racing, and exerted a strong influence on him in one other important respect. He was the adjutant of the Royal Horse Guards (the Blues) at the time and in 1928, when Bernard was twenty, persuaded him to join the regiment. Thus began an ambivalent relationship with the army which, despite a period of disenchantment during the next few years, cultivated a regard for order and precision which was to inspire his later stage-management of state occasions and great events on the Turf, specifically Royal Ascot.

Bernard's first impressions of the army were favourable enough. The Blues spent alternate years in London and at Windsor. They were at Windsor when Bernard Norfolk joined, and he found the barracks 'a very nice place and very near the park'. He was given an old black horse called George, who had been ridden formerly by Abel-Smith and knew the ropes thoroughly, as his charger and the regimental rugger fullback as his groom. The Blues were a small and friendly regiment, with no more than a dozen subalterns. The ceremonial duties were not too taxing and Abel-Smith, who saw no virtue in young officers hanging around the barracks or London with little to do, made a habit of sending them off on hunting leave whenever possible. Bernard had ample time to hunt and improve his riding, and on 31 March 1931 had his only race under N.H. Rules when he rode his mare Lady Castlederg into second place in a field of eight for the Royal Horse Guards Cup over 3 miles at the Household Brigade Meeting at Hawthorn Hill.

By that time, however, military life was losing its charm for Bernard Norfolk. What had been merely tedious and irksome became insupportable when he was sent on a course at the small-arms school at Hythe in August of the same year. Although he was able to set himself up in reasonable comfort at the Imperial Hotel, with a room overlooking the sea and a private bathroom, he found no merit whatever in the course or the company. At the opening lecture on 11 August the instructor told them that they were fortunate to be in Hythe at the best time of year – an unforgivable solecism on the eve of the grouse-shooting season. 'I had almost to be held in my seat otherwise there would have been a corpse,' he wrote to Rachel.

As if that were not bad enough, the instructor aggravated his offence by refusing to excuse Bernard from the final lecture so that he could drive the 3 miles to Folkestone racecourse to see his two-year-old Spearill run in the Saltwood Plate. The race was timed for 3.30 and Bernard, having dashed back to the hotel and changed in frantic haste, arrived at 3.55 to find that Spearill, having led for 5 furlongs, had failed to stay the final furlong and finished seventh. Three weeks later at Lewes, which had one of the easiest 5-furlong courses in the country, Spearill lasted just long enough to give Bernard Norfolk his first success as an owner on the flat by winning the Juvenile Selling Plate worth £142. Spearill's trainer Victor Gilpin did not think that she had much of a future in racing, and she was sold at the auction after the race for 200 guineas. Gilpin was right: she never won another race.

His frustrating experiences at Hythe convinced Bernard Norfolk that the life of a regular soldier, even the leisurely life of a subaltern in the Blues, was not for him. He resigned on 3 April 1933. Within the space of little more than four years after his resignation, and when he was still barely twenty-nine years old, he had thrust upon him as Earl Marshal the responsibility of organizing his first two state occasions, the funeral of King George V and the coronation of

King George VI. (He was to do six state occasions altogether, including the funeral of King George VI, the coronation of Queen Elizabeth II, the funeral of Sir Winston Churchill and the investiture of the Prince of Wales.) Although he had precedents to guide him – his father did four state occasions – his mastery of protocol, his ability to weld representatives of the armed services and many civilian bodies into an effective team, his theatrical sense, his insistence on meticulous planning and timing, combined to ensure that all these occasions were acclaimed as models of flawlessly staged pageantry. After the coronation of King George VI, D. B. Wyndham Lewis, writing in *The Bystander*, compared him to Cecil B. de Mille in his ability to arrange and control huge public spectacles.

Leaving the Blues did not retard Bernard Norfolk's growing interest in racing. Indeed, only six months later he was elected a member of the Jockey Club, the self-perpetuating body which had already been established as the principal authority in British racing for a century and a half, and which forty years on was to be confirmed by royal charter in its function 'to make, print and publish rules, regulations, advices and directions for the proper conduct of horse-racing, race-meetings and racehorse-training.' His feet were set firmly on the road which was to lead to three terms (1946–48, 1953–55 and 1965–67) as a Steward of the Jockey Club, and so to membership of a triumvirate of Stewards with virtually untrammelled powers to legislate and administer within the sphere of racing.

The base of his personal involvement in racing was broadening. As early as the autumn of 1930, when he was in Newmarket to stay with the Wolvertons and see Ut Majeur win a disappointing Cesarewich by 4 lengths, he was entering into discussions with Victor Gilpin to persuade him to move from the Clarehaven stables in Newmarket to Michel Grove on his Sussex estate. 'I told him that I must train with someone near my home. He is a very nice man and is an RC too,' Bernard wrote to Rachel. Gilpin needed little persuasion, because Clarehaven, where he had succeeded his father, had to be put on the market when his mother died. However, Saunders Davies-Scourfield, who had won the Oaks with Perola as long before as 1909, was the incumbent trainer at Michel Grove, and the realization of Bernard's plan had to await the death of Davies-Scourfield in 1934. Gilpin moved to Michel Grove the following winter.

Bernard Norfolk had horses with Gilpin from the time that the move to Michel Grove was planned. Spearill was one of the first of them, as was another filly whose name was to prove prophetic. This was Young Lavinia, by Gainsborough out of Passion. Bernard Norfolk was a keen fox-hunting man as well as a racing enthusiast, and for two seasons was Master of the Holderness Hounds, whose country was adjacent to his Yorkshire home at Everingham, 15 miles southeast of York. It was, however, while hunting with the Quorn in Leicestershire that he met Lavinia Strutt. They fell in love, and were married at Brompton Oratory on 27 January 1937.

Lavinia brought many great qualities to the marriage. The fact that she stood in for the Queen at many of the rehearsals and held her canopy at the coronation the same year was symptomatic of her own public spirit and determination to associate herself with her husband in all his public duties. Although she was not a Catholic, she respected his deep faith and supported him fully in his unique position in the British Catholic community. She was beautiful, intelligent, strong-willed, vivacious and energetic, bringing a sparkle to his life which had been missing. She was a fearless and skilful rider to hounds, graceful in movement and a good tennis player. She did not bear him a male heir, but she had four daughters who made up a devoted family circle in which he found happiness and tranquillity.

Lavinia was addicted to horse racing and had a profound knowledge of it, which is not surprising since her stepfather was the sixth Earl of Rosebery, one of the leading owner–breeders of the day, who won the Derby with Blue Peter and Ocean Swell. She possessed an exceptional flair for reading a race, analysing the performances of horses and understanding their characters. She immersed herself so thoroughly in Bernard Norfolk's own racing affairs that in time the cares of supervising growing numbers of horses in training and breeding stock devolved on her, leaving him free to enjoy their activites and concentrate on his manifold administrative duties on the Turf. She was the driving force in their successful stud and stable. In later years he never studied form or placed a bet. Lavinia placed an occasional bet for him and rendered a monthly account, taking pride in her ability to keep him in credit.

Lord Rosebery's wedding present to the Norfolks was his step-daughter's eponymous mare Lavinia, then five years old, who had won two little races for him over 5 furlongs at Edinburgh. Lavinia, by Bosworth out of Ann Hathaway, became one of the foundation mares when the Angmering Park Stud was formed, with Colonel Frank Holland as manager, in 1938. Without contributing a great deal to the evolution of the stud in the long term, Lavinia played her part by breeding the two winners Blue Angel and Minster Lovell. In her turn Blue Angel produced one of the first high-class horses to be bred at Angmering Park. This was the chesnut colt Caerlaverock, by Hyperion, who won the Newbury Autumn Foal Stakes as a two-year-old in 1951, and the Free Handicap at Newmarket the following year. Caerlaverock was very genuine, and his consistency kept him so high in the handicap that his winning opportunities were severely limited in the later stages of his racing career. He was placed in three successive big handicaps, the Rosebery Stakes, the Victoria Cup and the Kempton Jubilee, as a four-year-old. Eventually he was exported to Turkey as a stallion.

Lavinia Norfolk's sharp eye for a horse and shrewd business sense were responsible for the acquisition of one of the most successful mares in the early years of the Angmering Park Stud. The bottom fell out of the bloodstock market during the darkest days of the Second World War after the fall of France and the Dunkirk evacuation in 1940. There was no racing in England that year from June to September, and although the government allowed a few meetings to be held in the autumn, demand was very weak at the yearling sales which Tattersalls arranged at Newmarket on 15 and 16 October.

On the other hand, well-bred fillies are always a sound investment for an owner – breeder willing to ignore present difficulties and take a long view, and Lavinia was on the lookout for suitable fillies when she attended those sales. One filly she liked was a chesnut by Fair Trial out of Penny Rock, who was plain and rather small, with big ears, but a very good walker and attractive on her pedigree because Fair Trial was one of the most promising of the young sires of precociously fast horses. Lavinia bid up to 180 guineas for her; the hammer fell at that figure, but it was below the reserve price and she was unsold. Not to be put off, Lavinia sought out the filly's breeder, Major David Nicoll, at tea in the Rutland Arms and made a deal to lease her for her racing career.

The Fair Trial filly, named Honest Penny, came from a vintage crop which included such brilliant fillies as Sun Chariot, the winner of three Classic races, and Mah Iran. Honest Penny was able to hold her head high even in such august company. She won six races as a two-year-old, and gave her finest performance when she gave 8 lb and a beating of 1½ lengths to another fast filly, Gloria Mundi, in the Rous Stakes at Newmarket in September. Gloria Mundi was half a length in front inside the last furlong, but Honest Penny was as brave as she was speedy, and produced a final spurt in response to the urgent riding of Michael Beary, while Gloria Mundi cracked.

Honest Penny had one more race that season in the important Cheveley Park Stakes over 6 furlongs at Newmarket, but the distance was too far for her and she finished third to Perfect Peace and Lady Electra. As Bernard Norfolk wrote in a little monograph on Honest Penny which he produced for private circulation and presented to Lavinia in 1952: 'It answered once and for all the question that however fast you are over 5 furlongs it does not make you get six. She was kicked at the start which may have been why she did not quite show her usual dash.'

Honest Penny had five races as a three-year-old and showed that she had lost none of her speed when she won by 8 lengths on her first appearance at Salisbury in April. Although she was beaten in her other races she was a close second to Mehrali at Windsor and Hyland Brume at Salisbury. Not wishing to lose her at the end of her racing career, the Norfolks arranged with David Nicoll to extend the lease for three years, the terms being the payment of £300 a year and all expenses, including nomination fees. It was a very happy arrangement, as Honest Penny bred the three fast horses, Baccarat, Garrick and Silver Penny, who won fourteen races between them for the Norfolks. The best of the three was Garrick, who won the Queen Anne Stakes at Royal Ascot as a three-year-old. Honest Penny was an excellent broodmare and bred seven winners altogether.

Mares like Lavinia and Honest Penny, with others among whom Inquisition and Trouble were conspicuous, helped to establish Angmering Park as a regular source, and Bernard Norfolk as the breeder, of good if not quite Classic horses – though it was calculated

27

that Garrick was good enough to have been placed in the 2000 Guineas had he been entered. However, the Second World War brought fundamental changes to the overall structure of the Norfolk racing interests. Victor Gilpin rejoined the army at the outbreak of the war, and the decision was made to close Michel Grove and move the training operations to Arundel Park. The park provides one of the most peaceful and picturesque settings for thoroughbreds in England; their most disturbing experiences are likely to come from pheasants breaking covert or from browsing fallow deer. But the training facilities were far from comprehensive in the early days. Large-scale clearance of the ancient trees that dotted the park was necessary before the most rudimentary gallops could be laid out, and Bernard Norfolk would lend a hand with the work on summer evenings when his outside duties allowed. For years the training grounds within the park were supplemented by a longer gallop on the Downs above the village of Burpham on the far side of the Arun, until the installation of all-weather canters and gallops made it possible to concentrate all training in the park.

What began as a wartime expedient and a small private stable increased in an extraordinary manner during the next three decades. At first the training licence was held by Fred Bancroft; he was followed in succession by Willy Smyth and his son Gordon. Finally, with the dynamic John Dunlop at the helm, the Arundel Castle Stable developed into one of the principal public training establishments in the country, with nearly fifty different owners and a hundred horses at the time of Bernard Norfolk's death.

Bernard Norfolk had rejoined the army on the outbreak of war and went to France with the 4th Battalion, the Royal Sussex Regiment, in April 1940, returning by way of Dunkirk – though not in a fully combatant capacity, as he was in hospital with an injured knee when the fighting started. His soldiering days then were numbered, as the following February he received a telephone call from Winston Churchill asking him to 'do a job for him' as Joint Parliamentary Secretary to the Minister of Agriculture. 'I may say I have rather mixed feelings but I do not think one should refuse. It is a really interesting post, but I don't give myself more than three weeks,' he wrote to Rachel. In fact he remained in it until the end of the war.

Bernard Norfolk's Joint Parliamentary Secretary in the Commons was Tom Williams (afterwards Lord Williams of Bamburgh), who was the son of an illiterate Yorkshire miner and had earned his first money selling evening newpapers in Swinton after school hours. They quickly found that they were kindred spirits in many respects. 'We were an unlikely team, having emerged, as we did, from extreme and opposite ends of society. Oddly enough, we soon discovered, once he had emerged from his natural shyness and modesty, that we had a great deal in common. Horse racing was a special bond,' wrote Williams.

They travelled the country together addressing farmers' meetings, and substituting for each other when necessary. They formed a sort of comedy team at agricultural dinners. Bernard Norfolk would make fun of his colleague, describing him as the answer to a bookie's prayer, and Williams would reply by ribbing him for his natural instinct for confusing the geese and the swans in his own stable. They spent hours together debating the rival merits of Sussex and Yorkshire cricket.

From the point of view of the survival of British breeding Bernard Norfolk was the right man in the right post at the Ministry of Agriculture. He was able to attend the annual general meetings of the Thoroughbred Breeders' Association, of which his stepfather-in-law Lord Rosebery was president, for exchanges of views about the state of the industry and the vital question of rations for breeding stock. The compulsory ploughing-up of stud farm lands for food production was a matter of particular concern to breeders, and he was able to inform the annual general meeting in December 1943 of arrangements by which members of local War Agricultural Committees would inspect studs at the request of individual breeders for the purpose of settling grievances arising from ploughing-up orders.

In spite of his parliamentary duties, Bernard Norfolk found time to serve as a member of the Racing Reorganization Committee appointed to 'consider the whole future of racing in general'. This committee, under the chairmanship of Lord Ilchester, reported to the Stewards of the Jockey Club in February 1943, covering every aspect of the racing scene from catering to the licensing of Stewards' Secretaries. Some of the recommendations, such as the abrupt rejection of proposals for overnight declaration of runners, were reactionary; others, such as the need for control of the indiscriminate watering of courses, were remarkably farsighted. The section concerning 'The Racehorse' contained, under the heading 'Four Years Old and Upwards', the sentence: 'We think that greater encouragement should be given to owners to keep good-class horses longer in training, by the provision of races with substantial prizes for horses of four years and upwards.'

It foreshadowed precisely the doctrine of the Duke of Norfolk's Committee on the Pattern of Racing twenty years later – a doctrine whose implementation must be in the interests of the quality and variety of racing and of the evolution of the breed, but which is frustrated continually by the commercial incentives for early retirement and syndication of top-class racehorses as stallions.

The quarter of a century after the Second World War was the period when the fame and authority of Bernard Norfolk were at their zenith on and off the Turf. In racing he achieved a position near to indispensability as the sovereign's representative at Ascot, as Steward of the Jockey Club, as Steward of race meetings including Epsom and Brighton, as chairman of committees vital to the integrity and progress of horse racing. In his capacity of Earl Marshal he was the impeccable stage manager of state occasions, while he assumed a vast range of other public responsibilities as Lord-Lieutenant of Sussex, president of the Animal Health Trust, president of the Council for the Preservation of Rural England, chairman of the Territorial Army Council and manager of cricket tours abroad. His measured tread which added a proper air of solemnity to public processions, his impassive face with its heavy lids and semicircles of creased skin beneath the eyes, made him a gift for caricaturists and easily recognizable by people in all walks of life. He became a national institution.

He was appointed His Majesty's Representative at Ascot, an office which placed him in supreme control of all that pertained to the Ascot course and its racing arrangements, in 1946. He accepted the appointment on condition that Crocker Bulteel (afterwards Sir John Crocker Bulteel) joined him as Clerk of the Course. Bulteel was the most enlightened racing official of his day, combining great efficiency in administration with awareness of the need to appeal to the widest possible public and a farsighted and imaginative approach to race programming. His charm, sense of humour and willingness to listen to advice made him an easy man to work with, and he and Bernard Norfolk collaborated happily and effectively until his death ten years later. He was succeeded by Captain Nicky Beaumont, a man of similar qualities and an equally successful lieutenant for Bernard Norfolk.

These smoothly operating partnerships at the top of the Ascot chain of command facilitated the transition of Ascot racing from the single Royal Ascot meeting of four days' duration in June that had existed before the war to year-round operation and high-quality racing both on the flat and over jumps. The improvement of the course itself, and of the stands and amenities, was gradual and systematic. The will to spread quality through the whole Ascot programme was demonstrated by the introduction of the King George VI Stakes at the October meeting in 1946 and the Queen Elizabeth Stakes at the July meeting two years later. The international importance of both races was established immediately. The first King George VI Stakes was won by Souverain, the winner of the Grand Prix de Paris, then the principal French Classic race, from the Irish Derby winner Bright News and the Derby winner Airborne. The first Queen Elizabeth Stakes was won by the Italian horse Tenerani, who was to gain greater renown as the sire of the invincible Ribot, from Black Tarquin, who was to win the St Leger two months later, while Nirgal, one of the host of Boussac horses raiding English races at that time, was fourth. However, the real stroke of genius was made in 1951 when Crocker Bulteel, with the enthusiastic assent of Bernard Norfolk, decided to unite the two races as the main contribution of racing to the Festival of Britain celebrations. The race had £20,000 added to the sweepstakes (the Derby that year had £4250 added) and attracted nineteen runners including four runners from France and five Classic winners, though the English colt Supreme Court, unbeaten as a three-year-old, produced the decisive finishing speed to win from Zucchero, whose brilliance was often masked by a flawed temperament, and the best of the French horses Tantième.

The quality of the initial field immediately stamped the race as an international test of first-rate importance. Its success was such that there was no doubt that it had to be retained as a permanent part of the racing programme, and it became firmly entrenched as one of the two principal European middle-distance races in which the leading three-year-olds meet the best of their seniors; the other being the Prix de l'Arc de Triomphe on the first Sunday in October. The roll of winners speaks for itself. It includes the Derby winners Tulyar, Pinza, Royal Palace, Nijinsky, Mill Reef, Grundy, The Minstrel, Troy and Shergar; the mighty Italian horse Ribot, unbeaten in sixteen races; Right Royal V, one of the finest representatives of French breeding; Brigadier Gerard, who has been acclaimed one of the best horses bred in Britain in the second half of the twentieth century; and marvellous fillies like Aunt Edith, Park Top and Dahlia. Perfectly placed in the calendar, in midsummer when thoroughbreds are blooming, the King George VI and Queen Elizabeth Stakes became a vital tool of selection for the breeding industry.

Nor is the King George VI and Queen Elizabeth Stakes the only race at Ascot's new meetings which has provided signposts for breeders. The important mile race at the September meeting, formerly run as the Knights Royal Stakes, was renamed the Queen Elizabeth II Stakes, with a greatly increased prize, in 1955. It is the last important mile race of the English season in which the best of the three-year-old specialists meet their seniors, and has advertised the merits of a number of horses destined to make their mark as top-class stallions – for example, Derring-Do, Reform and Welsh Pageant. One brilliant member of each of the sexes – Brigadier Gerard for the males and Rose Bowl for the females – has won the race twice.

Meanwhile Bernard Norfolk defended the primacy of the Royal Ascot meeting, in terms both of pageantry and of a lodestone attracting the finest European thoroughbreds, jealously and steadfastly. His explicit opinion was that the interests of Royal Ascot were supreme, and that regulations made by authority for the proper control of ordinary meetings should not apply to it, certainly not if they conflicted with his own plans for its aggrandisement. His policy kept Royal Ascot far ahead of all its rivals in respect of the overall quality of racing. Under his guidance some Royal Ascot races attained a greater pre-eminence even than they had enjoyed before; specifically at the poles of distance running, with the Gold Cup as the paramount test of stayers and the King's Stand Stakes performing the same office for sprinters. Insistence on preserving Royal Ascot pageantry – the royal coach procession down the course before racing, the dress regulations which stipulated morning dress for men and dresses and hats for women in the Royal Enclosure – showed not only profound respect for tradition but a considerable measure of commercial prudence. Royal Ascot as an incomparable carnival of fashion and a unique social phenomenon attracted many thousands of paying customers who were indifferent to the standard of racing and otherwise never set foot on a racecourse. Bernard Norfolk's policies ensured the interdependence of the two aspects of Royal Ascot, social and racing, but the dependence of the racing was the greater because without the funds created by the social aspect the quality of Royal Ascot racing must have withered.

Only the race meeting at Goodwood in late July complemented Royal Ascot in its social content. Royal Ascot marked the climax of the London season; Goodwood its conclusion, when the social high flyers deserted London for the country, for Cowes and for the grouse moors. In contrast to Royal Ascot the Goodwood July meeting was informal, and was aptly described 'as a garden party with racing tacked on'. It was an ancient meeting, dating from the beginning of the nineteenth century, with long-established popular races like the Goodwood Cup and the Stewards' Cup. The course was laid out on the crest of the South Downs above Goodwood Park, with its magnificent beech groves, and Goodwood House, the country seat of the Dukes of Richmond.

Despite her lack of interest in racing, Bernard Norfolk's mother had seized on the Goodwood July meetings as opportunities to satisfy her love of entertaining on the grand scale. Goodwood was just nine miles from Arundel, and she refused to be outshone by the social splendour of Goodwood House. The lavishness of the Arundel Castle parties for Goodwood was renowned. Bernard Norfolk continued those parties after the Second World War because they formed an accepted part of his life, though certainly without his mother's enthusiastic commitment. He loved simplicity and a quietly ordered existence. Nevertheless, he did not do things by halves, and the postwar parties for Goodwood were models of faultless organization and liberal hospitality.

A novel feature of those parties was the Arundel Castle Private Sweepstakes. Each guest was invited to buy a cheap yearling at public auction – the maximum price was fixed initially at £500 – to run in the race of that title to be run at the next Goodwood July meeting as an additional race on the Thursday programme. The race was run annually from 1947 to 1963 and, in spite of the low cost of the runners, was often very keenly contested. The list of owners of the winners contained the names of most of the racing grandees of the period. The included Bernard Norfolk himself, who won with Geordie, the Duke of Devonshire, Lord Halifax and his son Lord Irwin, Bernard Norfolk's stepfather-in-law Lord Rosebery, Lord Sefton, Lord Allendale, Lord Porchester, Lord Derby and his brother Mr Richard Stanley, and Sir Humphrey de Trafford. At last the race became a victim of relentlessly changing times. The escalation of bloodstock prices, outstripping general inflation, made cheap yearlings with reasonable racing prospects increasingly difficult to find, and the older grandees less able or willing to pay the price.

The house parties for Goodwood had continued without interruption after 1962, when the Norfolks themselves moved from the castle, which was too vast and inconvenient for modern habitation, to a new house in the park. Arundel Park House was of stone in Georgian style, designed in the form of a central block of two storeys surmounted with a cupola and extended by two single-storey wings. Facing south, the main rooms overlooked a broad stone terrace and a croquet lawn to the coastal plain and the sea. The rear of the house gave onto the park and the training grounds. Bernard Norfolk kept an office in the castle and the younger guests were accommodated there during Goodwood week.

However, success in the Arundel Castle Private Stakes did not satisfy the ambitions that Bernard Norfolk, with Lavinia's eager prompting, nursed for his stud and stable in the years of postwar expansion. The Angmering Park Stud was producing good winners, like Burpham in the mile Britannia Stakes at Royal Ascot in 1949. During the next few years Eternal City, though a horse of only second-class ability, was a source of special pleasure. Some unkind critics had said that it would be impossible to train stayers with the limited resources at Arundel; and Eternal City won nine races over long distances up to the 2 miles of the Halifax Handicap at Ascot.

There was stamina enough in the Angmering Park stock. What was wanting was the kind of precocious speed that brings success in valuable two-year-old races, and a quick return on capital. To remedy this deficiency a policy of buying sprint-bred yearlings with signs of early physical maturity was devised. In this respect Lavinia's sure eye for a horse was invaluable. From the late 1950s a series of extemely fast two-year-olds that had been purchased, many of them inexpensively, at the yearling sales carried the Norfolk colours with distinction in important races. In 1959 Sound Track won the July Stakes, the next year Skymaster won the Middle Park Stakes, and a year later again Sovereign Lord won both the July Stakes and the Gimcrack Stakes, two of the longest established big two-year-old races in the calendar. In 1963 Ballymacad won the New Stakes (a race afterwards renamed the Norfolk Stakes at the express wish of the Queen to honour Bernard Norfolk's long association with the course), and the following year the indolent but, when roused, unusually talented Ragtime won a third July Stakes for the Norfolks and went on to win the Richmond Stakes at Goodwood. Conspirator and Golden Plume were two other bought colts who were multiple winners as two-year-olds during the same period without achieving success at the highest competitive level.

Many years later Lavinia Norfolk remarked that at that period it had been possible to buy yearlings of the right physical type and bred for the purpose of exploitation as two-year-olds for reasonable prices, but that this type of yearling had largely vanished from the market. There was less incentive to buy potential stayers, but Tudor Period, a half-brother by the Derby winner Owen Tudor to the Oaks winner Frieze, was bought at the Newmarket October yearling sales in 1958 and proved an excellent bargain when he won four races, including the Great Yorkshire Handicap over the St Leger course, and was second to Die Hard in the Ebor Handicap. Even Tudor Period did not have the same touch of class as the home-bred filly Predicament, who developed rather late to become one of the best three-year-old staying fillies in the autumn of 1966, when she won the Princess Royal Stakes over 1½ miles at Ascot and was second to Parthian Glance in two of the most important races for fillies of that kind, the Yorkshire Oaks and the Park Hill Stakes.

Meanwhile efforts were made to increase the element of high-class speed in the Angmering Park bloodstock. The most significant of the purchases made with this idea in mind was the mare La Fresnes, acquired for 17,000 guineas as a nine-year-old at the Newmarket December sales in 1962. She had the most illustrious pedigree and performance. Bred by Lord Derby, she was by Court Martial, twice champion sire and one of the strongest influences for speed in his time, out of Pin Stripe by Hyperion, winner of the Derby and the St Leger and six times champion sire. Pin Stripe's dam was Herringbone, who had carried the Derby colours to victory in the wartime 1000 Guineas and St Leger. La Fresnes herself had exceptional precocious speed. She was second to Weeber in the Queen Mary Stakes at Royal Ascot and the French filly Midget II in the two-year-old fillies' championship race, the Cheveley Park Stakes, at Newmarket in the autumn. Her best form was shown in two duels with Palariva, trained like Midget II in France and destined to become one of the best female sprinters seen for many years. La Fresnes and Palariva met twice, and La Fresnes finished in front each time. The first occasion was in the Molecomb Stakes at Goodwood, one of the fastest 5-furlong tracks in the country, where La Fresnes prevailed by a head in a bumping finish in the record time of 58.4 seconds but was disqualified for jostling. It was a different story in the Lowther Stakes at York a month later, for La Fresnes jumped off in front and had the legs of Palariva all the way to win decisively by 2 lengths. At the end of the season the authoritative *Bloodstock Breeders' Review* summed her up by saying that 'there was not a great deal of her, but she was lively, fast and very game'.

Like many fillies of her type, La Fresnes was not relatively as good at three years of age as she had been at two, though she did manage to win the Red Rose Stakes over 5 furlongs at Manchester by a short head in a field of three. Again, like many fillies of her type, she did not produce any offspring with anything like her own brilliance. Nevertheless, her influence on the fortunes of the Angmering Park Stud was to be profound in the longer term.

My own association with Bernard Norfolk began when I was invited to join the committee set up under his chairmanship by the Stewards of the Jockey Club in the autumn of 1964 to examine the Pattern of Racing in Britain. The only other member was Geoffrey Freer, the wisest, most experienced, wittiest and most respected of racing officials. Tall, aquiline, striking in appearance in the model of the first Duke of Wellington, Freer was well versed in almost every aspect of the racing scene. He was a former senior handicapper of a shrewdness exceptional even in a profession which has no room for the naive, a former stud manager and breeder, a former amateur rider with a deep affection for hunting and point-to-pointing, and a remarkably successful administrator and Clerk of the Course at several courses, notably Newbury, where he had shown a flair for imaginative innovation in race programming. The committee secretary was the amiable and efficient Brigadier Sidney Kent, the manager and secretary of the Turf Board and principal assistant to the Senior Steward of the Jockey Club.

We met for a preliminary briefing with Major General Sir Randle (Gerry) Feilden. Feilden and Bernard Norfolk represented the highest tier of the Turf hierarchy. The former was Senior Steward of the Jockey Club and chairman of the Turf Board; the latter a Steward of the Jockey Club and vice-chairman of the Turf Board. They worked together harmoniously in these posts, as they did on state occasions, when Feilden was one of the Earl Marshal's ablest lieutenants and was knighted for his services in connection with the coronation of Queen Elizabeth II. They were close friends, and Feilden was only the second owner, after Miss Grizelda Grant-Lawson, outside the family to have horses trained in the Arundel stable. Feilden applied to the affairs of the Turf the administrative skills he had developed in high staff appointments in the army and as chief of the N.A.A.F.I. He was energetic and industrious despite his appearance of being massively overweight; and he was friendly, patient and diplomatic to a degree which contradicted his outward air of military authority.

The terms of reference of the Duke of Norfolk's Committee on the Pattern of Racing were 'to make recommendations on the general programme of all races and stakes, with special attention to the top-class horses of all ages, the Prestige races and the improvement of the thoroughbred.' We met at frequent intervals during the winter of 1964–65 and the spring and early summer of 1965 and delivered our report in July.

Bernard Norfolk had great virtues as a chairman. He knew his own intellectual limitations, was content to stay within them and abstain resolutely from lightning responses and intuitive thinking. He was a patient listener, and resilient in argument in the open spaces between his own rock-hewn prejudices – for example, that the prize money for handicaps should be severely restricted and that the Ascot Gold Cup ranked in a special category of its own, only slightly inferior to the Classic races. Sometimes he would sit silent, with his eyes closed for minutes after the expression of a new or controversial idea. Finally, when his process of mental digestion was complete, he would open his eyes and say firmly, 'I accept [or I cannot accept] that.' As Feilden observed years later, 'His judgement was sound, and he had great common sense.'

Between meetings we exchanged memos based on independent thought and research. I found it disconcerting that if Bernard Norfolk approved of the contents of one of my memos he was liable to incorporate whole passages in the report without amendment or regard for the context. Other sections of the report he wrote himself. Lacking formal education, he found it much harder to express himself on paper than in speech, and had little talent for coherent argument. As a result the report in its final form involved a curious mixture of styles which, surprisingly, was never the subject of comment.

The preamble to the report defined the 'ideal racehorse' as a horse possessing more speed than the best specialist sprinter, but capable of dominating his rivals over distances from a mile to 1¾ miles at three years old and upwards. The duty of the Turf authorities was to provide the kind of overall racing programme calculated to promote this ideal type. The fundamental doctrine of the report was summed up in the sentence:

The Turf authorities must ensure that a series of races over the right distances and at the right time of the year are available to test the best horses of all ages, and they must attempt to ensure that the horses remain in training long enough and race often enough to be tested properly for constitution and soundness.

The recommendations of the report had both negative and positive aspects. On the negative side, the committee recommended that the value of two-year-old races should be limited, especially in the early part of the season; and that handicaps, races in which the weights carried by the horses are adjusted with the aim of equalizing their chances, should be limited in number and value because 'they put a premium on mediocrity'. On the positive side, the committee recommended that the two-year-old programme should build up to a series of championship tests over various distances in the autumn; that the three-year-old Classic races should be supplemented by regular weight-for-age races over distances ranging from a mile to 1¾ miles throughout the season; and that valuable races should be provided to tempt the best three-year-olds of each season to remain in training as four-year-olds. The report referred to the recommendations of the Racing Reorganization Committee of 1943, declaring that the situation had deteriorated in the meantime because the growth of stallion syndication acted as a spur to early retirement of high-class horses.

The report of the Duke of Norfolk's committee proposed and named five Classic, nine Prestige and thirty-four Feature races as those necessary to promote the development of the ideal racehorse. The Classic and Prestige races combined foreshadowed Group 1, and the Feature races foreshadowed Groups 2 and 3 of the later Pattern race system, if in skeletal form. The revolutionary aspect of the report was the insistence that the Turf authorities must take control of the whole racing programme and impose a 'pattern' on it to a degree undreamed of before. How revolutionary this idea was became apparent when the report was debated at a special meeting of the Jockey club on 20 July, with Sir Randle Feilden in the chair as Senior Steward. There was much discussion as to whether a committee charged with the responsibility of examining, amending and approving the annual programmes submitted by the various clerks of the course did or did not exist. Feilden attempted to brush the awkward question aside by moving on to the subject of apprentice races but Lord Rosebery, the formidable senior member of the club, would have none of this evasion. The following exchange occurred:

Lord Rosebery: Could we have an answer as to whether we have this committee or not.
Feilden: I promise you that the programmes will be vetted.
Rosebery: That is not an answer.
Feilden: I cannot find out what the committee is called. I will write to you.
Major Gibson: There is in fact a committee. I do not remember what it is called, but Lord Cadogan is the chairman.

★ ★ ★

No further progress towards elucidating the point could be made at the meeting. The fruitless discussion had exposed not only an astonishing ignorance at the highest level of the manner in which the ruling body of racing conducted its business, but also a lack of central race planning that was soon to be rectified (see page 13).

Little criticism of the philosophy of the report was voiced at the meeting. Rosebery and another elderly member of the club, Colonel Giles Loder, argued the rival claims of the Jockey Club Stakes, over 1¾ miles, and the Champion Stakes over 1¼ miles, to be the principal weight-for-age race of the autumn. Rosebery recalled that when Sceptre, one of the two greatest fillies of all time, had beaten the Triple Crown winner Rock Sand by 4 lengths in the Jockey Club Stakes of 1903, there had been an enormous crowd. Loder took his stand on a point of principle. 'I have always been brought up to believe that what you want on a racecourse is speed, and that anybody can breed a horse that stays 2 or 2½ miles.'

Throughout the debate Bernard Norfolk remained imperturbable and diplomatic whenever points of the report were referred to him. 'That is up to the club to decide,' he commented at a moment when a minor aspect of the report came under crossfire. From the outset it was clear that the prestige and authority that his name conferred on a committee report would brook no serious challenge, and that it would be left to the Stewards of the Jockey Club to take the measures necessary to implement the main recommendations.

More surprisingly the report found ready acceptance in the Levy Board, whose cooperation was required to provide the financial sinews for the promotion of the ideal racehorse. The chairman of the Levy Board was Lord Wigg, a former Labour Cabinet Minister who was totally out of sympathy with the traditions of inherited wealth and rank represented by Bernard Norfolk. However, Wigg eagerly embraced the philosophy of the Norfolk report and made its principal recommendations the basis of the Levy Board prize-money policy.

The next stage in the evolution of a programme to promote the ideal racehorse was the appointment of a new committee under the chairmanship of Lord Porchester to translate the ideas which inspired the Norfolk report into an actual series of races that would fulfil this purpose. The Porchester Committee delivered its report in May

1967, with a recommendation of 131 (later whittled down gradually to about a hundred in the light of experience) so-called 'Pattern races' which would be a comprehensive series of tests for the best horses of all types and ages. These races set the standard of British racing, and, in the words of the Racing Industry Committee of Inquiry of 1968, 'encourage everyone in the industry to breed, train and race horses which will run in these races both for the prestige they carry and the prize money attached to them.'

The idea of Pattern racing caught on amazingly. Within a few years the original British Pattern had been expanded to form the European Pattern, involving first Ireland and France and later Germany and Italy. There were significant moves towards partial integration of the national Patterns and the division of Pattern races into three groups to denote their degrees of importance. The United States followed the trend by nominating 'Graded Stakes' races with three grades corresponding to the European groups. Other countries quickly appreciated the advantages of the system and began to introduce their own groups and grades. The number of countries increased year by year, and by 1983 no fewer than twenty-nine countries contributed their schedules of Pattern races, divided into three groups or grades, to the booklet published jointly by the Turf authorities of Britain and France.

Although nobody would pretend that the standard of racing is as high in, say, Austria or Peru as it is in the principal racing and breeding countries, Pattern racing has been recognized universally as performing two invaluable functions. First, it indicates the races that are considered the most important in each country; and, second, it designates the horses of superior racing ability which will be preferred for subsequent breeding. The Pattern racing system has indeed become an essential tool for breeders in the selection process, and will always be the most lasting memorial to the services rendered by Bernard Norfolk to the evolution of the thoroughbred.

At the end of the 1960s Bernard Norfolk's prestige and authority were so solidly established as to seem impregnable. In the life of the nation he was the acknowledged master of ceremonial. On the Turf he was the archetype of the aristocratic establishment figure that had been dominant for nearly two centuries – personifying, to the majority of observers, the traditional primacy and integrity of the Jockey Club with a sureness unmatched even by Gerry Feilden, then in the midst of an unprecedented eight-year term as Senior Steward. No one else could have delivered an annual address to the jockeys about to ride in the Derby, warning against recklessness on the hazardous descent to Tattenham Corner, as he made a practice of doing after the disastrous Derby of 1962 when seven horses fell, beginning with the words, 'You have the honour to be riding in the greatest race in the world', without presenting an image of ludicrous pomposity.

Nevertheless, unqualified admiration for him was not universal. As Gerry Feilden shrewdly observed, he did not intend to be arrogant and to dominate people, but did so all unwittingly. Inevitably he ruffled feathers and aroused hostility in some quarters, perhaps more often among his peers in the racing establishment than among the rank and file who accepted his authority and his experience without question. His attitude to Stewards' Secretaries, the officials appointed to give to the Stewards of race meetings any help and advice relating to the conduct of the meeting and the Rules of Racing that they might require, was one of frosty tolerance. They should speak when invited, and not step an inch out of line. Undoubtedly this attitude caused resentment at a time when the influence of the Stewards' Secretaries was growing steadily. One prominent racing man of the period found him 'terribly dictatorial'. Those who shared that view did not subscibe to the proposition that he was unassailable or that his patronage conferred absolute protection against the impact of the Rules of Racing. There was a degree of friction capable of causing fire.

The first few months of the 1970 season were quietly satisfactory from Bernard Norfolk's point of view. By the end of June Chinatown, who won the Warren Stakes over the Derby course at the Epsom spring meeting, Gospel Truth, Dionysus, Star, Calaboose, Light Opera and Naval Rating had carried his colours successfully. All but Chinatown were home-bred at Angmering Park, and all but Dionysus were ridden by Ron Hutchinson, the stylish and utterly loyal Australian first jockey to the stable. Light Opera had looked very fast when she won the Kingsclere Stakes, a race always contested by some gifted two-year-old fillies, on her debut at Newbury in the last week of June, though a weak heart was to prevent the later realization of her talent; and the three-year-old Naval Rating had completed a double by winning the Childrey Maiden Plate an hour later.

If those victories were interpreted as harbingers of a successful mid-summer campaign, this interpretation was to prove entirely false. Bernard Norfolk's home-bred two-year-old filly Skyway, by Skymaster out of Emerald Isle, made her debut in the Weyhill Maiden Fillies' Stakes over 5 furlongs at Salisbury on 1 July. She broke quickly from the start, but soon lost her place and dropped back to nearly last of the field of fourteen. From this unpromising position she began to eat up the ground in the last furlong, finishing fastest of all to take third place behind Velvet Sheen and Royal Topper, beaten by a head and 1½ lengths. After the race John Dunlop, to his amazement, was summoned to a Stewards' inquiry. Mr Larch Loyd was in the chair; Lord Margadale and Brigadier Lord Tryon were the other two acting Stewards, and the Stewards' Secretaries Gerald Dawson and Philip Fielden were in attendance. Dunlop was shown the patrol film of the race and then asked by Loyd what were the instructions that he gave to Hutchinson. 'The instructions were that I told him to do his best. That is all my instructions were,' Dunlop replied.

Later Hutchinson was called in and asked what his instructions were. 'To try and hold my position and do the best I could, sir,' replied Hutchinson.

Further questioning by the Stewards concentrated on why Skyway had dropped back after starting well. Hutchinson explained that he could not keep up with Geoff Lewis, who made the running on Royal Topper, and Dunlop expressed the opinion that she had run very green. He went on, 'I was delighted with her running, from the way I thought she would run. My horses have been running well recently' – he had had five two-year-old winners including Light Opera during the previous week – 'but this filly has never done much at home.' He added that such fillies often do show much improvement when they appear on the racecourse.

When asked by Loyd for his opinion Gerald Dawson replied, 'I can't agree with Hutchinson's evidence from what I saw.'

After the Stewards had conferred alone Dunlop and Hutchinson were recalled and informed by Loyd, 'We are not entirely satisfied with the explanation given, and we have decided to refer the matter to the Stewards of the Jockey Club.'

Neither Bernard nor Lavinia Norfolk attended the Salisbury meeting because he was rehearsing the State Opening of Parliament and she was standing in for the Queen. Bernard Norfolk, as owner, had no responsibility for the running of Skyway; indeed, according to Gerry Feilden, he did not even know that she was running until the evening after the race when Dunlop told him about the inquiry. The Rules of Racing place firmly on the trainer the responsibility to ensure that adequate instructions are given to the rider of any horse in his care, and those instructions must assist the rider to take all reasonable measures throughout the race to ensure that his horse has a full opportunity to win or obtain the best possible placing.

That Bernard Norfolk did involve himself from the moment on the evening of 1 July when a telephone call from John Dunlop informed him that the case had been referred revealed a great deal about the man: first, his intense loyalty; second, his instinctive assumption that his trainer and his jockey, though leading members of their own professions, were in an old-fashioned sense his servants – and therefore criticism of them implied criticism of himself; and, third, his sense of outrage that he should be the object of what he regarded as an attack by his peers in the racing establishment.

The case was heard by the Stewards of the Jockey Club responsible for discipline (Lord Cadogan, Lieutenant Colonel John Hornung and Mr Jakie (later Sir John) Astor) in the Stewards' Room on Newmarket Racecourse on Wednesday, 8 July. Dunlop and Hutchinson arrived by private plane from Goodwood and were met by Bernard Norfolk, who accompanied them to the Stewards' Room with the intention of giving evidence on their behalf. There he received a sharp rebuff, for he was barred from the inquiry and forced to wait outside. The Stewards saw the film of the race and took oral evidence, and then gave their verdict, which was published in the *Racing Calendar*, the official organ of the Jockey Club. The verdict included these sentences:

The Stewards were satisfied that Hutchinson, after a good break, failed to persevere in the first part of the race so that he prejudiced his chances of winning. The instructions which the trainer J. Dunlop stated that he gave for the running of the two-year-old were, in the Stewards' opinion, contrary to the requirements of Rule 151 [describing the duties of rider and trainer to ensure the best possible placing of a horse in a race] and so were contributory to Hutchinson's riding in this race.

The Stewards suspended R. Hutchinson for 14 days starting on July 10th and imposed a fine of £500 on J. Dunlop.

Bernard Norfolk learned of the verdict with consternation. He sat down at Arundel Park that night and wrote to Dunlop:

Dear John,
I am deeply shocked by what happened today and feel terribly sorry for you. You may take what steps you wish so that people may know that our friendship and my confidence in you is unshaken. Not only have you trained the horses to a height of your trade but you have made the duchess and myself so happy in the happiest stable in England.
Yours ever,
Norfolk

He was not content to leave those steps to Dunlop. In the heat of his immediate reaction he gave an interview to Guy Rais of the *Daily Telegraph*, who visited him at Arundel, in which he alleged that there had been some kind of witch hunt inspired by jealousy. 'Why the Stewards acted in such a harsh way is beyond my comprehension,' he said. He went on to claim that it was an unwritten law that inquiries were not initiated into the running of two-year-olds on their first introduction to the racecourse. After reflecting on the damaging implications of his published remarks, however, he issued a general statement through the Press Association in which he said:

I made those remarks in good faith to defend the names of my trainer, John Dunlop, and my jockey, Ron Hutchinson, in both of whom I have complete confidence. If, however, I caused offence to anyone concerned in the Skyway case I unreservedly withdraw such remarks and offer an apology.

For Gerry Feilden, Bernard Norfolk's friend of long-standing and his collaborator in so much of Turf government, the Skyway case had been an intense embarrassment. Having feared an explosive row within the establishment, he heard of Bernard Norfolk's apology with profound relief, and issued a statement in which he expressed the hope that the case could now be considered closed. Years later he commented that he had set up the disciplinary machinery and had no alternative to letting it work; and he was convinced that the men concerned as Stewards, all honourable men, were purely doing their duty as they saw fit. But he added the enigmatic rider, 'Of course, the cases of Arthur and South Pacific had caused comment.'

The three-year-old Arthur, owned by Bernard Norfolk's mother-in-law Lady Rosebery, trained by John Dunlop and ridden by Ron Hutchinson, had made rapid headway in the last furlong to finish third in the Stroud Green Handicap at Newbury in April 1970, and had won the Scottish and Newcastle Breweries' Handicap at Newcastle next time out. The running of South Pacific to which Feilden referred had occurred five years earlier when Gordon Smyth, not John Dunlop, was the trainer at Arundel. A two-year-old owned by Bernard Norfolk, South Pacific won the Rowley Mile Nursery at Newmarket on 29 September after being unplaced in three previous races over 5 furlongs. No official action was taken in either case, and Feilden must have been aware that in no acceptable jurisdiction could insinuations about the running of those horses be accepted as valid testimony in the Skyway case.

It is tempting to argue that the rights and wrongs of the Skyway case are irrelevant; that Bernard Norfolk's reactions alone are germane to an understanding of his character. But his allegations of a witch hunt, though subsequently retracted, his postulation of an unwritten law that the running of a two-year-old on its debut was exempt from investigaton, his sense of injustice and betrayal by his peers in the Jockey Club, all obstruct the easy way out. The question has to be faced whether he was a man so wanting in judgement as to be disconcerted by purely imagined wrongs. John Lawrence (afterwards Lord Oaksey) devoted his racing article in the *Sunday Telegraph* immediately after the Jockey Club hearing wholly to the Skyway case, without giving a single word to consideration of the justice of the verdict. His theme was that 'the cause of firm, fair and impartial racing discipline has been in several ways substantially advanced' because the Skyway affair 'enabled the Stewards to dispose, courageously and I hope permanently, of the often-heard canard about one law for the rich, etc.' That was the entire basis of his argument in favour of the action taken by 'three honourable men', the Salisbury Stewards. It was a flimsy defence of the assumption that Bernard Norfolk's indignation was completely unjustified.

Bernard Norfolk was certainly wrong in claiming that two-year-olds first time out enjoy a dispensation from the Rules of Racing. On the other hand, there was no precedent for applying the letter of the law to a two-year-old filly, for the good reason that an impressionable or highly strung filly's prospects of continuing to race successfully may be prejudiced if she is punished when she has her first experience of competition on the racecourse. It is normal, accepted and indeed desirable practice for a filly to be treated with forbearance by her jockey in her first race, and this can be achieved without deliberately preventing her from winning if she is good enough. Equally, there are many two-year-olds of both sexes who, like Skyway, are physically mature enough to run but show little speed at home; the only way to find out whether they have any real ability is to give them a race in the hope that their competitive instincts will be roused, but a race of that kind is bound to be experimental.

There was an apparent absurdity in the censure of Hutchinson for failing to persevere in the early part of the race, since it deprived him of the option of riding a waiting race. The verdict could be covered, however, by the wording of Rule 151 which imposes on the rider the duty to take all the necessary measures 'throughout the race' to obtain the best possible placing at the finish. What those necessary measures are in individual cases is a matter of careful and difficult judgement – all the more difficult in the case of a jockey like Hutchinson noted for his quiet and patient style of riding. If Skyway, like hundreds of two-year-old fillies running for the first time each season, had been kept at the rear of the field throughout the race there is little doubt that she would have passed unnoticed. It was the fact that she was was taught a racing lesson and made to finish fast that drew attention. As Dunlop remarked at the Salisbury inquiry, 'She was the only animal who was really ridden out from the distance behind the first two.'

The *Sunday Times* racing correspondent Roger Mortimer took a different line from John Lawrence. Having stated that he could not remember such severe penalties being handed out in respect of a two-year-old, and a filly at that, making its first appearance, he wrote:

Skyway will never be of great account. It is worth bearing in mind that two of the fastest horses of the past 50 years were both defeated in minor races first time out – Abernant at Lingfield, Myrobella at Salisbury. Hyperion, unbacked and unplaced first time out, was shortly afterwards a well-supported winner at Royal Ascot. St Paddy and Royal Palace were unplaced first time out, and so was the brilliant Sir Ivor.

The difference between Skyway on the one hand and Abernant, Myrobella, Hyperion, St Paddy, Royal Palace and Sir Ivor on the other is that Skyway had only very modest racing ability whereas the rest were great racehorses. Events were to show that Skyway showed her best form first time out in the Weyhill Stakes. In its first weekly issue after the race *Timeform*, the publication whose ratings are esteemed universally as the most accurate commercial assessment of the individual merit of racehorses, rated Skyway at 90 accompanied by the symbol P, which conveys the editorial opinion 'that the horse is capable of form much better than he has so far displayed', while the winner Velvet Sheen was rated at 88 and the second Royal Topper at 76.★ But at the end of the 1970 season, when she had run five more times without winning, the rating of Skyway had dropped to 74 while Velvet Sheen had risen to 91 and Royal Topper, who was unplaced in three races after the Weyhill Stakes, remained on the 76 mark. Those final ratings amounted to a tacit admission that the result of the Weyhill Stakes fairly reflected the merits of the fillies concerned and that Velvet Sheen, not Skyway, made progress after that race.

Skyway was not good enough to be worth retaining in a stud or stable aiming at quality. She was submitted by Bernard Norfolk at the Newmarket December sales in 1970 and sold for 1900 guineas, a price which proved that no one discerned much latent ability in her. She joined the stable of Pat Rohan at Malton and ran once as a three-year-old, winning the Rutherglen Maiden Stakes over 1¼ miles at Hamilton on 16 July in a close finish with Rush Meadow and Belle Mourne. Neither Rush Meadow nor Belle Mourne ever

★The best two-year-old would normally have a rating of about 130, so the class of the fillies in the Weyhill Stakes was comparitively low.

won a race, and *Timeform* gave Skyway a rating no higher than 76 on the strength of her victory.

After the Weyhill Stakes *Timeform* took the extraordinary step of not only attaching the symbol P to Skyway but giving her a current rating 2 points above that of Velvet Sheen, who had beaten her by nearly 2 lengths at level weights. By the time she won a race a year later *Timeform* rated her 14 points lower, the equivalent of about half a dozen lengths, than her original rating. This testimony simply cannot be reconciled with the supposition that the way she was ridden in the Weyhill Stakes did not give her a full opportunity to win or obtain the best possible placing. It explains John Dunlop's contemporary view that the inquiry was nothing but a bad joke; it conveys an indelible impression that the verdict in the Skyway case involved a serious miscarriage of justice that was never admitted or corrected.

Bernard Norfolk's lasting indignation was no mere petulant reaction to an imagined wrong. His bitterness could not be assuaged. He expressed it publicly on the racecourse by sweeping past former friends whom he thought tainted by the Skyway affair without a glance or gesture of recognition. He felt betrayed by his peers in the racing establishment; and, which was perhaps even harder for him to bear, his pride was deeply wounded. Most of his pleasure in racing, much of his interest in numerous associated activities, had been destroyed for ever.

Some people close to him were convinced that the Skyway case killed him. Gerry Feilden, who knew him better than anyone else in the world of racing, believed that it hastened his death. The implications do not admit of precise reckoning. He suffered a heart strain when shooting with Jim Joel at Childwickbury at the end of the same year and was in bed for most of the winter. Although he recovered sufficiently to take up the reins again at Ascot and remain as Her Majesty's Representative for three more years, he was never a completely fit man again.

The last five years of Bernard Norfolk's life were clouded by sadness, ill health and disillusionment. Nevertheless, if they were years of impaired performance and latterly of obvious physical decline, then at least there was one period of remission when his old enthusiasm for racing and the fortunes of his own stud and stable were rekindled. The agent of that renewal was Ragstone, the horse of whom he was speaking when he said in a reply to an interviewer, 'I should imagine he is far and away the best I ever owned.'

Ragstone was a grandson of La Fresnes, the mare he had bought to augment the element of speed in the Angmering Park bloodstock. Like many mares who themselves possess exceptional speed, La Fresnes did not bear any offspring of racing ability comparable to her own. Her daughter Fotheringay, by the massive French champion Right Royal V, was a big filly with a plain head, and all she could achieve on the racecourse was to win one little race at Goodwood. But Fotheringay had the pedigree distinction of being inbred to Hyperion, one of the great stallions of the century, in the third remove, and when mated with stallions in which other powerful strains were dominant she was capable of producing highly talented performers. To Ragusa, a son of the mighty Ribot, she bred Ragstone; and to a later mating with Kalamoun, whose pedigree held double dosages of such potent influences as Nearco and Mumtaz Mahal, she bred the excellent middle-distance horse Castle Keep, though Bernard Norfolk did not live to see Castle Keep run.

In his early days Ragstone was somewhat on the leg and physically backward, but was unmistakably an athlete with the bearing of a class horse. He ran only once unplaced as a two-year-old, and did not run until the middle of August as a three-year-old, when he appeared in the Newtown Maiden Stakes over 1½ miles at Newbury. Experts commented favourably on his appearance in the paddock, but he was easy in the betting and started at 12–1. He did nothing wrong in the race, taking the lead inside the last furlong and staying on well to win from William Pitt and the odds-on favourite Admetus, a future winner of the Washington D.C. International. He had three more races that season and won them all. They were races of only passing importance, though he gave a brave performance to win the last of them, the Southfield Handicap at Newmarket in October, under top weight. It was as a four-year-old that he could be expected to develop his full powers and prove himself at the highest level of competition.

Although Ragusa had won the St Leger, Ragstone, with La Fresnes as his granddam, lacked the pedigree of a true stayer that is appropriate to a potential winner of the Ascot Gold Cup, the supreme test of stamina in the thoroughbred. Moreover, Ragstone was such a hard puller that it was difficult for any rider to conserve his stamina during a race. On the other hand, Bernard Norfolk's long dedication to the interests of Ascot had inflated the importance of the Gold Cup in his mind to such an extent that it had become for him the most desirable of all races to win. The Gold Cup had to be the objective for Ragstone.

The campaign opened auspiciously when Ragstone won first the Aston Park Stakes at Newbury and then the Group 2 Pattern race, the Henry II Stakes, at Sandown during May. The Henry II Stakes is the main preparatory race for the Gold Cup, but its distance is 2 miles exactly. There is an extra half mile against the collar to be faced in the Gold Cup, and nobody could take Ragstone's ability to stay it for granted. There would be horses like Lassalle, Authi and Proverb, whose stamina was fully proven, in the field.

A daring plan was devised to solve the problem. Hornet, a useful stayer who had won the Henry II Stakes himself two years earlier, had been purchased not for the conventional purpose of ensuring a fast pace, but with the highly original mission of regulating the pace so that Ragstone's doubtful stamina would not be overstrained. Ron Hutchinson, as usual, was to ride Ragstone; and Tommy Carter was given the vital tactical role on Hornet in the Gold Cup.

Carter was the most experienced lightweight jockey in the land, and an exceptionally accurate judge of pace. There was another pacemaker, Fire Bug, whose task was to give the greatest possible scope to the stamina of Authi, and Carter had to try and see that he did not fulfil that task too thoroughly. Carter was the definite winner of this battle of wits. He lost no time in sending Hornet to the front but then settled down at the steady pace which would suit Ragstone. Robert Jallu, the young French jockey on Fire Bug, lacked Carter's judgement of pace. Assuming that Carter's task was identical to his own, he was content to take up a position only slightly ahead of him and stay there.

Ragstone's eager competitive instinct made him take an extremely strong hold of his bit, but Ron Hutchinson, by exerting all his strength, was able to restrain him close behind the pacemakers. Hornet was beaten after 2 miles, but Fire Bug kept up the gallop till the straight where Lassalle, the 1973 winner, swept into the lead.

Hutchinson exercised patience until they were approaching the last furlong, and then called on Ragstone to accelerate. The response was magnificent. With a surge of speed and power that none of his opponents could match, Ragstone raced into the lead with the air of a sure winner. Although Proverb was cutting back his lead with every stride in the last 100 yards and Lasalle plugged on gallantly, Ragstone was not to be caught and reached the winning post with threequarters of a length to spare from Proverb, while Lassalle was a head farther behind in third place.

As the horses raced through the last furlong the Ascot crowd were anticipating Ragstone's victory with a growing roar of cheers. The race was followed by a spontaneous display of affection and rejoicing seldom seen on a racecourse. Elderly top-hatted gentlemen, suddenly remembering that they were among Bernard Norfolk's oldest friends, came running from the Royal Enclosure to the unsaddling enclosure to congratulate him. Expensively gowned ladies, clutching their ridiculous hats, ran too, and so did hundreds of more soberly dressed racegoers from the grandstand, impatient to express their delight. So many unauthorized people forced their way past the helpless gatemen into the enclosure that there was little room for Ragstone himself, or for Hutchinson, having dismounted, to carry the saddle into the weighing room. In the middle of the crowd of wellwishers thronging Ragstone, Bernard Norfolk stood flushed with victory, beaming his happiness.

A week later there was a celebration party in the Great Hall in Arundel Castle. The only outsider invited was Grizelda Grant-Lawson, who had been the first owner apart from the family to have horses in the stable. It was strictly a staff party embracing the Arundel stable men, the Angmering Stud staff and the estate workers. There was champagne and a lavish buffet supper. Bernard Norfolk made a gracious little speech of thanks to all those who had shared in Ragstone's development from conception to the day of triumph at Ascot. He stayed for a couple of hours and then went home to bed, leaving the party to continue, with dancing and an ample supply of drink, until the small hours.

Ragstone ran only once more, in the Geoffrey Freer Stakes over 1 mile 5 furlongs at Newbury in August. The aim was to establish him as a top-class middle-distance performer rather than the specialist stayer that breeders in the 1970s tended to shun. The going promised to be reasonably good, but less than an hour before racing was due to begin the skies darkened and a cloudburst deluged the course. There was debate whether it would be prudent to withdraw Ragstone; but he was the day's main attraction for the racegoers, and it was decided tht he must take his chance. The desperately wet conditions were all against him, and he was labouring as soon as the runners had turned into the straight. The mudlark Realistic was actually able to quicken and took command to win comfortably, while Ragstone finished a weary third 6½ lengths behind him. Worse still, he emerged from the race with symptoms of leg trouble that banished all hope of training him for the big autumn races. His racing career was over.*

Nevertheless, Ragstone had served his purpose nobly. Bernard Norfolk was ailing the next autumn, and was mostly confined to bed for his remaining months. Lavinia had taped the television film of the Gold Cup, and it was an unfailing source of pleasure to him to watch the race over and over again. He died peacefully on 1 January 1975.

Bernard Norfolk was in some respects enigmatic – a man of few or no academic gifts and poor education who could impress men of first-rate intelligence by the orderliness of his mind and his organizing ability. He was simple, direct and unostentatious. He was indifferent to, or at least only subconsciously aware of, his possessions and the outward signs of his wealth. His Canalettos, commissioned by the Howard family at a time in the eighteenth century when the English were the Venetian artist's principal patrons, were to him nothing more than a part of the way of life he had inherited and accepted as naturally as he took the stones of the castle for granted.

The greatest asset of his character, apart from his sense of duty and his sense of honour, was an inspired common sense. By instinct he may have been rigidly conservative, but in important matters his first reactions were often overturned by an extraordinarily prudent

*Ragstone retired to the Lavington Stud 6 miles from Arundel on the north side of the Downs. Three years later he slipped up on the road at exercise, suffered a hair-line fracture of the skull and had to be put down within a few weeks. Considering that he was given few good mares he showed signs of being a successful stallion.

wisdom. 'How would you like it if all and sundry were allowed into your club?' he demanded of an advocate of relaxation of the rules of admission to the Ascot members' enclosure. Yet within a year he had accepted and applied the advice which at first he had rejected so vehemently.

Gerry Feilden recalled that Bernard Norfolk declared inflexible opposition to the introduction of starting stalls, arguing that they would neutralize the deserved advantage accruing to a skilful and opportunist jockey at a barrier start. But within two years of their introduction he wrote to Feilden complaining of the absence of stalls at Wolverhampton on a day when he had a runner there.

His practical turn of mind often found the right solution to problems which had baffled men of better education or specialist knowledge. For years the problem of modernizing the old and inconvenient layout of the paddock, car parks, weighing-room block and stands at the Newmarket Rowley Mile course remained unsolved, although several expert committees were appointed to consider it. The solution sprang to Bernard Norfolk's mind one night after dinner at home. The only piece of paper to hand which was large enough for his purpose was a sheet of blotting paper. On it he sketched a new layout so obviously sensible and appropriate to the needs of the course that it was adopted with only small modifications and became the blueprint for one of the cheapest (£600,000) and most successful modernization schemes implemented on any British racecourse.

Nor were his contributions to the racing world and to his ceremonial duties bounded by his pragmatism. At times he showed flashes of creative intuition for which his critics failed to give him credit. His imaginative appreciation of the needs of press and television was demonstrated as early as the coronation of Queen Elizabeth II, when he set up a press relations bureau in the office of the Earl Marshal. And after the investiture of the Prince of Wales in 1969 Peter Dimmock wrote to him from B.B.C. Outside Broadcasts:

Having had the privilege of working at so many ceremonial occasions for which you have been responsible, I have come to anticipate perfection as the normal standard that you expect from all concerned. From the beginning, I so well remember your conception of how the ceremony and the castle should look on the TV screen, and you certainly provided those circumstances for us.

His idea of the perfection of the outward manifestations of traditional splendour, whether on state occasions or at Royal Ascot, was united with a marvellous sense of tact and sympathy with individual emotion; Mary Soames wrote to him after the funeral of Sir Winston Churchill:

I hope you will not think it an impertinence on my part if I try to express in some measure the very real gratitude I feel towards you for the splendour, and fitness, and beauty of my beloved father's funeral. I know the Queen commanded it, and I realize with deep emotion that the country wanted it to be so. I know there were many who played their parts – but it was you who from the first to the last ordered every detail.

The public demeanour of Bernard Norfolk was serious, phlegmatic, unbending. In private his solemnity was frequently relieved by a sense of humour which could transform his expression in waves of pure joy. On the other hand, his reputation for laconic wit was unfounded. When asked at a press conference before the investiture of the Prince of Wales what would happen if it rained on the day, he replied that everyone would get wet. 'Judging by the number of people who have mentioned this remark to me,' he said in an interview with Kenneth Harris of the *Observer*, 'it was regarded as some kind of witticism.' In fact it was no more than his idea of a straight answer to a straight question, accurately describing cause and effect. His sense of humour was uncomplicated, often teasing, sometimes gently sarcastic. To Rachel, on holiday in Cannes in 1928, he wrote a letter pretending that he had sent out a private detective to shadow her:

He will be wearing brown and white shoes, mauve socks, white flannel trousers rather short, a whitish pinkish shirt with a collar to match and a check bow tie, a yellow waistcoat and a red or green coat. Beware of this man. He may bite.

In his attitudes Bernard Norfolk was essentially the last British aristocrat, using the word not in the sense of a member of a hereditary ruling class, and not in the sense of a man set apart by intellectual

55

superiority, but of a man dedicated to the public good without thought of personal profit or reward. He played the roles for which birth and aptitudes ordained him with absolute dedication. It may be objected that he was born to a position of wealth and privilege in which he could afford to be indifferent to material advantage. The objection lacks force because there were plenty of men, in his own and in earlier times, who began life with similar privileges but never showed a fraction of his public spirit. Lord Wigg, with whom he once had an acrimonious disagreement on the subject of the proper relationship of the Jockey Club and the Levy Board and whose thinking was totally at odds with most of Bernard Norfolk's basic assumptions about society, had this to say in posthumous tribute in the House of Lords: 'He was a man of great honesty of purpose who saw his duty and did it to the best of his ability. He never dissembled, and to such a man much may be forgiven.'

Uttered by a man who was Bernard Norfolk's natural antagonist, those words were a true and generous epitaph.

As was proper for a man whose family had so long and paternalistic an association with Arundel, and as was fitting for a man of his unabashed and unaffected piety, Bernard Norfolk lay in state in the Cathedral Church of Our Lady and St Philip Howard for twenty-four hours before his funeral on 6 February. The coffin was draped with the Howard coat of arms and surmounted by the coronet of the premier duke and hereditary Earl Marshal and Chief Butler of England. The Requiem Mass at Arundel, which was attended by Prince Charles and Princess Alexandra, by Gerry Feilden and by many prominent members of the various communities he had served so well, coincided with Requiem Masses at the Brompton Oratory in London, at St Everilda's at Everingham Park in Yorkshire, and at St Andrew's in Dumfries. The Order of Service was identical in each case, but at Arundel cathedral only the service was followed by a Proclamation of the Style and Titles of the late Duke. This solemn rite was flawed by a single false and ironic touch. Garter Principal King of Arms began: 'Bernard Marmaduke Fitz Alan Howard, Duke of Norfolk . . .' But he had anticipated his cue, and at that point he was interrupted by a fanfare. He was forced to break off and wait for the end of the fanfare before beginning the Proclamation all over again. It was an error of a kind that Bernard

56

Norfolk himself, the master of ceremonial whether on State Occasions or at Royal Ascot where he did so much to construct a stage worthy for the presentation of the finest of modern thoroughbreds, would never have committed.

2

Edward,
Seventeenth Earl of Derby
1865–1948

The date was Saturday, 17 June 1933; the occasion annual Speech Day at Wellington College, the Berkshire public school founded in memory of the victor of Waterloo and at which Edward George Villiers, the seventeenth Earl of Derby, had been a pupil fifty years earlier. Derby, tall, heavily built and rotund, stood on a dais set beneath Lawrence's portrait of the Iron Duke in the dining hall and announced to his audience of delighted schoolboys and probably less enthusiastic parents, 'I have asked your headmaster to grant you an extra week's holiday this summer, and he has been kind enough to consent.'

F. B. Malim, the model of an ascetic pedadogue, sat unsmiling on the dais beside Derby. He had had no option but to consent, because Derby was not only the sole vice-president of the college – the president was the royal Duke of Connaught – but one of the last of the English aristocratic grandees, 'King of Lancashire' and a man of overwhelming authority in the life of the nation. But he could not have approved of this unprecedented inroad into academic routine, and even less of the, to his mind, utterly frivolous reason for it; for Derby had asked for the additional holiday to celebrate the victory of Hyperion, his masterpiece as the greatest English owner – breeder, in the Derby two weeks beforehand.

If Malim was the typical inflexibly stern headmaster, Derby was the image of avuncular benevolence. His smiling red face and somewhat unkempt moustache, his paunch encircled by a gold watch chain, his whole stance and demeanour seemed to radiate goodwill. He was probably the most popular man in the kingdom at that time. As the *Dictionary of National Biography* has noted: 'Derby possessed what Englishmen admire: geniality, generosity, public spirit, great wealth, and successful racehorses.' Like a younger man of similarly ancient lineage, the sixteenth Duke of Norfolk, he had accepted instinctively the obligations thrust upon him by his wealth and rank. He had discharged a wide variety of public duties almost from the day he left Wellington. He served as A.D.C. to his father, the governor-general of Canada, and after returning to England in 1891 was elected Conservative member for the Westhoughton division of Lancashire the following year. He became a junior lord of the Treasury in 1895, and on the outbreak of the second Boer War was appointed chief press censor in Cape Town and later private secretary to the commander-in-chief Lord Roberts. In 1901 he became financial secretary to the War Office, and two years later gained a seat in the Cabinet with his appointment as Postmaster General. He lost his seat in the conservative debacle in the general election in 1906, but succeeded his father as Earl of Derby two years later.

He was closely involved in many of the municipal and commercial activities of Lancashire in the years leading up to the First World War, and was elected lord mayor of Liverpool in 1911. He showed intense patriotic fervour throughout the war. He began by raising five battalions of the King's Regiment, which were encamped in his park at Knowsley on the outskirts of Liverpool. Later he became successively Director of Recruiting, Under-Secretary of State and finally, from 1916 to 1918, Secretary of State for War. His departure from the War Office was followed by his appointment as British ambassador in Paris where his amiability, his air of a forthright English nobleman, his lavish entertaining and his staunch support of the resurgent French horse racing made him extremely popular during his two-year term despite his inability to speak much French. On returning to England he became Secretary of State for War again in 1922; but after the Conservative defeat in 1924 he retired from political life for good and devoted the rest of his life to his many other public responsibilities.

His patriotism, his public spirit and the geniality which animated all his personal contacts endeared him to the nation. It used to be said that if some catastrophe wiped out the entire royal family Eddie Derby would be the only acceptable replacement as monarch. On the other hand, he possessed neither an original nor a powerful intellect. For this reason, and as a result of his reluctance to give offence, he was a prey to uncertainty in times of crisis. He tended to be swayed by the last piece of advice addressed to him. His vacillation was most evident during the controversy over plans to place the British army in France under French command during 1917 and at the beginning of 1918 which culminated in the dismissal of Sir William Robertson as Chief of the Imperial General Staff. Lloyd George, the Prime Minister at the time, recorded in his *Memoirs* that Derby resigned three times within twenty-four hours at the height of the crisis. At other times Lloyd George doubted Derby's loyalty. Finally Derby was replaced by Lord Milner and went to Paris.

Derby's critics questioned whether he was wholly dependable, and whether he was invariably as good as his word. This criticism has received some confirmation from the letters exchanged between Derby and George Lambton, who was trainer or racing manager for the Derbys, father and son, for forty years beginning in 1893.* Derby emerges from the correspondence as a man who was often indecisive, occasionally devious and even, in difficult circumstances, inclined to be hypocritical. If he had a strong vein of benevolence, he had too generous a share of human failings to be entitled to universal or unqualified respect.

Lambton was significantly reticent about the character of Eddie Derby in his memoirs, *Men and Horses I have known*, first published in 1924 when he was training for him. Whereas he was lavish in his praise of the charm, wisdom, kindness and quiet judgement of the sixteenth Earl, he qualified his praise of Eddie Derby by remarking that he was 'impulsive, and perhaps inclined to be hasty'.

The Derby family had a long racing tradition. The twelfth Earl gave his name to the premier Classic race, while the premier fillies' Classic race was named in honour of his Epsom house 'The Oaks'. He won the first race for the Oaks in 1779 with Bridget, and won the Derby

---

*The Derby – Lambton correspondence, covering the years 1917–45, was discovered by Michael Seth-Smith at Stanley House when he was engaged in research for a biography of Lambton. Seth-Smith used the correspondence as the basis for his book *A Classic Connection* (1983). The correspondence, contained in nine box files, is now lodged in the library of the National Horse Racing Museum at Newmarket.

eight years later with Sir Peter Teazle, otherwise known simply as Sir Peter. He was one of the leading, if also one of the most eccentric, racehorse breeders of his day.

Love of the Turf was as deeply ingrained in the fourteenth Earl, the scholar and statesman whose passionate oratory earned him the title of 'The Rupert of Debate'. He was Prime Minister for three short periods in the 1850s and 1860s, and found his principal relaxation in racing. He had a singularly happy relationship with his trainer, the great John Scott of Whitewall, and won the Oaks with Iris in 1851, the 2000 Guineas with Fazzoletto in 1852, the year of his first premiership, and the 1000 Guineas with Sagitta eight years later.

The tradition was broken by the fifteenth Earl, who had no interest whatever in racing. His absorbing interest was politics, and when he died childless and was succeeded by his brother in 1893 the family racing and breeding activities had been in abeyance for almost a quarter of a century. The sixteenth Earl lost no time in reviving them. That same summer he approached George Lambton, then at the outset of his career as a trainer, through his son and heir Lord Stanley to take charge of his horses. At first Lambton demurred, arguing that he was too young and inexperienced for such a heavy responsibility, but Stanley was insistent and soon overcame his objections. Lambton was the fifth son of the second Earl of Durham, and Derby and Stanley may have decided that it would be easier and more enjoyable to have their horses with a man who was their social equal. The next year the unconventional Duchess of Montrose decided to give up her large racing and breeding interests, and Derby was able to engage her extremely capable and experienced stud groom, John Griffiths. Before long Derby also bought the Duchess's Newmarket property, which became the nucleus of his Stanley House Stables and his Woodlands and Plantation Studs.

The dispersal sales of the Duchess of Montrose's Sefton Stud bloodstock were held in 1894. Acting on the advice of Griffiths, Eddie Stanley bought for his father the yearling filly Canterbury Pilgrim for 1800 guineas at the Newmarket July sales and the five-year-old mare Broad Corrie for 650 guineas at the Newmarket December sales. They were to prove foundation mares of inestimable value in the resuscitation of the Derby breeding operations at the old Knowsley Stud and at the new Newmarket studs.

Canterbury Pilgrim was by Tristan out of Pilgrimage. Tristan was a horse of marvellous soundness and constitution. Although he was no match for the American-bred Foxhall when they were both three-year-olds or for the two-years younger St Simon when he ran in the Ascot Gold Cup as a five-year-old, he continued racing until he was six and had won the Hardwicke Stakes and the Grand Prix de Deauville three times each and the Ascot Gold Cup and Gold Vase once each before he retired. Pilgrimage had one of the most extraordinary racing records of any thoroughbred as a three-year-old, as she ran only three times in 1878 but won both the 2000 Guineas and the 1000 Guineas and was second to Jannette in the Oaks.

The looks of Canterbury Pilgrim when she came up for sale were not striking, because she was small, had a short neck and was very low in the withers. However, Griffiths was adamant that she should be bought. She achieved little to vindicate the stud groom's judgement when she was placed in only one of her five races as a two-year-old. Moreover, she had a mean and spiteful nature. However, Lambton had a placid old gelding in the stable called Flare Up, and he became the perfect companion for Canterbury Pilgrim both at exercise and in the stable. Under his calming influence she improved rapidly in the spring of her three-year-old season, reappeared to beat the 1000 Guineas winner Thais in the Oaks and went on to win the Liverpool Cup, the Park Hill Stakes and the Jockey Club Cup. Canterbury Pilgrim became a broodmare of the utmost value for the sixteenth Earl of Derby and his son, producing two influential stallions in Chaucer and Swynford and five other winners.

The beneficial influence of Broad Corrie took longer to make itself felt. Her granddaughter Canyon (by Chaucer) won the 1000 Guineas for Eddie Derby in 1916 and became the dam of two Classic winners in Toboggan, winner of the Oaks, and Colorado, winner of the 2000 Guineas.

Lock and Key was a contemporary of Canterbury Pilgrim from the stud of the Duchess of Montrose, but she did not become the property of the sixteenth Earl of Derby until she was purchased privately as a four-year-old. She became the dam of Derby's first home-bred Classic winner Keystone II, successful in the 1906 Oaks.

In her turn Keystone II bred Keysoe (by Swynford), who won the St Leger in 1919. Keystone II was the great granddam of The Nile, who won the French 1000 Guineas in 1935, and of Lighthouse II, who was the second best two-year-old in France in 1939 and was shipped to England before the fall of France the next year and finished third in the Derby.

These three purchases were made on behalf of the sixteenth Earl. Within months of the acquisition of Canterbury Pilgrim, Eddie Stanley made a purchase on his own account of a filly also destined to make a notable contribution to the progress of the Derby breeding operation. This was Hettie Sorrel, one of the first horses sent to George Lambton to train. She had her first outing in a two-year-old selling race at Newmarket in July 1893, but improved so much that she won a maiden race and four nurseries during the autumn. Stanley bought her privately from another patron of the stable after her third victory. The influence of the family she founded spread far beyond the Derby studs in the course of generations; but her influence there was profound and lasting. Her great granddaughter Aurora was second in the 1000 Guineas in 1939, and became the dam of two top-class horses, Borealis and the great stayer Alycidon. Eddie Derby bred Alycidon, but did not live to see him finish second in the St Leger in 1948, or win the Ascot Gold Cup and the Goodwood and Doncaster Cups the next year.

Eddie succeeded to the title as seventeenth Earl of Derby on the death of his father in 1908. By then Canterbury Pilgrim's two sons who were to have such a vital impact on the evolution of the Derby studs had both been born; Chaucer, foaled in 1900, was already installed as a stallion at the Woodland Stud, and Swynford was a yearling.

Chaucer was no bigger than a pony, standing less than 15 hands, when he went into training, but he had exquisite quality and soon showed Lambton that he had plenty of speed. He was one of the best two-year-olds of 1902, winning the Gimcrack Stakes, but as a three-year-old became a victim of an epidemic of pink eye which swept through the stable and practically wiped it out as an effective force. Chaucer was unplaced in his four races that season. As a four-year-old he was still very nervous and delicate, though he made a partial recovery from his illness and won three small races. He continued to make progress the next year and won the Liverpool Summer Cup, then an important race, but it was not until he was six that Lambton was satisfied that he was back at his best and he gave his best performance by winning his second Liverpool Summer Cup after a sustained duel with another high-class horse, Velocity.

Lambton was convinced that Swynford had the makings of a great racehorse from the first moment he saw him as a foal but, in contrast to Chaucer, he grew into a big, plain, backward yearling and, though he showed great speed in his gallops at home, he disappointed Lambton bitterly in his races as a two-year-old and in the first half of his three-year-old season. It was not until he went to Royal Ascot as a three-year-old that he began to mature and justify his trainer's high opinion. He won the Hardwicke Stakes there and went on to win the Liverpool Summer Cup and the St Leger, in which he outstayed the Derby winner Lemberg and then repelled a late challange by Bronzino by a head.

As a four-year-old Swynford proved himself a great racehorse beyond all reasonable doubt. Lemberg beat him in the Coronation Cup, but on that occasion Frank Wootton played into the hands of his principal opponent by adopting waiting tactics in a slow-run race. Swynford was a galloping machine and invincible when he was allowed to force the pace. He got his revenge over Lemberg by wearing him down in the Princess of Wales Stakes and the Eclipse Stakes. His racing career came to an end tragically when he smashed a fetlock joint to pieces during a steady half-speed gallop at Newmarket in September the same year. His life was saved by one of the first of the veterinary miracles, and two years later he was able to join Chaucer at the Woodland Stud. By that time Chaucer had already proved himself as a stallion by siring Stedfast, who was second to Sunstar in the 1911 2000 Guineas and Derby, beaten by 2 lengths on each occasion. Stedfast became very upset during the preliminaries at Epsom and whipped round at the start, losing nearly 100 yards, and may have been unlucky to be beaten. Sunstar broke down and never ran again, but Stedfast was unbeaten for the rest of the season and won eight races. Stedfast won six more races, including the Coronation Cup and the Champion Stakes, as a four-year-old.

The achievements of horses like Chaucer, Swynford and Stedfast demonstrated that the Derby studs were well established as one of the finest sources of top-class horses in England, and the presence of those three as stallions at the Derby studs – Stedfast stood at the Plantation Stud – seemed good insurance for the future. Nevertheless Derby, Lambton and Walter Alston, Derby's stud manager for many years, were unanimous that the base of the broodmare band needed to be broadened for the purposes of further development of the studs as a high-class thoroughbred nursery and exploiting the potential merits of the young stallions. Accordingly a series of selective purchases were made at the beginning of the second decade of the twentieth century. There was careful avoidance of the fashionable top end of the market. Instead inexpensive mares with characteristics fitting them to fill specific roles in the Derby breeding operations were sought.

The first priority was given to a fresh injection of speed, and for this purpose the six-year-old mare Bromus was bought for 3200 guineas as a six-year-old at the Newmarket July sales in 1911. Bromus had won only one race, but her victory was gained in the important Seaton Delaval Plate over 5 furlongs at Newcastle. Moreover, in spite of the fact that she was by the Derby winner Sainfoin, she was inbred at the second and third removes to Springfield, the sire of both Sainfoin and her granddam Sunrise. Springfield was one of the fastest horses of the 1870s, winning the July Cup twice and the Champion Stakes.

Afterwards Derby mated Bromus repeatedly with his own stallions Swynford, Chaucer and Stedfast and as a result procured only one winner, the second-rate Hainault. But in the first stud season he owned her he sent her away to Polymelus, whose best performances included a second place in the St Leger and victories in the Cambridgeshire Handicap and the Champion Stakes. The produce was Phalaris, a horse destined to achieve immortal fame at stud and to be one of the decisive influences in the evolution of the modern thoroughbred.

Not that the future greatness of Phalaris was foreshadowed during his racing career, which covered the First World War years 1915–18. He was extremely fast. Lambton once tried him at level weights over half a mile with Diadem, a winner of the 1000 Guineas and the most brilliant filly of the day, and reported that it was a wonderful race between them all the way, but that at the finish he gave it to the filly by a nose. Phalaris ran in few important races except the 2000 Guineas, in which he was unplaced, and the 6-furlong Challenge Stakes, which he won. Nine of his fifteen victories were gained at 5 and 6 furlongs, and although he did win once over 1¼ miles he was essentially a sprinter. Derby's exclusive aim was to breed Classic horses, and on principle he declined to send his mares to sprinters. At one time during the racing career of Phalaris he would have been prepared to sell him for £7000 or £8000, but changed his mind and sent him to the Woodland Stud instead. It was an epoch-making decision not only for his owner's operations but for racehorse breeding throughout the world.

The second of this series of acquisitions involved Anchora, bought for 1300 guineas as a seven-year-old out of training at the Newmarket second spring sales in 1912. In some respects she seemed an unlikely prospect for a high-class breeding operation, as she was no better than a second-class stayer. Derby told Alston that he had looked up her pedigree and thought she would be a suitable mate for Chaucer. It is difficult to understand why he thought so unless he wished to produce a duplication of Hermit, a Derby winner and leading sire of winners seven times, who was the grandsire of Chaucer and also the sire of Anchora's maternal grandsire Hazle-hatch. Otherwise Anchora's pedigree was somewhat lacking in class. On the other hand, she was a fine strapping mare and had shown that she was exceptionally sound, brave and tough, as she had run in fifty-one races and won eight of them. For this reason she could be considered a good mate for a small, delicate horse of beautiful quality and pedigree like Chaucer.

Anchora was mated with Chaucer without delay, and the produce was the filly Scapa Flow. Although she moved well and had a perfect temperament, Scapa Flow showed practically no ability until the autumn of her three-year-old season. She was beaten in two selling races before she gained her first success over 1½ miles at Brighton, and went on to win further races at Stockton and Newmarket before the end of the season. She was improving so fast that Lambton expressed the opinion that she would have become as good as her dam, who had been similarly slow to mature, if she had been kept in training for another season or two.

Derby had had an unbreakable prejudice against keeping fillies in training after their second season since Keystone II had failed to hold her form as a four-year-old, and Scapa Flow was sent to stud and covered by Swynford's sire John O'Gaunt at that age. The produce was the bad-legged but useful stayer Spithead, whose principal victory was in the Chester Cup. After that Scapa Flow was mated with Phalaris in ten of the next twelve seasons, and this arrangement was terminated only by the death of Phalaris in 1931. The selection of Phalaris as her almost constant mate was vindicated by the production of the three top-class horses Pharos, Fairway and Fair Isle.

Pharos was one of the first crop of foals by Phalaris. Derby and his advisers had grave doubts about the ability of Phalaris to transmit stamina, and their misgivings seemed to be confirmed when Pharos was badly beaten over a mile at Pontefract on his first appearance as a three-year-old. Derby immediately wrote to Lambton: 'I still hope that on top of the ground he will be able to get a mile. It does look however as if it is quite certain that the Phalaris's will not stay and we shall certainly have to consider very carefully what mares we mate with him.' Nor was Lambton's reply reassuring: 'Pharos is a good horse, but not a great one, and better at 6 furlongs than 8.'

On the other hand, Lambton persevered with his preparation for the Derby, in which Pharos necessitated a reappraisal of himself and his sire by finishing second to Papyrus. Indeed, Pharos should probably have won but for the incompetence of his jockey Gardner. The best subsequent performance of Pharos was when he won the Champion Stakes as a four-year-old, and the distance of that race, 1¼ miles, was ideal for him.

Pharos was on the small side but perfectly proportioned. Fairway was longer on the leg and light of frame, but was not slow to mature and was a top-class two-year-old, winning the three important races, the Coventry Stakes at Royal Ascot, the July Stakes at Newmarket and the Champagne Stakes at Doncaster. The only real blot on his racing record was his failure in the 1928 Derby. The favourite at 3–1, he was mobbed by the crowd when he left the paddock to go out onto the course, became terribly upset and was unable to do himself justice, finishing twelfth behind Felstead. He rehabilitated himself by winning the Eclipse Stakes by 8 lengths, beating the French horse Palais Royal II in the St Leger and winning the Champion Stakes. He developed into a magnificent specimen of the thoroughbred as a four-year-old, when he won five of his six races including the Champion Stakes for the second time, and also the Jockey Club Cup over 2¼ miles. The plan had been to train him for the Ascot Gold Cup as a five-year-old, but he developed tendon trouble in the spring of 1930 and had to be retired to the Woodland Stud.

After Fairway had raced no one could say that the progeny of Phalaris were necessarily deficient in stamina. However, Fair Isle, the third of the top-class products of the Phalaris–Scapa Flow mating, did not possess the same stamina as Fairway and also had a delicate constitution. She had speed, class and courage, and these assets were enough to bring her a narrow victory in an extremely hard-fought race for the 1000 Guineas. Her exertions on that occasion took a heavy toll of her constitution, and she was able to finish only fourth behind Rose of England in the Oaks.

Gondolette, the third in this series of acquisitions, was bought for 1550 guineas as a ten-year-old at the Newmarket December sales in the same year that Anchora was purchased. Her racing form had been moderate, for two of the three races she had won as a two-year-old had been selling races; one of those races had been the Juvenile Selling Plate at Epsom on Derby day, a race won by another filly destined to become famous as a broodmare, namely Doris. On the other hand, she was known to have some breeding value because she had been represented by two winning offspring at the time of sale; one of those, Great Sport, had won two races, including the Rous Plate at Doncaster as a two-year-old that year. However, the primary reason for choosing her was unconnected with her racing ability or her breeding record, but was the fact that she offered the opportunity of inbreeding to Pilgrimage through matings with Swynford and Chaucer, her sire Loved One being a son of Pilgrimage.

Gondolette was in foal to Minoru when Derby bought her, and the produce was the filly Serenissima. After that she was mated exclusively with Swynford and Chaucer, and the reason for her purchase was proved to be extremely sound when her unions with Swynford produced the Classic winners Ferry, who won the 1000 Guineas in 1918, and Sansovino, who won the Derby six years later.

On his form as a whole Sansovino could not be regarded as one of the best of Derby winners, but he was a big strong colt, able to gallop through some of the wettest and worst going ever seen on Derby day far better than any of his rivals, and he won by 6 lengths from St Germans. Sansovino was the first horse to carry the 'black, white cap' colours of the Earls of Derby to victory in their eponymous race since Sir Peter 137 years earlier, and Eddie Derby permitted himself a little jig of triumph as he waited in the pouring rain for Tommy Weston to ride Sansovino back to be led into the winner's enclosure.

Sansovino never rose to the same heights again, and was beaten by St Germans in the Coronation Cup over the Derby course a year later. Nevertheless, his place in the annals of the Turf, and particularly of the Derby family's connection with racing, was secure. His Epsom victory epitomized the arrival of Eddie Derby at the very summit of achievement as an owner–breeder. He had written to Lambton at the end of the 1923 season:

To be head of the winning owners and breeders: to have the racehorse of the year which has won more money than any other [Tranquil]: to have the winning stallion: and to have all four stallions in the first 25 [Swynford 1st, Stedfast 8th, Phalaris 12th and Chaucer 24th]: is a record which I should think has never been equalled, and certainly never beaten, and it is to you that all this is due.

Derby's eminence was consolidated in 1924 when, thanks mainly to Sansovino and Pharos, he was second in the lists of winning owners and breeders. Tranquil, who won the 1000 Guineas and the St Leger and had stakes earnings of £20,707 in 1923, had confirmed the wisdom of the purchase of Gondolette, because Tranquil was by Swynford out of Serenissima, the Minoru filly Gondolette was carrying at the time. A year before Tranquil was born Serenissima produced the filly Selene to a mating with Chaucer. Selene was small – so small that Lambton struck her out of the Classic races, for which horses had to be entered as yearlings in those days, at the earliest opportunity. That proved to be a bad mistake. Selene became one of the best two-year-old fillies of 1921, finishing second in the Queen Mary Stakes at Royal Ascot and winning the Cheveley Park Stakes at Newmarket. As she was out of the Classic races Lambton took the step, unusual in the case of a three-year-old filly, of entering her in the Coronation Cup, and she was second to the four-year-old colt Franklin. She could almost certainly have won the St Leger, which was won by the second-class Royal Lancer. Instead she won the 'Fillies' St Leger', the Park Hill Stakes, and went on to beat a high-class field for the Hampton Court Great Three-Year-Old Stakes. By the end of the season she was so superior to her remaining contemporaries that Lambton was eager to keep her in training for another season. However, in this instance Derby, so often undecided, was adamant that her stud career should begin without delay. 'I see the temptation . . . but I have definitely decided not only is she to go out of training but that she is to be covered next year as I disagree with Walter's proposal to give her a rest for a year. I think it is absolutely unnecessary,' he wrote to Lambton.

What Selene might have achieved if she had raced as a four-year-old is a matter for guesswork, but Derby was certainly right to overrule Alston's wish to rest her. Selene's initial mating to Phalaris produced Sickle, who was one of the best two-year-olds of 1926 when he won three races and was second a head behind the subsequent Derby winner Call Boy, to whom he was conceding 3 lb, in the Middle Park Stakes. The next year Sickle confirmed his high class by finishing third to Adam's Apple and Call Boy in the 2000 Guineas. The mating to Phalaris was repeated immediately and the second time produced the equally talented Pharamond, who won the Middle Park Stakes. Both Sickle and Pharamond were exported to the United States and exerted a beneficial influence there.

As far as Selene was concerned, the best was still to come. In 1929 she was mated with the wartime Triple Crown winner Gainsborough and the produce was a diminutive but perfectly formed chesnut colt with four white feet, who was given the name of Hyperion. His small stature had been handed down through his genealogical tree from Canterbury Pilgrim, to Chaucer, to Selene. Lambton had learned his lesson, and this time did not strike Canterbury Pilgrim's descendant out of Classic engagements on account of his size. Indeed, as early as March of his two-year-old season Lambton was remarking in the notes of the horses in training he sent to Derby: 'Hyperion. Wants more time but goes well and a nice horse.' Although he was a May foal, Hyperion developed so rapidly that he was able to go to Royal Ascot after one preliminary race at Doncaster and gain a brilliant victory in the New Stakes. He won by 3 lengths from the filly Nun's Veil, whose experienced trainer Fred Darling had considered her sure to win. His time of 61 seconds was two fifths of a second faster than that of Gold Bridge, the best three-year-old sprinter, in the Granville Stakes over the same 5 furlongs on the same afternoon. He did not show the same scintillating form in his three subsequent races that season, but the fact that a colt bred purely for middle-distance racing should possess such brilliance augured well for the future.

Hyperion wintered well. Lambton stated in his notes to Derby in the early spring: 'Hyperion. Has grown a little and everywhere. Could not look better.' All efforts were concentrated on getting him to the peak of fitness for Derby day. He won his preliminary race, the Chester Vase, without much trouble, and dealt with his rivals at Epsom in most decisive fashion, winning by 4 lengths from King Salmon in the then record time of 2 minutes 34 seconds. Again Eddie Derby, beaming his happiness, was in the enviable position of waiting for Tommy Weston to ride back to him on a Derby winner, and leading him into the unsaddling enclosure, this time in the sunshine of a pleasant June afternoon.

Hyperion won the St Leger with sure authority but his three-year-old season, in which he was unbeaten in four races, ended on a discordant note when Derby, after much heart-searching, decided to dismiss Lambton. A few years earlier when Lambton had ceased temporarily to train Derby's horses he had been retained as racing manager while Frank Butters did the training, but this time the breach was complete. Colledge Leader was appointed as Lambton's successor, but the new arrangement began badly when Hyperion, after winning his first two races as a four-year-old, failed to stay in the Ascot Gold Cup, and was beaten by a short head by his solitary opponent, the three-year-old Caithness to whom he was conceding 29 lb, in the Dullingham Stakes on the Newmarket July Course. Thus the racing career of Hyperion ended in anticlimax, but nothing could take away the glory of his performances in the New Stakes and in the Classic races. A true gentleman of a horse, he retired to the Woodland Stud and became one of the mainstays of British Classic breeding and a potent influence on the top-class Thorough-bred all over the world.

Apart from the burgeoning of the families founded by Anchora and Gondolette, the most persistent factor in the success of Derby's breeding in the period between the two world wars was the amazing

71

fruitfulness of the nick between Phalaris and Chaucer mares. A nick, as defined by Sir Charles Leicester in his book *Bloodstock Breeding* (1957), is said to exist when a certain line of blood appears to have an affinity for, and to produce exceptional results when mated to, another specific line. When mated with Chaucer mares Phalaris sired Fairway, Pharos, Fair Isle, Sickle and Pharamond, whose deeds have been described already, and other top-class horses like Colorado, who won the 2000 Guineas and the Eclipse Stakes and was third in the Derby, the Eclipse Stakes winner Caerleon, and Warden of the Marches, who won the Champion Stakes and was third in the St Leger. All those horses except the last-named were bred by Derby, who owned both stallions, and it is also true that Phalaris was in his prime as a stallion at a time when many Chaucer mares were in their prime as producers. It is tempting to conclude that proximity and opportunity contributed to the success of Phalaris on Chaucer mares. Nevertheless, the researches of Leicester showed that Chaucer mares were mated with many other good stallions without attaining anything like the same rate of success. There really was an affinity between Phalaris and Chaucer mares for which there was no logical explanation and which, by no other agency than pure chance, provided a huge bonus in favour of Derby's breeding operations for more than a decade.

The only trouble with a nick, as Adrian Scrope, Derby's stud manager for the last dozen years of his life, pointed out long afterwards, is that as the scope for exploiting it dwindles inevitably with the passing of time, the breeder who has been the main beneficiary is left high and dry. He has to experiment with new pedigree combinations in his attempt to maintain the momentum of his breeding operations. There was no evidence that the efficacy of the Phalaris–Chaucer cross was projected in the next generation of their descendants; and for Derby the consequent dilemma was aggravated in the middle and late 1930s by diminishing returns, in terms of class, from the once dominant Anchora and Gondolette families.

One other strain of long standing in the Derby studs was helping to eke out the deficiency of high-class performers by bearing fruit after lying dormant for a couple of generations. This sprang from a mare appropriately named Bridget. This latter-day Bridget had been purchased for only 840 guineas as a six-year-old in 1894 and bred Santa Brigida, winner of the Yorkshire Oaks and third in the

Oaks for the sixteenth Earl. This Bridget's notable descendants were Tide-Way (by Fairway), winner of the 1000 Guineas in 1936; Heliopolis (by Hyperion), winner of the Princess of Wales's Stakes and third in the Derby in 1939; and Sun Stream (also by Hyperion), winner of the 1000 Guineas and the Oaks in 1945 – all out of the Swynford mare Drift.

Despite the providential resurgence of the Bridget family there would have been an unmistakable falling-off in the overall standards of the Derby bloodstock during the Second World War but for the benefits of an earlier infusion of French thoroughbred strains. Derby had developed a keen interest in French racing while he was ambassador in Paris, when he had considered it his duty to support the recovery of the thoroughbred industry from the ravages of the First World War and the suspension of all racing in France. At the same time he was flattered by the enthusiastic appreciation which his support received from the French racing community, who welcomed him as a symbol of everything that was most sporting and admirable in their concept of an English nobleman.

Derby's first Classic victory in France was with Frisky, who won the French 1000 Guineas in 1922. He also entered into partnerships with the American Ogden Mills and his daughter Lady Granard, winning the Grand Prix de Paris with Cri de Guerre and Capiello, the French Oaks with En Fraude and the Prix de l'Arc de Triomphe with Kantar. He also made a substantial investment in French breeding. He sent Pharos to spend most of his stud career at the Haras d'Ouilly in Normandy, a move which enabled Pharos to make his name as an international stallion and sire such great and influential horses as Nearco and Pharis II. He also maintained a French breeding operation of about a dozen mares at Jean and Elisabeth Couturié's Haras du Mesnil in the Sarthe. Lambton, after visiting Le Mesnil at Derby's request, reported that both yearlings and foals were wonderfully clean in the legs and joints. 'I should say you could breed hard stuff at that stud,' he concluded. In 1935 Derby won the French 1000 Guineas with the Le Mesnil-bred The Nile, and other good horses bred for him there included Shining Tor, who had undoubted class though finally condemned as 'an absolute thief', the Prix du Cadran winner Nepenthe and Lighthouse II.

The Couturiés' own breeding also had a direct impact on Derby's bloodstock and his later Classic success. In 1926 Jean Couturié sent

73

a filly by Rabelais to the Deauville yearling sales and Derby bought her for 95,000 francs on the advice of his beloved only daughter Victoria, who was to be killed in a hunting accident the following year. This filly, Ranai, was small, but had useful precocious speed and won races over 4 and 4½ furlongs in France as a two-year-old. Afterwards Derby sent her to stud in England. Clearly there were no great expectations of her as a broodmare, as she was not sent to leading stallions in her early years at stud. However, she bred winners consistently, and in 1938 she was upgraded and sent to Fairway, with the result that she bred the Derby winner Watling Street. Two years later another mating of Ranai with Fairway produced Garden Path, who became the first filly to beat the colts in the 2000 Guineas since Sceptre in 1902. It was a bold decision by Derby's trainer Walter Earl to direct her to the 2000 Guineas, but as her time for the mile on the Newmarket July course was three fifths of a second faster than that of Picture Play when winning the 1000 Guineas the previous day, it is fair to assume that Garden Path could have won either race. The decision to challenge the colts again in the Derby did not meet with success, and Garden Path was unplaced behind Ocean Swell.

Another of Derby's acquisitions from France was Aileen, purchased privately as a ten-year-old in 1928 from Jean Couturié's cousin, the Duc Decazes. Aileen had been an exceptionally tough performer, winning eleven races on the flat and four over hurdles. She was in foal to Tricard when Derby bought her, and the resulting colt Trickster was gelded and exported to Ceylon. After that Aileen's stud record became disastrous. She produced dead fillies in 1930 and 1931, and was not covered in the latter year. She was barren to her matings of 1932 and 1933. As a measure of despair she was sent in 1934 to Schiavoni at the Thornton-le-Street Stud in Yorkshire, which had been added to the Derby group of studs for the main purpose of rearing the weaned foals. Schiavoni lacked nothing in pedigree, as he was by Swynford out of Serenissima and was a full brother of Tranquil. But he had none of Tranquil's class; he did not run until he was four owing to leg trouble, and the best of his five victories gleaned from three seasons in training was gained in the Liverpool Spring Cup, in which he carried the light weight of 7 st 7 lb. However, he justified his retention as a stallion by getting Aileen in foal. The produce was the filly Schiaparelli, who as a performer was no better than a useful stayer, winning five races at distances of about 1½ miles as a three-year-old. As a broodmare Schiaparelli was an instant success, because her first mating was with the Eclipse Stakes winner King Salmon and produced Herringbone, winner of the 1000 Guineas and the St Leger in 1943.

Derby's ventures in French breeding paid rich dividends in terms of both his own operation at Le Mesnil and connections which provided mares like Ranai and Aileen, who helped to revitalize his English studs at a time when some of his old thoroughbred families seemed to be in decline. During the Second World War and the German occupation Derby's bloodstock in France were transferred to the name of the Marquis de St Sauveur, who managed his racing interests there, in order to avoid forfeiture by the Germans. Pharos had died in 1937, but St Sauveur moved Derby's remaining stallions Plassy and Fair Copy to his own stud, the Haras de Bréville near Caen. During the Normandy invasion in 1944 British Paratroops landed on part of the stud. In the ensuing chaos Plassy disappeared and was presumed to have been seized by the Germans, and Fair Copy got loose and was later found in a butcher's orchard and brought home to England. When the war ended Derby's French operations were in disarray and he was disinclined to make the effort and the investment required to revive them.

Indeed Eddie Derby was an old and a tired man in the summer of 1945. He died on 4 February 1948, when only Alycidon was on hand to remind the British racing community of the glories achieved by Derby-bred horses bearing the black and white colours during the past half century.

It is necessary to make a brief expedition into the usually arid field of statistics in order to convey the magnitude of the achievements of the seventeenth Earl of Derby as a breeder. The objective of every owner–breeder aspiring to produce top-class horses is to win the Derby first and foremost, and after the Derby the other four Classic races. For much of his life Eddie Derby stood out as the Englishman most likely to attain those aims. His record in the Classic races speaks for itself, as he bred sixteen winners of twenty Classic races in a span of twenty-nine years. His Classic victories were:

1000 Guineas: Canyon (1916), Ferry (1918), Tranquil (1923), Tide-Way (1936), Herringbone (1943) and Sun Stream (1945).
Oaks: Toboggan (1928), Sun Stream (1945).
2000 Guineas: Colorado (1926), Garden Path (1944).
Derby: Sansovino (1924), Hyperion (1933) and Watling Street (1942).
St Leger: Swynford (1910), Keysoe (1919), Tranquil (1923), Fairway (1928), Hyperion (1933) and Herringbone (1943).

He was first in the list of winning owners in Britain six times and first in the list of winning breeders nine times. Stallions that he had bred and retained for stud duty dominated the list of sires of winners in the British Isles time after time. Hyperion was leading sire of winners six times, Fairway four times, Phalaris twice and Swynford and Pharos once each. Pharos was also top of the sires list in France once. Of the Derby-bred and retained stallions who were first in the list of sires of winners, Colorado was second twice and Chaucer once. The marvellous results of 1923 have been mentioned. Other years in which the dominance of Derby's stallions was specially marked were 1925, when Phalaris and Swynford were first and second; 1936, when Fairway, Pharos and Bosworth were first, third and fourth, 1939, when Fairway, Hyperion and Caerleon were first, second and fourth; 1942, when Hyperion and Fairway were first and second; and 1944, when Fairway and Hyperion were first and second.

The beneficial influence of Derby stallions has not been confined to the British Isles or even to Europe. Hyperion has been one of the most potent and enduring factors in Classic breeding all over the world in the second half of the twentieth century. Swynford founded a powerful Classic dynasty through his son Blandford. Pharos's son Nearco is a pervasive and universal influence in Classic pedigrees as the male-line ancestor of great stallions like Northern Dancer, Royal Charger and Nasrullah. The Fairway male line lived on in the Derby winners Grundy, Troy and Shergar. Phalaris's son Sickle stands at the root of the flourishing American male line that leads through Native Dancer to Raise A Native, Exclusive Native and Mr Prospector. It is clearly true that strains emanating from the studs of the seventeenth Earl of Derby were the cornerstones of top-class racehorse breeding everywhere in the second half of the twentieth century.

One of the most striking features of the success of the breeding operations of the seventeenth Earl of Derby is that he achieved it with many fewer mares than some of the other breeders who have dominated the Classic scene at various stages of thoroughbred history. He had twenty-six mares in 1914, thirty-one in 1930 and twenty-six in 1947, and a broodmare band of this size is not large in relation to the worldwide influence that Derby's breeding has exerted.

The potency of the Phalaris–Chaucer nick was certainly a matter of luck, but it would be absurd to attribute the whole, lasting dominance of Classic breeding by the Derby studs to this single essential ingredient of every successful breeding enterprise. There is plenty of evidence of the vital contribution made by intelligent planning and practical efficiency to the progress of the Derby studs. Success sprang, to a degree found in few breeding operations, from purchases of fillies and mares chosen for their suitability as mates for the home stallions. An equally important factor was Derby's judgement in the selection of the men to serve his racing and breeding interests, and his readiness to accept their expert advice. His engagement of John Griffiths, and purchase of Canterbury Pilgrim when Griffiths urged him to do so, set the tone of his policy. His engagement of Lambton as trainer and Walter Alston, and later Adrian Scrope, as stud managers also were inspired choices. Lambton and Alston worked together harmoniously for many years. Lambton was charming and urbane as well as thoroughly professional, and had a sense of style expressed in the angle at which he always wore his favourite squashed and battered homburg. His intimate knowledge of the way generations of Derby's horses behaved in training and on the racecourse made an invaluable contribution to the team's deliberations, though he made a rare and surprising blunder, in view of his experience with her ancestors, when he struck Selene out of her Classic engagements.

Alston was exceptionally well read in the literature of the thoroughbred, was pragmatical in his approach to the problems of breeding and was a slave to no crack-brained theories. He was very definite in his opinions and required tactful handling. As Lambton once wrote to Derby: 'The difficult part of the situation is that he [Alston] thought, and still thinks, that everything is absolute perfection and that it cannot be improved on.' As he grew older and became increasingly a martyr to asthma his formerly tight grasp of every aspect of stud management began to falter. When Scrope took over, after a short interval during which Jack Paine held the reins, he found the paddocks at Thornton-le-Street deplorably neglected. The yearlings leaving there to go into training tended to be light of bone and to have compacted feet, the classical signs of horse-sick paddocks. Scrope advised Derby that £40,000 needed to be spent to put the stud right and Derby agreed, with the admonition that he expected to see results from such heavy expenditure. The results were not slow in coming and took the form of the Second World War spate of Classic winners.

Alston's practice was to submit each autumn a list of proposed matings for the next covering season, and these were discussed by Derby, his wife Alice and Lambton before the list was finally settled. Alice Derby had a profound understanding of horses in general besides detailed knowledge of thoroughbreds and their pedigrees. Scrope followed the same practice, though Lambton was no longer the trainer. He found that Derby would usually accept his recommendations, though he had to be prepared to give a logical reason for each proposed mating. An example of this was the mating of Aurora with Brumeux in her first stud season in 1940. Brumeux had been a good stayer who gained his principal victory in the Jockey Club Cup over 2¼ miles, but he had been virtually ignored by breeders, and stood at a fee of £24 19s. However, Scrope liked him because he was one of the few sons of the French Classic stallion Teddy available in England, and had the stamina and toughness that Aurora lacked. Derby was persuaded and the produce of the mating was Borealis, a top-class middle-distance horse who was third in the St Leger and won the Coronation Cup.

This kind of mating was in the tradition of the matings of Anchora to Chaucer and Gondolette to Swynford which prepared the way for breeding some of Derby's most talented horses. Beside this strictly practical attitude, there are two more theoretical aspects of Derby's mating policies that must be emphasized. One was the judicious use of inbreeding, and the other was the repetition of matings deemed to be fraught with special promise. It may be no more than coincidence that no breeder in the history of the thoroughbred in Britain has embraced the idea of inbreeding with greater enthusiasm, or applied it more persistently, than Eddie Derby's great-great-grandfather. The twelfth Earl's first experiment in inbreeding involved his Derby winner Sir Peter and his threequarters sister Wren, a winner of fifteen races. This experiment was successful and produced four valuable offspring. In later experiments, however, he used less and less gifted stallions and mares and achieved progressively worse results. Eddie Derby carefully avoided the same mistake and never ventured into matings of stallions and mares as closely related as Sir Peter and Wren. His inbreedings used only individuals of the highest racing class and proven breeding value like Galopin and his son St Simon, and Pilgrimage and her daughter Canterbury Pilgrim. Of his sixteen individual Classic winners, only three – Herringbone, Swynford and Toboggan – did not have a duplication of one of those four ancestors at least as close as the third and fourth removes. All his Derby winners were inbred; Sansovino was inbred to Pilgrimage in the third remove, and Hyperion and Watling Street both had duplications of St Simon in the third and fourth removes.

Derby expounded his theory of repeating matings to Elisabeth Couturié on one of his visits to Le Mesnil to see his French-based bloodstock. The theory was drawn from the scientific fact of the genetic variability of the thoroughbred which means that the potentially most favourable results of any given mating may not be realized in either the first or the second offspring of it. Derby was convinced that a well-thought-out mating must be put into practice at least three times in order to give it a fair chance of success.

The repeated matings of Gondolette with Swynford and Scapa Flow with Phalaris show that he practised what he preached. The benefits of this mating policy were most strikingly demonstrated in the case of Canyon, who was inbred to Galopin in the third and fourth removes and won the 1000 Guineas in 1916. Canyon had two series of matings with Phalaris. The first mating of the first series produced Halcyon, an ordinary sprinter; on the second occasion she was barren; and the third mating produced the brilliant Colorado, winner of the 2000 Guineas. The first mating of the second series produced the second-class miler Yosemite; on the second occasion she was barren; and the third mating produced another top-class performer, the Eclipse Stakes winner Caerleon.

Eddie Derby was said to have two ambitions; to win the Derby and to be Prime Minister. He achieved the former three times, but the fulfilment of his political aspiration was denied him. He was insufficiently firm of purpose, not decisive enough in thought or action to attain the highest office of state. His weaknesses were concealed from the majority of his countrymen, who were aware only of his manifest national and local patriotism, his magnanimity in public affairs and the grandness of his way of life. Nor did his weaknesses debar him from an unprecedented, and probably unrepeatable, degree of success and influence as an owner–breeder of thoroughbreds. Yet in some of his relationships on the Turf he betrayed those flaws of character just as clearly as he did in any of his transactions in the wider field of politics.

His difficulty in making decisions and adhering to them was evident in his hesitancy over the release of Steve Donoghue for the 1921 Derby. Derby had first claim on the services of Donoghue, the master jockey at Epsom at the time, but his Derby candidate Glorioso was a forlorn hope. Jack Joel and his trainer Charles Morton made overtures to Derby to release Donoghue to ride their strongly fancied candidate, and eventual winner, Humorist, but Derby temporized repeatedly, alternately encouraging and dashing their hopes, before giving his consent at the last moment. Even then he summoned Morton to his box at Epsom on Derby day and read him a lecture on the rights of an owner to the services of his retained jockey, saying peevishly that this was the first and last time he would ever agree to release his jockey for the Derby.

Derby was of course perfectly entitled to argue that the jockey he retained should ride for him. What was less admirable was his vacillation and his ungraciousness after he had agreed to release him.

Derby was equally changeable in his attitudes to Tommy Weston, who rode his first two Derby winners Sansovino and Hyperion. In the early 1930s he began to think that Weston had lost his nerve, and in the middle of 1932 wrote to Lambton complaining of the jockey's 'extraordinary reluctance to go up to the tapes' and insisting that he could not retain him for another season; but he changed

The sixteenth Duke of Norfolk walks to the paddock with the Queen on Derby day at Epsom, where he acted as a steward for many years. They are followed by the Queen Mother

Above: Ragstone, ridden by Ron Hutchinson, in the park at Arundel. The best horse bred by the sixteenth Duke of Norfolk, Ragstone won the most important European stayers' race, the Ascot Gold Cup

Right: Lord Derby, here pictured at an official dinner

Facing page:
Above: Lord Derby's Hyperion, winner of the Derby and the St Leger in 1933, while in training at Stanley House, Newmarket. He became one of the most influential stallions of the twentieth century

Below: Lord Derby's Swynford, winner of the St Leger in 1910. His life was saved when he broke a leg in training the next year, and he became a leading Classic stallion

Phalaris, though limited in stamina as a racehorse, became a
dominant factor in classic breeding throughout the world

his mind, and Weston justified the reprieve by riding Hyperion confidently to victory in the Derby and the St Leger the next year.

There is no doubt of Derby's affection for Lambton, and his generosity to his principal trainer during his frequent periods of ill health was remarkable. But he never had the same warm feelings towards Lambton's wife Cicely, whom he suspected of meddling in the running of the stable, especially when Lambton was away, and of working betting coups on his horses. The fact that Lambton invariably began his letters to Derby 'My dear Eddie', whereas Cicely began hers 'My dear Lord Derby', or even 'Dear Lord Derby', conveys the fundamental difference between the two relationships.

Derby's suspicions were aroused acutely in 1931 when Caerleon won the Eclipse Stakes at 25–1 and Lambton was summoned by the Sandown Stewards to explain the horse's improved form compared with his inconspicuous running in his previous races that season. Although the explanation was accepted, Derby did not easily forgive the slur on the integrity of his stable and surmised that Cicely had had a substantial bet on the horse. The idea festered in his mind and two years later, at the end of the season in which Hyperion won two Classic races, he finally decided to dismiss Lambton. The letter of dismissal made great play with Lambton's health problems and, in giving the news that he had appointed Colledge Leader as his successor, summed up on a note of pure humbug: 'Your skill has been backed up by your pluck and enthusiasm during the last six months, when you have, in the training of Hyperion, had the biggest triumph of your always successful career, but to continue at that pressure would be too great a sacrifice of yourself.'

If Eddie Derby was guilty of insincerity at this time, he could hardly be acquitted on a simultaneous charge of deviousness. He had prepared a memorandum for the dismissal, anticipating every objection that Lambton might make with his own counter-arguments. He gave away his true reason for making the break when he wrote down this riposte to a possible suggestion that Lambton should continue as trainer with an assistant to take over most of the arduous routine work:

I was told on very good authority that nobody would accept this position as long as Cicely had the influence she has and gave the orders which she did do, nominally through you, though there is no doubt in the summer she took an authority with regard to the stables which personally I resented at the time.

Lambton had to go, though the timing, in the year of Hyperion's triumph, and the manner of his dismissal did Derby little credit. His departure, and the death of Walter Alston the same year, marked the end of an era. For although Derby had seven Classic victories still to come, none of his later horses, with the exception perhaps of Herringbone, founded dynasties or families or exerted worldwide influence on the same scale as Swynford, Phalaris, Pharos, Fairway, Hyperion, Scapa Flow and Selene. The relatively small influence of Derby's horses bred after Hyperion was no doubt largely a matter of the fluctuating fortunes of breeding a genetically variable animal. There was no fresh nick to replace the fortuitously prolific Phalaris–Chaucer cross, no obvious scope for inbreeding to individual horses and mares as dominant as St Simon and Pilgrimage. The fact remains that the age of the supreme greatness of the Derby studs which lasted from the second to the fifth decade of the century was the product of a team of which John Griffiths – until his death at the end of the First World War – Lambton and Alston were the wise and experienced members, and with whom Derby must share the credit for the achievements of his breeding.

3

Elisabeth Couturié
1904–82

In the summer of 1908 William Chanler, an American seeking to set up a breeding operation in France, called at Le Mesnil on the outskirts of the village of Savigné l'Evêque and 8 kilometres from the city of Le Mans in the Sarthe. Le Mesnil, a 1000-hectare property owned by Jean Couturié and his stepmother, comprised a turreted chateau dating from the seventeenth century, large areas of woodland and some general farming land, with a dairy herd and extensive cultivation of potatoes, maize and asparagus. It was practically virgin land as far as stud farming was concerned, though for years Jean Couturié had kept one or two half-bred mares to supply himself with horses for his favourite pastimes of hunting and steeplechasing.

During lunch Chanler asked him 'Do your cows give a good milk yield?' And when Couturié replied in the affirmative he added, 'What makes for good milk yield also makes bone in thoroughbreds. If you will build ten boxes I will send you a stallion and some mares.'

This chance conversation led to the foundation of a stud which was to become one of the most famous thoroughbred nurseries in the world under the control first of Jean Couturié and his stepmother, then of Jean Couturié and his wife Elisabeth, and finally of Elisabeth Couturié alone for thirty-four years after the death of her husband in 1948. There was a golden age in the 1950s and 1960s when Right Royal, the finest product of Le Mesnil, won the French 2000 Guineas, the French Derby and the King George VI and Queen Elizabeth Stakes and Le Mesnil-bred colts won the Grand Criterium, the foremost two-year-old race in France, five times in the space of nine years. During the last three and a half decades of her life, when the fortunes of Le Mesnil lay entirely in her hands, her idealism, her tireless crusading for quality and integrity in every aspect of Turf affairs, made Elisabeth Couturié the keeper of the conscience of French racing. She was, as Guy de la Brosse wrote in the magazine *L'Eperon*, the '*Grande Dame des Courses* in the best sense of the term'.

Chanler was as good as his word. Not that the Le Mesnil venture brought him much joy or profit. The stallion Olympian was a complete failure and the mares he sent from America bred him few winners of note. On the other hand, the patronage of Chanler had an absolutely vital formative influence on Le Mesnil as a thoroughbred stud. One of the original mares was Simper, who in 1910 had a daughter called Grignouse. Eight years later Grignouse in turn produced a filly by the local stallion Helicon. This filly was born with a twisted leg and Chanler, who had no time for cripples unfit to race, gave orders that she should be put down. However, the filly, a light chestnut in colour, was otherwise attractive and showed a lot of qaulity, and Couturié pleaded for her life and that he should be allowed to buy her. Chanler acceded to his request, but refused to accept any payment for a filly in his estimation worthless. So La Grelée, as she was named came to Couturié as a gift, and became the priceless foundation mare of the Haras du Mesnil.

Helicon was not a top-class racehorse. His three victories were gained in the Hastings Plate over 1¼ miles at Newmarket and the North Derby of 1½ miles at Newcastle as a three-year-old, and the Redcar Welter Handicap over 1¼ miles the following year. Nor did he shine brightly as a sire of winners. But he did exert a powerful and enduring influence as the sire of two great broodmares. They were Hélène de Troie, who bred the French Oaks winner Adargatis and La Troienne of worldwide fame; and La Grelée who, as Elisabeth Couturié remarked many years later, 'bred us nothing but Classic horses'.

The best of the offspring of La Grelée was Rialto, a chestnut with four white legs by St Simon's son Rabelais, who stood at the Haras de Montfort only six miles from Le Mesnil. Rialto, foaled in 1923, was sold to Jean Stern as a yearling and, although he did not win a Classic race, showed form of undoubted Classic standard. He won nine races, eight of them in succession, including the now Group 1 Prix d'Ispahan, and was second in the Prix de l'Arc de Triomphe. After he had finished racing Stern returned him to the care of Jean

Couturié, and he became the first of a long line of great stallions to stand at Le Mesnil. Stern also began the practice of keeping mares at Le Mesnil, where numerous high-class performers including the French St Leger and Arc winner Biribi, the Grand Criterium winner Pantalon, the Prix d'Ispahan winner Sanguinetto (by Rialto), the Grand Prix de Deauville winner Saint Preux and the Prix du Cadran winner Hern the Hunter were bred for him before the Second World War.

The only Classic winner bred by La Grelée was Roahouga who was successful in the French 1000 Guineas, but Alcyon won the Prix d'Ispahan, Romeo was second in the French 2000 Guineas and fourth in the 2000 Guineas, and Phébé was third in the French 1000 Guineas.

La Grelée bred ten winners altogether and Phébé nine. It was thanks to Phébé that the influence of the La Grelée family was woven like a continuous thread through the whole history of Le Mesnil down to the death of Elisabeth Couturié. One of the family's most brilliant members was Tahiti, a filly of nervous disposition who had a goat as her constant companion; she won the French Oaks and was second in the French 1000 Guineas. Tahiti was the great granddam of Rex Magna, who was by Right Royal and brought great joy to the last years of Elisabeth Couturié's life by winning the French St Leger for her in 1977 and returning to Le Mesnil as a stallion. It was not only at Le Mesnil that the La Grelée family flourished. Scions of the family bred elsewhere included Argument, winner of the Washington D.C. International in 1980, and Kingston Town, a horse of towering ability in Australia at the same period.

Although Chanler had given away a filly who was to become a marvellous broodmare, La Grelée, he was not entirely without compensation. Grignouse, the dam of La Grelée, also bred him the colt Grand Guignol to another mating with Rabelais, and Grand Guignol had enough ability to win the now Group 2 Prix Noailles at Longchamp as a three-year-old. From the point of view of the evolution of Le Mesnil, the patronage of William Chanler was also vital because it established an American connection which resulted in a long and close relationship with the Widener family. Joe Widener, who was one of the leading owner–breeders in the United States, England and France during the 1920s and 1930s, sent mares to Le Mesnil before the end of the First World War and had an early Classic victory with a colt bred there when Pendennis, by Rabelais, won the French 2000 Guineas in 1920. Before the outbreak of the Second World War he had raced half a dozen other top-class horses bred at Le Mesnil, namely Confidence, Astronomer, Fastnet, Victrix, Castel Fusano and Gossip.

When Lord Derby was appointed British ambassador to France in 1918 he lost no time in involving himself in French racing. He began to keep some mares at Le Mesnil and as early as 1922 won the French 1000 Guineas with Frisky. Frisky proved an excellent foundation for his breeding interests in France, and returned to Le Mesnil and produced for him Turbulent, who won the Grand Criterium and the Prix d'Ispahan, and Nepenthe, who won the principal French test of stamina, the Prix du Cadran. Before the outbreak of the Second World War, horses bred for Derby at Le Mesnil had included a second winner of the French 1000 Guineas, The Nile, and other high-class performers like Shining Tor, who won Deauville's big mile race, the Prix Jacques le Marois, and the versatile filly Ad Astra, who won the now Group 1 Prix Morny over 6 furlongs at Deauville as a two-year-old, and was second in the French Oaks the following year. Nor was the influence of Le Mesnil beneficial to Derby's interests in France only. The Le Mesnil-bred Ranai, purchased for him by his daughter Victoria as a yearling at Deauville in 1926, was taken to England where she bred two wartime Classic winners, the 1942 Derby winner Watling Street and Garden Path, who was successful in the 2000 Guineas two years later.

By the mid-1920s Le Mesnil was established as a high-flying commercial breeding enterprise with wider international associations than any comparable stud in France.

Jean and Elisabeth Couturié were married on 20 January 1927. They had a family connection because his stepmother was her aunt. They had an additional link through the close involvement of both their families with horses. Elisabeth's father, Charles Raoul-Duval, was passionately fond of equine sports, particularly polo, hunting and racing; her mother Beatrice was the youngest of twelve children of Richard Tobin, who emigrated from Ireland to Chile as a young man, moved on to California in 1847 and, after working at first as secretary to the Archbishop of San Francisco, set up in legal practice on his own and then founded the Hibernia Bank. The Tobins were an ardent polo-playing family, and the Raoul-Duvals spent most of their winters foxhunting in Leicestershire.

Elisabeth was ten years old and on holiday with her Tobin relations in California when the First World War broke out. She stayed there for the duration of the war, receiving her education at the Convent of the Sacred Heart at Menlo Park and spending most of her spare time riding the Tobin polo ponies. She returned to Europe at the end of the war and completed her education at the Convent of the Sacred Heart at Roehampton. Important results of her unconventional upbringing were that she was completely bilingual in French and English, was a first-class horsewoman and, by the time she came of age, had an exceptional insight into, and appreciation of, the national characteristics of the French, the English and the Americans. These were valuable assets in the kind of life she was destined to lead.

Elisabeth Raoul-Duval was a lovely girl, with soft, naturally curling fair hair and a singular sweetness of expression. She was also a fine athlete. She excelled at tennis, playing in the various European international tournaments in the 1920s and winning the ladies singles in the Spanish championships at San Sebastian the year she was married. In those days tennis was strictly amateur, and Elisabeth's reward was a silver cup presented by the Queen of Spain.

In addition to her beauty and her intelligence, Elisabeth possessed a strength of character which was matched by her husband's. Jean Couturié broke his left leg badly jumping over a stream at the age of seven and the local doctor, wrongly diagnosing a congenital bone weakness, kept the leg in plaster for three years. When the plaster was at last removed the leg was terribly wasted and permanently shorter than the other. But he was a boy of invincible determination and, in defiance of this disadvantage, became one of the leading amateur steeplechase riders in France, riding skilfully and fearlessly over the formidable obstacles at Auteuil. Although he was exempt from military service and was ineligible for a commission, he insisted on enlisting as a private soldier in the First World War and served as chauffeur to the general commanding the 4th French Army Corps. He was decorated with the Médaille Militaire.

The union of two such strong personalities might have been inflammatory, but in fact the twenty-one years of married life of

Jean and Elisabeth Couturié were spent in happiness and harmony. They were deeply in love; moreover, they were mutually absorbed in the various equine activities centred at Le Mesnil. She gave up tennis as soon as she was married in order to concentrate on the horses. Jean kept a pack of hounds, and the winter off-seasons for stud farming were spent hunting roebuck in the woods near Le Mesnil and in the Forêt de Bercy, one of the most splendid oak forests in France, situated 25 miles to the south, where he had a hunting lodge. But mostly it was the development of the Le Mesnil stud interests that occupied their time and attention. Elisabeth wrote of the early years of their marriage:

I was almost at once passionately interested by breeding and racing. There was so much to learn. Human contacts were innumerable and most enriching. The horses themselves were beautiful and easy to love. The sporting side of the racing world was fascinating. Everybody spoke the same language; the given word was sacred and signatures were not necessary, even for very important deals. Great horses were always given generous admiration in every country and the 'Sport of Kings' was also the most democratic, especially in France where all those who contributed to the sport found immediate reward for success.

Jean and I were able each day to share a wonderful and exciting life. From the foalings at the stud to the gallops in the woods; from the visits to the stables at Chantilly to the races at Longchamp; the journeys abroad, the sales – what more could one ask for? We also had all those who worked with us and who composed a big and united family. They were just as emotionally involved as we were ourselves, and their professional conscience was unfailing even in difficult moments. We all shared together our joys and our sorrows. The farms worked in close collaboration with the studs. Yes, if it could all begin again, I would ask for the privilege of living the same life.

This was the philosophy which was to animate not only her attitudes to horse racing and stud farming but also her approach to the management of the whole Le Mesnil estate. She refined it over the years and late in life reduced it to a simple equation: 'Horses + Love + Courage + Hard Work + Hope = Happiness.'

During the dozen years between her marriage and the outbreak of the Second World War Elisabeth had the opportunity vastly to expand her knowledge of thoroughbreds in general and of top-class international breeding in particular. The boarding mares at Le Mesnil, besides those belonging to the Couturiés themselves, represented some of the choicest European strains, while men like Derby and Widener, who were frequent visitors to Le Mesnil, were walking repositories of wisdom and experience in matters concerning the thoroughbred. It was quite a daunting task for a hostess, not long married and still in her twenties, to entertain a man as grand as Derby, forty years her senior. But there were lighter moments and Derby, with his comfortable girth and rubicund geniality, never failed to put her at her ease at awkward moments. Once when Derby was staying and all the guests had gone upstairs to change for dinner, she heard sounds of anxiously raised voices and frantic footsteps in the passage. Putting her head round her bedroom door, she managed to catch the attention of Lord Derby's valet and inquire what the trouble was: Lord Derby was stuck in his bath.

Half an hour later, when the guests had assembled in the drawing room, Elisabeth felt she must say something to Derby on the delicate subject and murmured an apology for the narrowness of the bath. But Derby immediately put her at her ease by replying in his most blandly reassuring tone, 'My dear lady, don't give the matter another moment's thought. It was the first time I've seen my toes for twenty years.'

At other times there were many discussions of the theory and practice of breeding and of the individual problems of the boarding mares. As Derby kept the high-class stallions Pharos and Plassy at other French studs he had ready-made answers to the questions of mating many of the Le Mesnil-based mares. On the other hand, those two stallions were not suitable in all cases, and once when the choice of outside stallions was being considered Elisabeth suggested diffidently the name of Tourbillon, the French Derby winner of 1931, who was regarded as one of the most promising young stallions (Tourbillon was to become a truly great Classic stallion). Derby replied that he would love to use him, but could not do so because Tourbillon, being by the 'half-bred' Derby winner of 1914, Durbar II, was ineligible for the *General Stud Book* and all his progeny would be similarly excluded; that was a kind of mating which no breeder with his main stud and racing interests in England could contemplate.

Elisabeth was left pondering deeply on the question of *General Stud Book* exclusiveness. That conversation was the genesis of much of her later thinking on the inconsistencies of the rules of entry to various stud books. In the last twenty years of her life she was to become one of the leading crusaders for a policy of clearing away archaic regulations and basing stud records on merit rather than foolish notions of pure blood.

The Couturiés saw Joe Widener for the last time at Deauville in August 1939. The outbreak of the Second World War brought immediate changes to the happy and tranquil life at Le Mesnil. Elisabeth packed off their two small daughters, Sylvia and Marguerite, in the care of their governess, Wallie, to a cottage in County Waterford where they remained for the duration, being thus spared the rigours of wartime France just as Elisabeth herself had been during the First World War. All the stud staff of military age were called up for a newly formed cavalry regiment, and eighteen hunters, including Jean's favourite hunter, Merry Pal, were requisitioned. None of the horses survived the fighting of June 1940.

The farm lorry and the Couturiés' Citroën car also were requisitioned, but the Lincoln Zephyr was converted from petrol burning to steam propulsion by means of a charcoal-fired boiler and provided locomotion for essential stud purposes and for attending the races in Paris throughout the war. With only a short interruption during the summer of 1940, when the Couturiés fled to the south in front of the advancing German armies, Le Mesnil continued to operate as a top-class thoroughbred nursery.

The Couturiés returned to Le Mesnil when the situation had stabilized after the signing of the armistice by the Vichy government. Elisabeth, whose Catholic faith sustained her throughout the tribulations of the war, had left badges of the Sacred Heart in every room of the Chateau and in every cottage on the estate before their departure. On their return she found that other French families, fleeing from northern France, had occupied the farms, living off the produce and caring for the animals. Although the Germans had stolen many famous horses, including Clairvoyant and Corrida, from other studs, all the Le Mesnil bloodstock were intact and in perfect condition. The family silver, hidden under the Christmas ornaments in a cupboard set in the panelled walls of the drawing room, had not been touched and never was discovered even when the Germans requisitioned the house during the final stages of the occupation. 'The Sacred Heart badges had worked marvels,' Elisabeth commented in her wartime diary.

The Germans encouraged the continuation of racing throughout their occupation of France, partly because they realized that it was essential to maintain the standard of French bloodstock, which in turn they regarded as a source of improved stock for their own thoroughbred industry; and partly as a recreation calculated to absorb French interest and energies which might otherwise have been diverted to the Resistance. But the situation at Le Mesnil was complicated, and full of menace for the Couturiés, because they had mares and young stock belonging to Derby, Stern and Widener. In 1940 the Germans issued an order that anyone having in their custody property of Englishmen or Jews must declare it, and this was extended to the property of Americans when the United States entered the war at the end of 1941. The Couturiés decided not to declare Derby's horses, which had been transferred to the name of the Marquis de Saint Sauveur, one of the most respected figures in French racing; to claim that Stern's horses had been sequestered by themselves in discharge of unpaid keep bills; and that the Widener mares were held against expenses incurred in shipping twenty horses in training to the United States shortly before the American declaration of war.

The first crisis arose when Major Pulte of the Altenfeld Stud, who was in charge of a commission for the purchase and confiscation of valuable French bloodstock, visited Le Mesnil and said that he knew they had horses belonging to a Jew. The Couturiés argued that in the circumstances it would be a deep injury to themselves to take them. Later Pulte summoned them to his headquarters in the Majestic Hotel in Paris and informed them that he accepted their story, but would like to buy some mares. This crisis was resolved satisfactorily when Pulte agreed to buy Fidra, a mare of Derby's pronounced unfit for further breeding, for 100,000 francs, whereas a previous arrangement had been made to sell her to a local butcher for 10,000 francs.

However, that incident was succeeded by a second and worse crisis when the Couturiés were summoned to 72 Avenue Foch for an interview with the Gestapo. The interrogator began by demanding, 'Since when have you had the horses of the Jew Stern? Don't you know that it is a criminal offence to hide Jewish property?'

They told him about the settlement of Stern's debts, but he greeted the story with a cynical laugh and the threat that he would institute a complete investigation of all their activities. When they arrived home they burned all the archives concerning the Stern and Widener horses and concocted some false papers designed to corroborate their story. In due course two thoroughbred experts hired by the Gestapo went to Le Mesnil to conduct the investigation but one of them, Buhman, confided when his colleague was out of the room that he had been a guest of the Wideners in Florida before the war. The Gestapo confiscated the Stern horses and took control of the Widener horses, and the Couturiés were under constant surveillance for the rest of the German occupation, but they were convinced that the merciful coincidence of Buhman's acquaintance with the Wideners saved them from arrest.

The Couturiés were present on the terrible day, 4 April 1943, when Longchamp was bombed. American aircraft were bombing the Renault factories at Boulogne-Billancourt, which adjoins the Bois de Boulogne, when German anti-aircraft guns sited in the middle of the racecourse opened fire. The Americans attacked the guns, and bombs fell around the stands where crowds were already gathering for the start of the afternoon's racing. More than 150 civilians were killed. With a display of immense physical and moral courage, the Longchamp Stewards announced that the meeting would be held, and that all the proceeds would be distributed to the families of the dead racegoers.

After the initial tragedy, the day became one of triumph for Le Mesnil. The big race was the Prix des Sablons (since renamed the Group 1 Prix Ganay and one of the greatest French races for horses older than three-year-olds), which resulted in a deadheat between the Le Mesnil-bred colts Arcot and Tornado. Arcot, owned by Lord Derby, carried the Saint-Sauveur colours, and Tornado, owned by Joe Widener, carried the black and white lozenges of the Couturiés.

Elisabeth went on repeated missions as a courier taking messages to unoccupied France, and assisted in the escape of many prisoners and persons wanted by the Germans. It is not clear whether the Germans got wind of these activities, but as the battle of Normandy approached its climax in the summer of 1944 the Couturiés heard through underground channels that they were marked down to be shot as hostages the next time the electric cables were cut by the Resistance and that the Germans intended to blow up the house, from which the Couturiés had been evicted in April of that year. It was with inexpressible emotion and gratitude, therefore, that they watched the Germans leave in too much of a hurry to carry out their threat, and American tanks advancing across the open fields south of Savigné l'Evêque.

The Liberation brought the lifting of fear and repression, and an unalloyed joy to the Couturiés and all who had helped them to keep the Le Mesnil stud operation going in difficult times. Yet, significantly, the experience which Elisabeth found most moving in the first days of freedom was the sight of a truckload of American tank crews at mass in the little church of Savigné l'Evêque. When mass was over they remounted the truck and were driven back to rejoin their unit and continue the advance.

The reputation of Le Mesnil for producing top-class racehorses was fully upheld during the war. Arcot and Tornado were the best four-year-olds of 1943, and other Le Mesnil-bred horses that were born or raced in the war years included the Prix du Cadran winner Hern the Hunter, the Prix du Conseil Municipal winner Galene, the French 2000 Guineas winner Dogat, the Prix Ganay winner Basileus and the Grand Prix de Paris winner Avenger; and, most important of all, the wonderful little Wild Risk who, uniquely for a horse who was French champion hurdler twice and had only second-class form on the flat, became a great Classic stallion.

Nevertheless, the end of the war brought radical changes. Derby was an old man and disinclined to rebuild his breeding interest in France. Jean Stern salvaged what was left of his broodmare band and launched his own breeding operation at the Haras de Saint-Pair-du-Mont in the beautiful hilly countryside 20 miles south of Deauville. Joe Widener had died in 1943 at the age of seventy-one, and his heir Peter was neither in the best of health nor certain that he would be able to continue racing and breeding on the same scale as his father. Finally Jean Couturié, utterly exhausted by the nervous and physical strains of the war, died in 1948 at the age of sixty-two. The old order of the 1930s could never be recreated at Le Mesnil.

The Couturiés had no son and Elisabeth was left in control of the stud and estate – alone, but absolutely determined to preserve the traditions of Le Mesnil and apply the doctrine she had learned in conversations with Derby and Widener: always strive to breed Classic horses. To assist her in this aim she had, first and foremost, members of the wonderful family of La Grelée. They were to be reinforced by judicious purchases from time to time. However, the most valuable recruitment to Elisabeth's own broodmare band was to come not from any purchase but as a result of a gift. When Peter Widener decided to take home his mares from Le Mesnil in 1945 he also offered two of them to the Couturiés as a present in recognition of his family's long, happy and successful association with Le Mesnil. The mares concerned were the eleven-year-old Barberybush and the six-year-old Flying Colours. The offer was eagerly accepted.

Each of these gift mares had a far-reaching beneficial influence on Elisabeth's fortunes as a breeder. Flying Colours bred a total of ten winners of whom two, Fontenay and Le Mesnil, were top-class performers. Fontenay won two races afterwards classified Group 1, the Prix de la Forêt and the Prix Ganay; and Le Mesnil, whose name clearly indicated the high hopes that were reposed in him from an early age, won two Group 2 races, the Prix Greffulhe and the Prix Hocquart, and was second in the Prix de l'Arc de Triomphe. The daughters of Flying Colours did not achieve the same distinction on the racecourse, but had enough breeding value to support the family as a living force in the stud for the remainder of Elisabeth's lifetime.

The acquisition of Barberybush was to have even more dramatic repercussions. By Ksar, the first great racehorse bred in France after the First World War, out of Pervenchères, she was a sister of Wood Violet, the granddam of Wild Risk. Barberybush had produced the excellent Basileus, who was by Victrix, before she came into Elisabeth's possession. In 1950 Elisabeth decided to repeat the mating with Victrix but, fearing that Victrix might be losing some of his fertility at sixteen years of age, she also had the mare covered by the five years younger Tornado on the same heat period. Barberybush duly conceived and the following year gave birth to a small filly who was given the name of Bastia.

Bastia was born in the same year as Tahiti. The two fillies were brought up together and were sent into training with Etienne Pollet at Chantilly at the same time. Their achievements as racehorses were in marked contrast. Whereas Tahiti was a Classic winner, Bastia, who had a nasty temper, never won a race. On the other hand, Bastia did serve a useful purpose by leading her famous stable companion in her gallops, and even made the pace for Tahiti when she won the French Oaks. As Pollet remarked, 'When one has a filly as good as Tahiti it is necessary to sacrifice one less good to help her in her work and make her running when she needs it.' Bastia was not so devoid of ability that she could not have won a small race if that had been the prime requirement.

Bastia returned to stud at Le Mesnil. Her first foal, Chêne Bope, showed good form as a two-year-old. Elisabeth decided to send her next to Owen Tudor, the ageing Derby winner of 1941, at Newmarket. By then Owen Tudor was out of favour with many English breeders, but Elisabeth had strong reasons for selecting him. First, he was a Derby winner at a reasonable price; second, he was a son of Hyperion, and Hyperion-line stallions were rare in France as a result of the separation of the two breeding industries during the war; thirdly, Hyperion had emerged as one of the most potent influences on Classic breeding in Europe; and fourthly, Owen Tudor had done her a good turn already by siring the very fast filly Lovely Rose.

At about 7 p.m. on Sunday, 23 March 1958, the stud groom Pierre Delangle called Elisabeth and told her that Bastia was about to foal. Elisabeth liked to be present at the births whenever possible, and on this occasion she hurried to the foaling box. Years later she wrote:

Bastia was rather violent in character and her reactions were often brutal, but as soon as her foal was born she thought of nothing else but caring for him. He got on his legs very quickly after his birth with a strong graceful movement. Unlike most foals he did not wobble and went straight to suckle, showing a great desire to live. He was a very big, dark bay, with two small white socks on his hind legs. He had good limbs and a head showing great character. At once Pierre and myself realized that we had to do with a really unusual foal.

The foal was Right Royal, a name chosen from a poem by John Masefield. He grew and developed amazingly, and by the time he

went into training with Pollet in the autumn as a yearling he stood
16.1½ hands and had the physique of a three-year-old. Despite his
size he had a light and supple action and, to Elisabeth's astonishment,
Pollet proposed to run him for the first time in a maiden race over
5 furlongs at Le Tremblay in April. She had already appreciated that
the trainer considered him a Classic horse when he had replied to
her question concerning his progress, 'I must see him on a racecourse
to believe it.'

Right Royal won the Tremblay race eaily, and went on to win
the races now classified Group 1, the Prix de la Salamandre and the
Grand Criterium, and be given top weight in the French two-year-
old Free Handicap.

As a three-year-old Right Royal fully substantiated his claim to
be regarded as a great racehorse by winning five consecutive races
– the French 2000 Guineas, the Prix Lupin, the French Derby and
the Prix Foy in France, and the King George VI and Queen Elizabeth
Stakes in England. The measure of his excellence was that he beat
Match, afterwards acclaimed one of the best international performers
of his day, in the Prix Lupin, and St Paddy, the winner of the Derby
and the St Leger the previous year, in the big race at Ascot. His
victories were decisive in every case. He was undoubtedly past his
best when he was beaten into second place by the Italian colt
Molvedo in the Prix de l'Arc de Triomphe. When Right Royal left
Chantilly at the end of his three-year-old season to go to stud at Le
Mesnil, Pollet told Elisabeth that during the two years he had been
in training he had never caused him the slightest worry – neither in
his health, nor his limbs, nor his character.

For most of his career at stud Right Royal was kept fit by being
ridden out daily. His personality gradually became more masterful
and he would brook no interference with his routine, but with
patience and firmness his stallion man Henri Foulard was able to
manage him. He was only fifteen when he reared up, fell over
backwards and broke a leg so badly that there was no alternative to
have him painlessly destroyed. He was buried under a willow tree
in a tiny walled space situated between two stallion paddocks. The
grave is marked by a rectangle of granite chippings and a plain
granite headstone giving his name and the dates of his birth and
death.

The vast majority of great racehorses are disappointments as stallions for the simple reason that exaggerated hopes are reposed in them at the outset of their stud careers. On the racecourse a horse stands or falls by his own prowess; but at stud he is dependent on the quality and suitability of his mates, from whom his progeny derive half their genetic inheritance. Right Royal, the greatest racing product of Le Mesnil, was no exception to the general rule. His progeny did not sweep the board in the principal European races in the manner predicted. Nevertheless, he was certainly no failure. His progeny included Prince Regent, winner of the Irish Sweeps Derby, Ruysdael, winner of the Italian Derby; Right Away, winner of the French 1000 Guineas; Rex Magna, winner of the French St Leger; and a score of other high-class horses among whom In the Purple and Rangong distinguished themselves as leading sires in New Zealand.

The male line of Right Royal was carried on at Le Mesnil by his son Versailles, who had neither the prodigious stature, nor the athletic ability, nor the strong will of his sire. Versailles, who sprang from an old Le Mesnil family that had supplied Derby's great mare Ranai, was the kindest of stallions. He bred a few good horses like Suvannee, who was second in the French 1000 Guineas, and Viteric, who won the now Group 2 Criterium de Maisons Laffitte. He had an additional claim to fame, because he figured prominently in a breeding experiment which occupied a great deal of Elisabeth's attention during the last years of her life.

The racing career of Right Royal marked the climax of the golden age of Le Mesnil which extended throughout the 1950s and well into the 1960s. Tahiti, Le Mesnil and Lovely Rose were three of the top-class Le Mesnil products of that era. Others were Tyrone and Neptunus, who both won the Grand Criterium as two-year-olds and went on to win the French 2000 Guineas the following spring. Tiepoletto also won the Grand Criterium, and during the following winter was earmarked for the 1957 Derby, a race not normally included in the plans for Couturié horses. Unfortunately, Tiepoletto sprained a ligament early in April and the plan to send him to Epsom had to be abandoned, but he recovered in time to run second in the Grand Prix de Saint Cloud at the beginning of July. Antares, who was second in the French Derby, Fontenoy, Tosco, Toscanella,

Tracy, Demi Deuil, Principino and Cupid's Doll also were notable representatives of Le Mesnil breeding in the golden age.

No stud without continuous heavy investment on the highest international level can keep up such a hot pace indefinitely. That kind of investment was impossible at Le Mesnil, which was dependent on generating its own financial resources. Inevitably there was some falling-away in the late 1960s and the 1970s, and the French racing community lost the habit of waiting eagerly each season, as they had done in the golden age, for the advent of Le Mesnil-bred two-year-olds born to dominate the important autumn two-year-old races. However, it would be wrong to write of a general decline, for Le Mesnil continued to turn out performers of superior merit with a regularity that should have been the envy of other studs of comparable status. This secondary period was dignified by such gifted fillies as Lastarria, Dame des Ondes and Suvannee; and by talented colts like Ribécourt, who won the Group 1 Gran Premio d'Italia and the French Group 2 races the Criterium de Saint Cloud and the Prix Kergorlay; Trepan, who won the Group 2 Prix Dollar but suffered two disastrous disqualifications after finishing first in important English races; and Rex Magna.

Rex Magna had a special place in Elisabeth's affections. He was by her beloved Right Royal and came from his last crop of foals. Moreover, he resembled Right Royal closely in his dark bay colour and in many quirks of personality. In addition, he was a great grandson of Tahiti, the best filly ever bred at Le Mesnil, and so was a descendant of La Grelée. Rex Magna looked a lively proposition for the French Derby when he won the Prix Greffulhe at Longchamp in April as a three-year-old, but shortly after that race sustained a hairline pastern fracture when he put his foot in a hole on the gallops. He was out of action for six months, but came back in the autumn to win the Prix Royal Oak, then the French equivalent of the St Leger, beating the Queen's Oaks and St Leger winner Dunfermline. Rex Magna followed in his father's footsteps to take up a stud career at Le Mesnil.

Rex Magna was the last top-class horse to win for Elisabeth Couturié on the flat, but he was not her last winner of a big race. This honour belonged to Bison Futé, who won the Grande Course de Haies d'Auteuil, the French Champion Hurdle, over 5100 metres on 21 June 1981.

A favourite saying of Elisabeth was: 'All the Le Mesnil horses can jump if you want them to.' Her theory was that Jean, with his long experience of riding in steeplechases and in the hunting field, instinctively had the image of a good jumper in his mind's eye whenever he was selecting bloodstock. Of the twenty-seven mares in her last private stud book, compiled in 1981, no fewer than seven had run over jumps and six had won jumping races. This is a proportion which would not be approached in any other stud whose primary purpose was the production of Classic horses, with no specialized production for jumping at all.

There was a certain ambivalence in her attitude to jumping and jumpers. 'It is a hard and dangerous business which demands tremendous qualities of courage and patience,' she remarked in her speech at the dinner given in honour of Bison Futé in November after his victory in the Grande Course des Haies. She was referring specifically to Bison Futé's jockey Dominique Costard and trainer Jacques de Chevigny, a former champion amateur rider. But she would have applied the words equally to the horses who run successfully over hurdles and fences, believing that they had the courage and toughness which were often neglected by breeders but which must be preserved in the breed. On the other hand, she considered that prize money for jumping races in France had been boosted to crazy heights which could not be justified in view of the fact that the most valuable races could be won by geldings who were useless for breeding. The first prize for the Grande Course des Haies won by Bison Futé was 450,000 francs, as much as the French 2000 and 1000 Guineas and the Grand Prix de Paris. 'The prize money for jumpers is there and I cannot afford to ignore it.' she concluded.

She made a practice of sending a contingent of jumpers to the winter meeting at Pau, in the northern foothills of the Pyrenees, staying herself at her villa at Hossegor on the Atlantic coast and visiting the course when she had runners. She was the leading owner at the meeting with a regularity that must have been exasperating for her rivals. She had a succession of big winners there inlcuding Olympique, Apollo Quatorze, Amenti and Bison Futé himself, who won the Grand Course des Haies de Pau on the way to his more resounding victory in the corresponding race at Auteuil.

Bison Futé became a hurdler by accident. He was most attractive as a young horse and was thought to have a bright future on the flat, but he was a rig and was in such pain as a two-year-old that it became necessary to have him operated on for the removal of the testicle which had not descended. The operation pulled him down so badly that he spent more than six months convalescing at Le Mesnil. When at last he was fit to go back into training the prospects of a glittering career on the flat had vanished, and a career over obstacles was the only option. He sustained triumphantly a tradition of Le Mesnil-bred hurdlers which had been established by the two French Champion Hurdle victories of Wild Risk almost forty years earlier.

The approach to Le Mesnil lies through a double avenue of tall over-arching plane trees. At the end of the avenue white wrought-iron gates give on to a circular driveway and lawn in front of the chateau.

The chateau, though compact and charming in its general aspect, has undergone too many alterations to the roof and the turrets at the corners of its rectangular plan to be a harmonious whole. However, it is enhanced by its setting which has a tranquil perfection of its own. A stream meanders through watermeadows against a backdrop of spreading woods, and curls round the front of the chateau. There is a miniature waterfall, a lake with swans and a tiny island reached by a wooden footbridge, an ancient mill converted to agricultural use and a vast walled garden from which Elisabeth could supply not only the chateau but all the stud staff with vegetables. The walled enclosure also contained a disused hard tennis court – symbol of her conversion from the world of athletic to the world of equine sport.

The chateau was not merely Elisabeth's residence, it was the heart of the entire Le Mesnil operation. Her bedroom and small sitting room adjoined the stud office, occupied by two permanent secretaries, and the accountant's office was on the other side of the first-floor passage. The bedrooms of the *stagiares*, stud working pupils who at different times included men destined for prominence in racing like Francois Boutin, Alain de Royer-Dupré, Jeremy Hindley,

Henry Cecil and Michael Wyatt, were on the second floor. A side-board in the hall and a grand piano in the ground-floor sitting room displayed many Le Mesnil trophies; the conservatory was lined with Eugene Péchaubes pictures, resembling painted photo-finish strips, of the great Longchamp victories of the 1950s and 1960s; and the panelled walls of the drawing room at the back of the house were hung with portraits of Le Mesnil heroes like Right Royal, Le Mesnil, Tiepoletto and Neptunus, besides the great broodmare Polamia owned by the Wideners.

Elisabeth's personality pervaded the house. She loved to talk, ceaselessly expressing her ideas about the condition of the thorough-bred and the thoroughbred industry, the state of the world, declining moral standards and the threat of communism to society and to religion. But her conversation was not a constant moan, nor did it consist purely of prophecies of doom. Always she could find inspiration in individual acts of courage, of resourcefulness, and of piety and in the achievements of dedicated research workers; most particularly, she rejoiced in the devoted relationship of men and women in all walks of the thoroughbred community to the horses in their care. From her favourite low armchair in the sitting room, with the leather-cased telephone at her elbow, she could dominate a roomful of guests perched above her on upright chairs and bow-window seats.

The lives of the *stagiares* were governed by one invariable rule apart from the requirement to observe a rigorous work routine – they must be tidily dressed, with jackets and ties, and punctual for meals. Lunch and dinner were formal occasions, usually with several guests and often attended by her daughter Marguerite and son-in-law Comte Bertrand de Tarragon, who assisted in the stud management besides serving as a Steward of the Société d'Encouragement for many years. The food was simple but plentiful, always faultlessly cooked and served. All the main ingredients (meat, poultry, eggs, fruit and vegetables) came from the Le Mesnil farms, for she had a deep suspicion that most of the food bought in shops was contaminated by chemicals or tainted by factory farming. Above all she had a horror of the use of hormones and steroids in cattle and poultry rearing.

Her belief in the virtue of pure food was not confined to human diet. Indeed, the essence of her philosophy of raising thoroughbreds at Le Mesnil was insistence on proper feeding, and in her scale of values environment was exalted firmly above genetic influence. She like to tell the cautionary tale of the famous Normandy stud whose produce showed a grave deterioration of racing performance as two-year-olds. Finally a nutrition expert advised that the lush Vallée d'Auge pastures had been allowed to grow too long, and the young stock had been bloating themselves with grass with the result that they had no appetite to eat an adequate ration of oats. The paddocks were then mown short, and the produce quickly regained their precocious powers.

There was no danger of making the same mistake at Le Mesnil because the poor soil did not allow a sufficient growth of grass. 'The grass here is just a salad,' Elisabeth used to say. Instead the Le Mesnil young stock were encouraged to eat substantial quantities of oats even before they were weaned. The paddocks were equipped with mangers inside small enclosures, railed at a height which would admit only the foals so that the mares could not deprive them of their feed. The yearlings were fed oats at the rate of adult horses, while their development was assisted by the stud's own water supply rich in calcium and other trace elements. The yearlings were broken and taught to canter on a sandy track 3000 metres in circumference laid out in the woods, so that muscles and sinews were well developed before they were sent to the sales or into training. This was the regime that contrived the shining record of achievement by Le Mesnil horses in the Grand Criterium and the French 2000 Guineas.

Although this emphasis on feeding and early physical training was the hallmark of the Le Mesnil method, Elisabeth was fully aware of the crucial importance of the genetic inheritance of each thoroughbred and therefore of the intense study that must be applied to correct matings. There was evidence of this selectivity in her choice of Owen Tudor and the consequent breeding of Right Royal. She had much faith in Ribero, the winner of the Irish Sweeps Derby and the St Leger in 1968, at the beginning of his stud career. Ribero, who stood at the Sandringham Stud, proved a disappointing stallion, but Elisabeth's faith was rewarded by breeding one top-class horse by him, by name Ribécourt. She rescued Breakspear from obscurity at stud in Ireland and installed him at Le Mesnil, having been attracted to him first because he was a fast son of the prepotent Bold Ruler, whose influence in France was rare at the time, and secondly because he was a great grandson of Confidence, a Le Mesnil-bred winner of the Grand Prix de Deauville. Breakspear died of cancer at the age of eleven, but not before he too had bred one top-class horse for Elisabeth, namely Trepan.

Nevertheless, she seldom repeated matings from year to year, or for a series of years, and it is difficult to discern a definite plan or system in her selection. She once remarked, 'Many of my best matings come to me during the sermon in church,' but did not explain whether she attributed this to divine inspiration or to the opportunity afforded for quiet contemplation of all the factors involved in matching the characteristics of stallion and mare.

A corollary of Elisabeth's belief in the overriding importance of environment in the first eighteen months of the life of a thorough-bred was her conviction that skilful individual attention from trainer and lad was the key to the realization of the horse's potential racing ability after it had left the stud. The trainer should continue a logical process of development from the stage reached on the sandy tracks of Le Mesnil. For this reason Etienne Pollet, who trained all the Couturié horses during the golden age, was the ideal trainer in her eyes. Pollet had marvellous judgement of the character and capabilities of young horses; was exceptionally patient; had an expert and devoted staff; trained mostly for owner–breeders and had their interests as his first priority; and refused ever to accept more than sixty horses in his yard so that he was able to supervise each of them personally.

In later years she became progressively more disenchanted with the encroachment of commercialism into racing and breeding. She objected to the extension of the interests of some of the leading trainers into breeding, ownership and the buying and selling of horses so that they had obtained a considerable measure of control over the whole bloodstock industry; she found the incursion into breeding of immensely rich men lacking background knowledge and understanding of horses equally objectionable; and she deplored the inflation of stallion values and the attitude of mind which gave precedence to the sales prospect of a yearling over his potential class as an actual racehorse. Her own guiding principle was that the breeder should strive to produce a Classic winner with no thought

103

to its value on the yearling market; and it is true that some of the best Le Mesnil horses failed to fetch their modest reserves at Deauville and went into training as her property, though she was happy to sell shares in them when their promise became apparent in order to defray some of the escalating training costs in the 1970s.

She was convinced that following fashion among stallions meant a complete lack of discrimination by mare owners and buyers at the yearling sales. Naturally she crowed over the results of 1979 when the cheaply produced horses Le Marmot (by Amarko), Dragon (by Phaeton), Viteric (by Versailles) and the Le Mesnil-bred Pareo (by Armos), all by unfashionable stallions, were among the leading performers in Europe. By way of comment on these results she wrote: 'Many new owners know very little about the game and do not take the trouble to find out. Undoubtedly breeding will suffer from this state of affairs and a great many good stallions will not have a chance to show their value.'

Her antipathy to excessive commercialism took her to the opposite extreme of praising the small breeder as the sole champion of her ideals. In 1977 she wrote to Jacques Wimpfheimer, the wise and fair-minded chief of the American Thoroughbred Owners' and Breeders' Association: 'The small breeder with only a few mares is the backbone of the racing industry because they love their mares and breed because they have the vocation to do so.' But she drew this sharp retort: 'Undoubtedly it is true that the small breeders are very important to the racing industry, but are they the backbone? Are not those big breeders who do attempt to breed for class as well as for the market really the backbone of the industry?'

However, they found themselves in complete agreement with regard to another controversial subject, which was the restriction of a proportion of French races to native-bred horses. Elisabeth declared that France had the finest racecourses and the finest overall racing programme in the world for testing the highest class of thoroughbred, with a level of prize money that attracted the strongest international competition. The Pattern races must be open to all, but the French breeding industry, with its relatively small output, must be protected in many of the less important races if it were to survive. Wimpfheimer did not dissent from this view; indeed, it was in line with the thinking that supported protective measures for the local breeding industries in the majority of American racing states.

Elisabeth, though critical of the uglier aspects of French racing and breeding in the last dozen years of her life, was at the same time a fierce defender of the reputation of the French thoroughbred and its enduring virtues. She admitted that the French thoroughbred could not match the British for precocious speed or the American for the brilliance generated by continuous heavy investment, but remained sure that foreign breeders would always have to return to France at regular intervals to replenish their stocks of toughness and stamina.

The French fiscal system and ever rising social charges, she believed, had driven many of the large studs out of business and were forcing small breeders to send their mares and colts to the butchers to meet their costs and tax bills. At the same time the impact of capital-gains taxes applied to racehorses, the treatment of racehorses as 'external signs of wealth' for taxation purposes and high training fees were discouraging the entry of new French owners into racing. 'The sales went quite well,' she wrote after the Deauville yearling sales in 1980, 'but not a French buyer in sight.'

Elisabeth had two contrasting perceptions of the thoroughbred. One was romantic, seeing the thoroughbred as a creature of beauty and spirit to be admired with a mystical fervour; the other was more pragmatic, seeing the Thoroughbred as a breed of horses whose infinite complexity and uncertain origins invited constant study and analysis. 'What I am really trying to find out is the truth about many things which are still obscure,' she once wrote. These two perceptions were fused in the experiments with white horses which claimed a great deal of her interest during the last dozen years of her life.

On 2 June, 1963, a white thoroughbred colt was born on a small stud in the vicinity of Le Mesnil. White thoroughbreds are extremely rare and are wholly distinct from greys, which may be born bay or chestnut with only a few grey hairs, but become progressively more grey in time and sometimes end up completely white in old age. This white horse, who was given the descriptive name of Mont

Blanc II, had blue eyes, pink skin and a pure white coat except for a few black spots round the poll and anus.

Mont Blanc's parents Murghab and Tharsine were bays. The nearest grey horse in his ancestry was that paragon of speed The Tetrarch, who appeared twice in the fourth remove of the pedigree of Murghab. Contrary to the opinion firmly held by Elisabeth, Mont Blanc could not have inherited his white coat from The Tetrarch. Tetrameter, the son, and Tetrabbazia, the daughter of The Tetrarch, who appeared in the pedigree of Murghab, were chestnut and bay respectively, and as the gene for greyness is dominant and therefore always expresses itself when it is present, neither of them could have inherited it; and as they had not inherited it they could not have transmitted it to their offspring and descendants. The whiteness of Mont Blanc could only have been due to a mutation.

Mont Blanc was sold as a yearling and sent to be trained by Walter Nightingall at Epsom. Two years later he proved himself a useful second-class middle-distance performer by winning races at Lingfield and Epsom and finishing third in the Brighton Derby Trial. Afterwards he returned to France as a stallion at the Haras de la Chaise at Bruère-sur-Loire, within easy reach of Le Mesnil.

Whiteness in animals often exercises an extraordinary fascination on the human mind. Herman Melville in *Moby Dick* attributed 'an elusive something' to whiteness, 'which strikes more of panic to the soul than that redness which affrights in blood.' In *Idle Days in Patagonia* the great naturalist, W. H. Hudson, took a kindlier view of whiteness, but argued that it must have some quality above rarity, conspicuousness and abnormality to account for the intense interest it excited. He wrote:

Among savages the distinguishing whiteness is sometimes regarded as supernatural: and this fact inclines me to believe that, just as any extraordinary phenomenon produces a vague idea of someone acting with a given purpose, so in the case of the white animal, its whiteness has not come by accident or chance, but is the outward sign of some excellence of the intelligent soul distinguishing it from its fellows.

There is no reason to suppose that the whiteness of Mont Blanc aroused feelings of terror in Elisabeth, but it certainly did fill her with an intensity of interest and an almost supersitious awe which

Hudson would have recognized. And the coincidence that she had a grey pony with blue eyes called Fanny was enough to persuade her that it was worth arranging a series of matings with the aim of establishing a strain of white horses.

Fanny stood only 13 hands and her origins were unknown, but she had the quality to indicate that she had Arab blood. She had spent her working life as a child's pony and pulling a trap, and her docile and willing character made her ideal for those tasks. She had reached the age of fifteen when she was first mated with Mont Blanc in 1970, and to Elisabeth's delight she became pregnant and in due course produced a white filly who was given the name of Blanche Neige. The next year Fanny was mated with Mont Blanc again, and this time the produce was the white colt Glacier. Fanny had fulfilled her breeding function to perfection.

The next phase was to mate Blanche Neige when she was three years old to her own sire, Mont Blanc, and again success was achieved when the produce was the white colt, White Glory. A year later the brother and sister, Glacier, then a four-year-old, and Blanche Neige, were mated and this time the produce was the white filly, Boule de Neige. The progress of the experiment had been threatened by the fact that Glacier and Blanche Neige inherited their sire's bad temper and became so savage that eventually they had to be put down, but the situation was saved when Boule de Neige grew up as quiet as a lamb.

Elisabeth had established her desired white strain. The next and final phase of the experiment was to outcross the strain in order to increase the thoroughbred genetic content. The resident Le Mesnil stallion Versailles, a bay horse by the dark bay Right Royal out of the chesnut Décor, was chosen. Boule de Neige was mated with Versailles in 1979 and 1980 and each time, to Elisabeth's delighted astonishment, the produce was a white foal – first the filly Fleur de Lys and the second time a colt.

These results inspired Elisabeth to proclaim triumphantly that she had produced a breed of white horses that would breed true in this regard, irrespective of the colour of their mates. Her enthusiasm had run away with her. On the other hand she had proved that the mutant white gene was heritable and dominant, and had conducted successfully an intriguing experiment of a kind for which no other breeder had ever been prepared to spend time, trouble and money.

It has to be assumed that the greyness of Fanny was an irrelevance, as no link between grey and white in thoroughbreds has been proved; while it must also be assumed, in the absence of corroborative evidence, that Fleur de Lys and her brother were hybrids in respect of colour.

It had been Elisabeth's aim not merely to create a breed of white horses but to prove that they were capable of competing successfully with thoroughbreds on the race-course despite their admixture of non-thoroughbred blood from Fanny. She had not been sanguine about the prospects of Fleur de Lys, but considered that her brother was much more racing-like and had planned to put him into training in Ireland. Her death when he was a yearling extinguished hopes of realizing that ambition.

In her mind the aim to establish a white strain had been confused by an obsession with stud-book anomalies which had been simmering since the days when Derby had declined to send mares to the then, by *General Stud Book* standards, 'half-bred' Tourbillon; in the last years of her life this obsession merged inevitably with her interest in white horses.

Her preoccupation with stud-book anomalies ran along two parallel lines. In the first place, she was implacably opposed to the kind of stud-book exclusiveness that was pushed to extreme lengths in the 'Jersey Act'* which, from 1913 to 1949, had the effect of barring most American thoroughbreds, and their descendants in other countries, from admission to the *General Stud Book*; and, in the second place, she made favourable comparison of the racing regulations in Britain, where non-thoroughbreds were permitted to run against thoroughbreds in all races, even the Classic races, with the regulations in France, where non-thoroughbreds, even those with properly documented pedigrees like A.Q.P.S. and Selle Français,†

---

*She persisted in stating that the 'Jersey Act' was an Act of Parliament whereas it was simply a motion proposed by Lord Jersey, approved by the Jockey Club and implemented by Weatherbys, the owners of the *General Stud Book*.

†The French saddle horse breed which contained a high proportion of thoroughbred blood. Selle Français were permitted to run against thoroughbreds in races over obstacles and included many top-class chasers like Isopani and Jasmin II, winners of the Grand Steeplechase de Paris in 1981 and 1983 respectively.

were banned from running against thoroughbreds on the flat in all but a few minor races.

Foreign non-thoroughbreds likewise were banned in principle from running against thoroughbreds in French flat races, and Elisabeth was particularly incensed by apparent inconsistencies in the application of this rule. For example, the British non-thoroughbred sprinter, Gay Mairi, was permitted to run against thoroughbreds on the flat, and her son, Montgomery, became one of the leading French sprinters; but the excellent Irish non-thoroughbred stayer, Bigaroon, twice winner of the Irish Cesarewitch, was not allowed to run in the time-honoured French test of stamina the Prix Gladiateur, although his entry had been accepted and he actually arrived at Longchamp.

While the *General Stud Book* rules were amended to admit a few mares previously regarded as non-thoroughbred under strict safeguards after 1968, the *French Stud Book* authorities still declined to introduce any means by which non-thoroughbred mares could graduate. Elisabeth believed that all forms of exclusiveness were utterly misguided and inimical to the interests of thoroughbred evolution because they denied the breed access to fresh sources of excellence, and, in France at least, even denied non-thoroughbreds the right to demonstrate their prowess on the racecourse. She missed no opportunity, in speech or in print, to chip away at outworn notions of 'purity of blood' in the context of the thoroughbred.

She recruited two curiously assorted allies in this long-running compaign. One, Patrick Saward, was a marvellous example of how the thoroughbred may mesmerize persons with absolutely no prior racing connections, for he was a parcels clerk in British Rail; the other, Marie Kaminski, was a Polish-born research worker at the Laboratory of Enzymology at Gif-sur-Yvette near Paris.

Saward, who was something of a recluse, had collected one of the best reference libraries in England for his chosen subject and had an unrivalled knowledge of stud-book lore and history. Elisabeth quickly recognised his genius for research, befriended him and, although he had never been out of England before, invited him to Le Mesnil, took him to the races at Longchamp, entertained him to dinner on a *bateau mouche* on the Seine, gave him rare books for his collection, helped him to get articles published in French racing and breeding periodicals and exchanged letters with him frequently on the subject that engrossed them both. From him she learned of many uncorrected errors in various volumes of the *General Stud Book*; of new families with short pedigrees admitted in volume 2; of the preface to the little-known volume of 1827, a precursor to the definitive volume 3 of 1832, which made the never-to-be-repeated admission that the *General Stud Book* was compiled too late for the first editor to obtain proper accounts of early pedigrees. The preface included this paragraph:

Indeed the *English Stud Book*, although so ably commenced, was begun too late, as appears from the imperfect accounts of many of the old stallions and mares in the first volume,. . . and there appears now very little chance of obtaining further particulars.

If the origins and identity of the foundation stock were thus in doubt, Saward argued, then it was ridiculous to talk about purity of breed and keep any horses possessing racing merit out of the stud book.

The work of Marie Kaminski, who also visited Le Mesnil and was in frequent correspondence with Elisabeth, was in the field of bloodtyping and fully confirmed the doctrine of Patrick Saward concerning purity of blood. For Kaminski's analysis of genetic markers in blood types disproved any idea that the thoroughbred boasted a pure descent, and indicated that the breed had mixed origins. Kaminski concluded:

It is possible to state definitely that a similar bloodtype is found among thoroughbreds, half-breds and even ponies. The three breeds showing the same bloodtypes among a number of individuals are mainly the thoroughbred, the Anglo-Arab and the Selle Français.

The documentary and the scientific evidence supplied by Saward and Kaminski respectively was precisely the proof Elisabeth was seeking for her theories. In the circumstances she found it a ludicrous exaltation of the *Almanach de Gotha* principle that thoroughbred families which had not produced a high-class winner for many generations were entitled to remain in the *General Stud Book*, while gifted representatives of non-thoroughbred families were excluded. In the last ten years of her life she was an enthusiastic advocate of the idea of forming a new international stud book in which all

meritorious performers, and meritorious performers only, were
entitled to a place.

Although she was a member of the Commission of the *French Stud
Book** and had a close link with the corridors of power in the
Société d'Encouragement through Bertrand de Tarragon, Elisabeth
Couturié, with her incessant probing of anomalies and inconsistencies in the rules and regulations affecting the breeding industry, was
often a thorn in the flesh of the racing establishment. Nevertheless,
her profound knowledge and immense fund of experience, her
marvellous record as a breeder of top-class horses, her unquestioned
integrity and her sheer force of character gave her unrivalled
authority in the French thoroughbred community. Her pre-eminence at last received due recognition with the award of the Légion
d'Honneur in 1977. The award was made on the recommendation
of Henri Blanc, the head of the Service des Haras, for her supreme
contribution to French breeding, but it was thought that her acts of
courage in the Resistance, for which she received five awards
including the Croix de Combattant, were also taken into
consideration.

The ceremony was performed on 12 February at Le Mesnil at her
request, because she wished to be 'among those who, for many
years, have collaborated with me, have made this distinction possible
and deserve it just as much as I do.' Hubert de Chaudenay, the
President of the Société d'Encouragement, pinned the Légion
d'Honneur on her breast in the walnut-panelled drawing room,
praised her as a great ambassadress for French breeding, and
concluded his speech with these words: 'Let me say that it is not
only you and not only your staff, it is all French thoroughbred
breeding, all that is most noble and glorious, that is honoured
today.'

Her wish to receive the decoration at Le Mesnil epitomized her
affectionate and matriarchal relationship with her staff. It was said
that she bred not only horses but also her stud workers at Le Mesnil.
It was one of her most deeply felt beliefs that as soon as a worker

*The *French Stud Book*, in contrast to the privately owned *General Stud Book* in England, is
the property of the government and is administered by the Service des Haras of the Ministry
of Agriculture, with representation for breeders on the Commission.

had demonstrated his competence and willingness to stay in his job he must be given a house. Only in that way, she insisted, could he be made to feel secure and dedicate himself to the horses and the interests of Le Mesnil. She had no faith in stocks and shares, and did not believe in keeping large sums of money in the bank. She preferred to plough profits back into the stud, to build or improve houses for the staff, and to support the children's home maintained by her daughter Marguerite.

Her passionate determination to uphold the traditions and the greatness of Le Mesnil never faltered. In the spring of 1982 she embarked on a large-scale forestry programme, planting 10,000 seedlings, mostly poplars and American oaks, in clearings in the woods; and on the afternoon of 23 June she drove her Citroën Quatre Chevaux round the bumpy farm tracks on a tour of inspection, noting with satisfaction that the young trees had taken root and were making vigorous growth. She died peacefully in hospital at Le Mans eleven days later.

After her death a single sheet bearing a quotation from Abraham Lincoln was found among her papers. It contained the following passage:

You cannot bring about prosperity by discouraging thrift. You cannot strengthen the weak by weakening the strong. You cannot help the wage earner by pulling down the wage payer. You cannot further the brotherhood of man by encouraging class hatred. You cannot help the poor by destroying the rich. You cannot keep out of trouble by spending more than you earn. You cannot build character and courage by taking away man's initiative and independence.

Lincoln's words expressed the essence of the philosophy which had guided her own life, inspired her management of Le Mesnil, and made her unique among the breeders of her time.

Above: Fanny, the grey pony who was the starting point of Elisabeth Couturié's experiments in breeding white horses, with her white foal by Mont Blanc II. The chateau of Le Mesnil is in the background

Right: Elisabeth Couturié with her husband Jean on the steps outside the front door of Le Mesnil on a hunting morning

Above: Rex Magna, the last top-class flat race horse bred by Elisabeth Couturié, in playful mood outside his box at the Le Mesnil stud

Right: Right Royal V, winner of the French Derby and the King George VI and Queen Elizabeth Stakes and the best horse bred by Elisabeth Couturié, in his prime as a stallion at Le Mesnil

Facing page: Marcel Boussac leads in Galcador after his victory in the Derby in 1950. Rae Johnstone is in the saddle

Above: Tourbillon, winner of the French Derby for Marcel Boussac in 1931. He became a great classic stallion and one of the pillars of Boussac's breeding policy

Below: Pharis II was acclaimed the most brilliant horse bred by Marcel Boussac after winning the French Derby and the Grand Prix de Paris in 1939. He was confiscated and taken to Germany during the Second World War, but was repatriated after the war and became a champion sire in France

4

Marcel Boussac
1889–1980

In Proust's *Time Regained* the narrator, Marcel, after years in a sanatorium, returns to Paris and attends an afternoon party at the house of the Princesse de Guermantes. Many of his old acquaintances are present, and he is disconcerted to find them all subtly changed, as if they had come to the party in fancy dress.

The Prince, receiving his guests, still preserved that air of a jolly king of the fairies he suggested to my mind the first time I saw him but now, having apparently submitted to the disguise he had imposed upon his guests, he had tricked himself out in a white beard and dragged his feet heavily along as though they were soled with lead. He seemed to be representing one of the ages of man. His moustache was whitened as if the hoar-frost in Tom Thumb's forest clung-to it. It seemed to inconvenience his stiffened mouth, and once he had produced his effect he ought to have taken it off. To tell the truth, I only recognized him by reasoning out his identity with himself from certain familiar features.★

Similar thoughts might have run through the head of anyone seeing another Marcel, Marcel Boussac, in the Ascot paddock before the King George VI and Queen Elizabeth Stakes on 22 July 1978 on his last visit to an English racecourse. The pathetically frail and shambling figure supported on a stick, the deeply lined face expressing a desperate melancholy, could be identified with the man whose dapper appearance and purposeful stride on a comparable occasion thirty years earlier would have struck British onlookers with awe

★Stephen Hudson's translation (1931).

113

only because certain familiar markers remained – the bowler hat, the fawn light overcoat, and the neatly gloved hands.

The changes in Boussac's appearance reflected not only the passing of time but the cataclysmic decline in his fortunes. For a decade after the Second World War the Boussac studs and stable dominated European racing, and the declaration of a Boussac runner for a big English race usually spelt disaster for the home contingent. There were setbacks of course, as when Arbar suffered a head defeat by Sayajirao in the 1947 St Leger and Coronation V was beaten by a neck by Musidora in the Oaks two years later. But mostly the Boussac colours of orange jacket and grey cap were to the fore, with the climax in 1950, when he won the Derby with Galcador, the Oaks with Asmena and the St Leger with Scratch II in England, besides the French 1000 Guineas and the Irish Oaks with Corejada.

In the early 1950s the Boussac thoroughbred empire seemed absolutely secure and permanent. But the seeds of decadence had been sown, and they germinated with such devastating suddenness in the second half of the decade that the Boussac supremacy disintegrated. In 1956, to the casual eye, the Boussac legions seemed to be advancing as relentlessly as ever. That year Apollonia won the French Oaks, Philius the French Derby and Janiari the Prix Vermeille, while Floriados was second in the Grand Prix de Paris; and Boussac was leading owner in France with 60 per cent more prize money attributed to him than to his nearest rival Mme Léon Volterra. The Boussac stable, however, was weak in two-year-olds, and the best of them, Ambar, was placed no higher than fourteenth in the French Free Handicap. The next year the significance of Ambar's undistinguished position became clear as Boussac dropped to fifteenth place in the list of winning owners. Though few would have been bold enough to say so at the time, the era of Boussac domination was over. From then until the final collapse twenty years later, the number of top-class horses bred and owned by Boussac did not reach double figures; the best of his winners were Arbencia in the 1957 Prix Vermeille, Abdos in the 1961 Grand Criterium, Astola (deadheater) in the Prix Vermeille the same year, Crepellana in the 1969 French Oaks, Dankaro in the 1974 Prix Lupin and Acamas in the 1978 Prix Lupin and French Derby. For most owner–breeders that number of victories in races of the championship grade would have represented success on a scale barely dreamed of; but it represented a precipitous decline for Boussac. As he remarked in his speech at the annual press conference of the Société d'Encouragement in 1968: 'It is essential not to forget that once one has attained the front rank, to descend to the second is a sympton of decay.' He was referring to the condition of French breeding in the light of the successes of foreign-bred horses in races like the Grand Prix de Saint Cloud and the Prix de l'Arc de Triomphe that year, but the words were equally applicable to his own case.

By the time he went to Ascot in July 1978 Boussac had to face not only the decline of the quality of his bloodstock. In addition, his industrial and textile interests had collapsed, he was personally bankrupt and his affairs were in the hands of the liquidator. It was only by courtesy that Acamas, who had been purchased jointly by the Aga Khan and Tim Rogers, was allowed to carry his colours for the last time in the King George VI and Queen Elizabeth Stakes. Acamas, a small horse possessing the elegance that was the hallmark of the Boussac breed, ran a fine race, but hung to the left badly in the straight and was beaten by 1½ lengths by Ile de Bourbon. Thus was he denied the consolation of a last great victory for his colours which would have tempered the humiliation of his downfall on the Turf and in industry. He died a broken man on 21 March 1980.

Yet Marcel Boussac in his prime had enjoyed a prestige on the European Turf which had no parallel in the twentieth century. That prestige sprang from the quantity and the quality of his successes. In less than sixty years he won 1800 races, of which 140 were races classified as Group 1 in the Pattern race system introduced in 1970. He won the French Derby twelve times (with Ramus, Tourbillon, Thor, Cillas, Pharis II, Ardan, Coaraze, Sandjar, Scratch II, Auriban, Philius and Acamas). He won the French Oaks five times, the Prix de l'Arc de Triomphe six times and the Grand Criterium, the most important French two-year-old race, nine times. He headed the list of winning owners in France nineteen and the list of French breeders seventeen times. He was the leading breeder in both France and Britain in 1950.

Contemporary observers were incredulous that so much achievement could be swept aside and so many of the glories of the years of prosperity condemned to oblivion. The Haras de Fresnay-le-Buffard, Boussac's principal stud, incorporates a charming manor house commanding a view of a wide sweep of lawn, a small lake with swans, and clumps of giant beeches. A low flat-topped mound is the graveyard of thirteen of the great Boussac stallions and mares. The graves are arranged in a semicircle, each marked by a rectangular rosebed. But there are no headstones, nothing to identify the *Chefs-de-race* buried there. Tim Richardson, the stud manager for the Greek shipping magnate Stavros Niarchos who bought Fresnay-le-Buffard from the liquidator, tried hard but unavailingly to elucidate the mystery. When he questioned the old studmen who had worked for Boussac he found that each had a different recollection of which grave was which. They could not even agree as to the names of the horses in the graveyard.

Those anonymous graves symbolize the transient nature and final extinction of a Turf empire which lacks fitting memorials not only for the superbly talented individual horses which it produced over a period of half a century, but for the grandeur and originality of its conception. The single-minded application of a whole philosophy of breeding on a monumental scale to the Boussac studs was unprecedented and is surely unrepeatable. The daring idea that Boussac conceived and put into practice was nothing less ambitious than the creation of a breed of horses segregated from and superior to the rest of the thoroughbred population.

Marcel Boussac was not academically inclined. On leaving school at the age of seventeen he refused to enter a university or any of the schools of administration which prepare sons of members of the French establishment for careers in the civil service, finance and industry. Instead, he went straight into his father's business, leaving it three years later to found what was to become an immense chain of textile factories. Government contracts aided the expansion of his business during the First World War; and at the end of the war he seized an opportunity to buy up large surplus stocks of French Air Force parachute silk at bargain prices, which gave him a profitable foothold in the quality end of clothing manufacture. New factories were opened in all the regions of France to make the Boussac enterprises a complete vertically integrated textile manufacturing business, beginning with the raw materials and embracing all the processes of spinning, weaving, dyeing, printing and bleaching to the final production of finished articles of clothing and retailing. He launched the famous designer Christian Dior, whose genius breathed new life into the world of high fashion and stimulated the market for quality garments. A total of fifty-five factories employed more than 25,000 people. Boussac scorned to 'go public', and his enterprises never had a Stock Exchange quotation. He preferred to keep the entire business within his own paternalistic control, and his enormous textile empire owed nearly everything to the vision, drive, organizing ability and entrepreneurial skill of its creator.

He first took an interest in thoroughbred breeding in 1914, when he entered into partnership with Count Gaston de Castelbajac, who owned eight broodmares at his stud at Saint-Antoine-la-Forêt in the department of the Seine-Inférieure. It was not an auspicious time to begin breeding racehorses, because the formation of the partnership was followed by the outbreak of the First World War which disrupted the industry and led to the temporary cessation of racing in France apart from a few *épreuves de sélection* run at Chantilly. Nevertheless, the Castelbajac connection proved extremely fruitful in the long term and provided Boussac with some of his best foundation mares. After the war, in 1919, he embarked on breeding on his own and on a much larger scale with the purchase of Fresnay-le-Buffard from a breeder of trotters who had let the stud to two American thoroughbred breeders, Clarence Mackay and Charles Carroll. He bought the Clarence and Carroll band of twenty broodmares at the same time. Fresnay-le-Buffard, situated 6 miles south of William the Conqueror's birthplace, Falaise, on a plateau between the valleys of the Orne and the Dives, had magnificent pastures, a private supply of calcium-rich water drawn by windpumps from deep wells, and a complex of stud buildings clustered round the manor house, some built in the pale honey-coloured Falaise stone and some in traditional Norman half-timbered style.

One of the neighbouring studs was the Haras du Gazon, owned by the American Herman B. Duryea, who had won the 2000 Guineas in 1912 with Sweeper II and the Derby in 1914 with Durbar II, who was described as 'half-bred' under the terms of the so-called 'Jersey Act' introduced the previous year for the purpose of regulating admission to the *General Stud Book*. However, Durbar II was eligible for the *French Stud Book*, and this difference in stud-book rules was to have far-reaching consequences for Boussac's breeding in particular and for the evolution of racehorse breeding in general.

Herman Duryea died in 1916. His widow decided to maintain the stud, but to sell the produce as yearlings instead of putting them into training. It was as a result of this change of policy that in 1919 Boussac was able to buy ten Duryea-bred yearlings privately for 100,000 francs and, except in the following year when Mrs Duryea leased the yearlings to another French owner, Boussac persisted in the same practice until 1925.

The years 1919 to 1926 were the formative period of the Boussac thoroughbred empire. The Castelbajac mares, the mares already at Fresnay-le-Buffard and the fillies obtained from the Haras du Gazon were the kernel of the operation. To them were added fillies like Zariba, Likka and Hélène de Troie bought in France; mares like Desmond Lassie, Primrose Lane, Casquetts and Sweet Picture bought in England; and Astérus, purchased as a yearling colt in France, who was to have a dynamic impact on the evolution of the Boussac bloodstock, especially as a sire of broodmares. By 1926 the acquisitions were practically complete, and after that the broodmare band was augmented from outside sources hardly at all until the Second World War, when a few well-bred mares were available at bargain prices owing to the exceptional circumstances.

The mares at Fresnay-le-Buffard in the mid-1920s were an exceptionally varied group by the standards of the time, and might have been a model for what was later to be called the international outcross. Numerically they could have got out of hand very quickly through the multiplication of their daughters, granddaughters and later descendants. Boussac held this tendency tightly in check by strict pruning, so that the number of mares, which stood at twenty-eight in 1920, had increased to no more than fifty-four by 1925 despite all the additions in the intervening years. Any filly or mare unlikely to improve quality and fit into Boussac's concept of a top-class breeding operation was culled ruthlessly. Indeed, only three of the Mackay and Carroll mares remained in 1925. Boussac had made a careful choice of a force adequate for a concentrated assault on the highest peaks of achievement in the thoroughbred universe. The events of the next thirty years were to demonstrate how skilfully his plans had been laid.

In thoroughbred breeding, as in business, Marcel Boussac was very much his own man. He did not believe in divided responsibility. One of the most striking aspects of the growth and one-time domination of his breeding operation was that it was achieved by a man without deep family roots in the world of the thoroughbred and lacking prior experience of working with horses and stud management. He sought little advice except from Réné Romanet, a man of sharp intellect and boundless diligence, and a profound student of thoroughbred bloodlines. Romanet, if anyone besides Boussac himself, supplied the rationale for his breeding policies and may, albeit unwittingly, have helped to sow the seed of Boussac's ultimate downfall by an attitude to the problems of breeding which was too intellectual and too little tempered by practical considerations.

Réné Romanet had begun his working life as a civil servant, but developed an interest in, and began to write articles on, the esoteric subject of thoroughbred breeding as a young man. His brother Maurice was secretary general of the Société d'Encouragement, and Réné succeeded him in that office when Maurice was called up for military service at the beginning of the First World War. He remained secretary general until his death in 1945 and founded a dynasty. His son Jean, who took the title of director general, succeeded him at the Société d'Encouragement, and in the 1970s and 1980s Jean's son Louis was his heir apparent as assistant director general. The family connection held firm, because Jean Romanet was the chief executive during the fourteen years that Boussac was president of the Société after the Second World War. The influence of Réné Romanet can be discerned in many of Boussac's acquisitions in the formative period, because their choice indicated that a mind with a comprehensive knowledge of bloodlines was at work.

However, Boussac's first Classic winner owed nothing to the advice of Romanet. This was Ramus, winner of the French Derby in 1922. Ramus, by St Simon's son Rabelais out of Only One, was a product of the Castelbajac partnership and was bred before Romanet came on the scene. Ramus was not one of the best of the Boussac French Derby winners either in ability or character. He gained his Classic victory by a short head from Kefalin, and that very hard race undermined his will to win. He was fractious and lost many lengths at the start of the Grand Prix de Paris, and although he made up a lot of ground, could not catch Kefalin. After that he stubbornly refused to exert himself on the racecourse. Ramus was kept for stud, but was poorly patronized and was a failure as a sire. On the other hand, Only One's family made a lasting contribution to the progress of Boussac breeding; her family thrived at Fresnay-le-Buffard and her great grandson Scratch II won the French Derby and the St Leger in 1950.

Two other Castelbajac mares did excellent service for Boussac. One of them, Lasarte, was the dam of Thor, who gave Boussac his third French Derby victory in 1933. No more than Ramus could Thor be called one of the more distinguished of French Derby winners. He too was a failure at stud. He was sold to the French National Stud Service, but became savage and suffered the indignity of being gelded at the advanced age of seventeen. The remaining Castlebajac mare, Diana Vernon, had an enduring beneficial influence and her high-class descendants who raced for Boussac numbered more than a score. The best of them were the brilliant filly Coronation V and Dankaro, one of the last good horses bred by Boussac.

Although the Mackay and Carroll bloodstock made an important contribution to Boussac's breeding, that contribution came from a very narrow base. The score of mares which came with Fresnay-le-Buffard were subjected to such a rigorous winnowing process that Boussac in the end retained only Ballantrae and two of her daughters. Ballantrae had an extraordinary career. Bred in England, she won the Cambridgeshire Handicap with the light weight of 6 st 8 lb as a three-year-old in 1902, and had spent some of her stud career in the United States and there bred Mediant, who was sent to England and won the big sprint handicap the Stewards Cup. Ballantrae was twenty years old when she came into the possession of Boussac and two years later, as a result of a mating to Teddy, produced the filly Coeur à Coeur, her last foal. Coeur à Coeur was not good enough to win a race, and her daughter Loika, by the First World War Triple Crown winner Gay Crusader, won only one small race as a two-year-old. Boussac became disenchanted with the family, and sent Loika, in foal to Tourbillon, to the Newmarket December sales in 1936. Fortunately Loika failed to fetch her reserve; for the foal she was carrying was Djebel, the exquisitely elegant, talented and durable colt who gained a great reputation on both sides of the Channel at the beginning of the Second World War.

As a two-year-old Djebel was sent to England to win the Middle

Park Stakes, then considered the championship test for horses of that age. He was not given a rating in the English Free Handicap although he had beaten Tant Mieux, who was placed top of the handicap, by 2 lengths; paradoxically he was placed top of the French Free Handicap, in spite of the fact that he had won only one of his four races in his native country. He returned to England the following spring and gained another 2-length victory in the 2000 Guineas from Stardust and Tant Mieux, displaying a superbly free, skimming action and matchless acceleration in the last furlong. The plan was for Djebel to visit England again to run in the Derby, but this was thwarted by the German offensive leading to the fall of France. He was able to resume his racing career in France in the autumn of 1940, when he won the substitute French 2000 Guineas run on the Parisian steeplechase course of Auteuil, and continued to run until he was five, when he showed his best form and won the Grand Prix de Saint Cloud and the Prix de l'Arc de Triomphe.

The purchases of Mrs Duryea's yearlings from the Haras du Gazon had an immediate impact on Boussac's fortunes as a racehorse owner. The first batch purchased in 1919 included the two best French two-year-old fillies of the following year, Durzetta and Durban. They met in their last two races that season, the Grand Criterium over a mile and the Prix de la Forêt over 7 furlongs at Longchamp. Durban won the former race easily, but Durzetta got her revenge in the Prix de la Forêt in which they both proved too good for their older opponents. They trained on well as three-year-olds without showing the same superiority over their contemporaries. Durban won the Prix Vermeille, a fillies race run over 1½ miles in September and later classified Group 1, and Durzetta was second in the French Oaks.

Durban and Durzetta represented precisely the mixture of English, American and French strains Boussac was seeking. The two fillies were very closely related. Durban was by Durbar II out of Banshee by Irish Lad, out of Frizette by Hamburg, out of Ondulee by St Simon; while Durzetta was by Durbar II out of Frizette. Ondulee was a granddaughter of the excellent filly Shotover who won the Derby in 1882. They were inbred to St Simon, the greatest of English stallions, as Durbar II was by Rabelais, the best of St Simon's sons to stand in France. They were also inbred to the great American stallion Hanover, the sire of Frizette's sire Hamburg and of Durbar's granddam Urania. The maternal grandsire of Urania was the French horse Mortemer. However, Mortemer occupied a relatively distant position in the pedigree of Durban and Durzetta, so that they were ideal outcrosses for strains that were prominent in France in the 1920s.

Durban and Durzetta raced so successfully that when they were three-year-olds Boussac went to the same source and bought Durban's yearling full sister Heldifann, and in 1922 bought Durzetta's yearling full sister Frizelle. Without possessing the same Classic ability as Durban and Durzetta, Heldifann had plenty of speed and won three races over 5 furlongs including the Prix du Couvert, later a Group 3 race, at Longchamp. By contrast Frizelle never ran. This tightly knit quartet of mares collectively formed a strain which endured throughout the whole of the Boussac breeding operations. Durzetta's was the least notable branch of the family, though even that produced three top-class horses in Golestan, Norval and Djelta. Durban was the dam of Boussac's second French Derby winner Tourbillon, and Heldifann was the ancestress of Boussac's last French Derby winner Acamas. These two branches of the Frizette family were united successfully at the very end of Boussac's breeding operations, for the stallion Labus, a scion of the Durban branch, was mated twice with Acamas's dam Licata and the produce were Akarad, winner of the Grand Prix de Saint Cloud, and Akiyda, winner of the Prix de l'Arc de Triomphe. In the meantime Frizelle had excelled her sister Durzetta by becoming the granddam of Boussac's fourth French Derby winner Cillas and his tenth French Derby winner Auriban.

Tourbillon was not the most attractive of yearlings, and his form as a two-year-old in 1930 was below top class. He won a race at Chantilly and the Zukunftsrennen at Baden-Baden, but was unplaced behind Indus in the Grand Criterium. However, he made tremendous improvement during the following winter, and had developed into a magnificent type of colt when he began his three-year-old campaign with a victory in Prix Greffulhe over 10½ furlongs at Longchamp in April. He went on to win successively the Prix Hocquart, the Group 1 Prix Lupin and the French Derby, in which his victory by 2 lengths from Bruledur and Barneveldt seemed completely decisive. However, his series of races in the spring may have taxed his strength more than had been realized. In any case Barneveldt turned the tables on him in the Grand Prix over the additional distance of 3½ furlongs a fortnight later, and Tourbillon finished only third, though less than a length behind the winner. Some observers were inclined to blame Tourbillon's defeat on faulty riding tactics by his rider Charlie Elliott, but the truth was that Tourbillon was losing form progressively, and Barneveldt increased his winning margin to 6 lengths when they met again in the Prix du Président de la République at Saint Cloud a week after the Grand Prix. Tourbillon was in need of a rest, and he seemed to be back in form when he ran in the French St Leger (Prix Royal Oak) in September. He beat Barneveldt all right, but was unable to resist the late challenge of the thorough stayer Deiri, who beat him by a neck. He started favourite for the Prix de l'Arc de Triomphe on the strength of that performance but broke down during the race and finished unplaced.

The Arc was Tourbillon's last race. Boussac sent him to stud, and he became one of the chief agents of his supremacy in Classic breeding in the middle years of the century.

Two of the fillies Boussac acquired from other sources in France were related in the same degree as Durban and Durzetta. They were Zariba, foaled in 1919, and the six years younger Likka. Their pedigrees were of such a special kind that they could have been selected only by someone who had made a deep study of bloodlines, and the guiding hand of Réné Romanet can surely be detected in their purchases. They were both by the French Derby and Grand Prix winner Sardanapale, one of the stoutest stallions in France, and came from the family of Dame Masham, whose virtues would not have been apparent to anyone versed only in European racing. Zariba and Likka traced their descent from two daughters of Dame Masham, Fairy Gold and Ferelith. Fairy Gold, the granddam of Zariba, was the dam of Fair Play, who sired America's greatest thoroughbred, Man o' War, and of the Belmont Stakes winner Friar Rock. Ferelith was the great granddam of Likka. The relationship was all the closer because St Lucre, the dam of Zariba, and Ferula, the granddam of Likka, were both by St Simon's son St Serf.

Zariba, purchased for 45,000 francs as a yearling at the Deauville sales in August 1920, had top-class speed and won three races afterwards classified Group 1 – the Prix Morny and the Prix de la Forêt as a two-year-old, and the Prix Jacques le Marois over a mile at

Deauville the next year. She became a great broodmare, producing four top-class performers – the filly Corrida (by Coronach) and the colts Goyescas (by Gainsborough), Abjer (by Astérus) and Goya II (by Tourbillon). On the other hand, most of her offspring were afflicted by disastrous bad luck. Goyescas, an excellent middle-distance horse whose victories included the Champion Stakes in England, broke a fetlock joint when contesting the Prix du Président as a five-year-old and had to be destroyed; Abjer, a very fast horse who also made a visit to Newmarket to win the Middle Park Stakes, died after only two seasons at stud; and Corrida, a brilliant filly who won the Prix de l'Arc de Triomphe twice, disappeared during the Battle of Normandy in 1944 and left only one living foal, the French Derby winner Coaraze. Only Goya II, who won the Gimcrack Stakes at York and the Prix des Sablons (afterwards the Group 1 Prix Ganay) at Longchamp, had a normal span of life. Having raced until he was six, Goya II did very well during his seven seasons at stud in France, siring the French Derby winners Sandjar and Good Luck and the Oaks winner Asmena, before he was exported to the United States. The excellence of Goya II, and the promise shown by Abjer and Corrida during their brief stud careers, indicated how adversely the tribulations of the family must have affected the fortunes of Boussac's breeding. The continuation of the family story was left to Zariba's daughter L'Espérance, whose racing form was relatively moderate. L'Espérance played her part nobly, and was the ancestress of Boussac's only Derby winner Galcador, besides the French Derby winner Philius and the French Oaks winner Crepellana.

Boussac acquired Likka privately as a foal. She was nothing like as good a racemare as Zariba, and merely won two small races as a three-year-old. Her important contribution to the progress of the Boussac studs was as the dam of the great broodmare Astronomie. Astronomie even surpassed the achievements of Zariba by producing six top-class offspring. They were the great stayer Marsyas II (by Trimdon), the Grand Prix de Paris and Prix de l'Arc de Triomphe winner Caracalla II (by Tourbillon), the Ascot Gold Cup winner and St Leger second Arbar (by Djebel), the Oaks winner Asmena (by Goya II), the Prix d'Ispahan and Prix Jacques le Marois winner Arbele (by Djebel) and the Prix Hocquart winner and Grand Prix de Paris second Floriados (by Djebel). Asmena's paternal and maternal granddams were, of course, the closely related mares Zariba and Likka.

The influence of Likka did not persist anything like as long as that of Zariba. Although Asmena bred two good horses in Kurun and Ardaban, and Arbele had a more than useful daughter confusingly named Arbela, that was the sum of it.

Like Zariba, Hélène de Troie passed into Boussac's hands when he was beginning to collect his broodmare band in 1919, but she was three years old at the time. Her sire Helicon was generally undistinguished, but was also the sire of the Le Mesnil foundation mare La Grelée. Hélène de Troie had won one race as a two-year-old, but had no worthwhile form as a three-year-old. She contributed to the growth of the Boussac breeding empire as the dam of Adargatis (by Astérus), who became his first winner of the French Oaks in 1934. Adargatis was the dam of the marvellously gifted Ardan, whose six consecutive victories as a three-year-old included the French Derby and the Grand Prix de Paris. He went on to win the Prix de l'Arc de Triomphe, and raced until he was five, winning sixteen of his total of twenty-three races.

The Adargatis branch of the family began to wither after the triumphant career of Ardan. It is one of the ironies of breeding that Hélène de Troie's relatively moderate daughter La Troienne, who was by Astérus's sire Teddy and therefore very closely related to Adargatis, made a more lasting contribution to the breed. Like her dam, she won only one race as a two-year-old. Boussac weeded her out and sold her to the United States, where she founded the great family which has been the source of scores of high-class performers from Bimelech and Black Helen to Buckpasser and Allez France.

Boussac's English mares were bought cheaply even by the depressed standards of the boodstock market in the years following the First World War. He bought Desmond Lassie as a seven-year-old for 200 guineas at the Newmarket December sales in 1920; Primrose Lane as a seven-year-old for 500 guineas at the December sales the next year; Casquetts as an eight-year-old for 600 guineas at the December sales in 1921; and Sweet Picture as a yearling for 750 guineas at the Newmarket July sales two years later. They all made a lasting contribution to the progress of his breeding. Primrose Lane, for example, was the ancestress of the top-class miler Djelal, the dual Champion Stakes winner Dynamiter and Abdos, who won the Grand Criterium in 1961 and became an influential broodmare sire.

Casquetts, however, was the English mare who played a crucial role in the evolution of Boussac's breeding. Her name was taken from a group of rocks and a lighthouse seven miles west of Alderney, but there was nothing rocklike about her credentials, and at a first glance it is difficult to see why Boussac and Romanet should have selected her. She herself never ran; her sire Captivation ran only once, finishing unplaced in the Imperial Produce Stakes at Kempton as a two-year-old; and her dam Cassis also ran only once, finishing unplaced in a selling race as a two-year-old. Captivation had been at stud since 1904 and had been represented by his first runner of any class, the Irish St Leger winner Kircubbin, in the year Casquetts was purchased. The aspect of her pedigree which must have appealed to Boussac and his adviser was that Cassis was a great-granddaughter of Jenny Diver, the dam of the Oaks winner Jenny Howlet, the granddam of the Oaks winner Musa and the great-granddam of the Oaks winner Mirska and the French Derby winner Montmartin. Casquetts was a member of a flourishing Classic family.

Boussac sent Casquetts to the 2000 Guineas winner Clarissimus, who was standing in France, in her first covering season after she had joined his stud. The produce was Carissima, who showed high-class form by winning two important fillies' races, the Prix de Malleret and the Prix de Minerve, and was second in the French Oaks. She bred eight winners, but it was not until she was thirteen that she produced, as a result of a mating to the Derby second and then leading European Classic sire Pharos, her masterpiece Pharis II. The name of Pharis II will always shine brightly in the annals of French racing on account of his sensational performances in the French Derby and the Grand Prix de Paris. He was a colt who was always slow to warm up, and was far back in the field turning into the straight at Chantilly in the French Derby. Then he stumbled so badly that he was brought to his knees, and his position seemed hopeless. However, his rider Charlie Elliott quickly got him balanced, and in the last two furlongs he was able to produce such an astonishing burst of speed that he swept past the leaders to win by 2½ lengths from Galerien. He overcame even greater difficulties in the Grand Prix, in which he became hopelessly shut in by a wall of beaten horses well after turning into the short Longchamp straight. There seemed to be no way out, even though he was full of running, and one English spectator turned to his companion on the stand and said, 'That's the unluckiest loser we shall ever see.' But Elliott managed to extricate him with a little more than a furlong to go, and once he was clear he began to overhaul the leaders with lightning speed. Tricameron was in front inside the last furlong and his rider Charles Bouillon said afterwards, 'I heard Pharis coming up behind me, but when I looked round he had already gone past.' Pharis's finishing speed was so overwhelming that he went away to win by the same margin as at Chantilly.

That year, 1939, there were two brilliant three-year-old colts in Europe, Pharis II and Blue Peter, who had won the 2000 Guineas and the Derby in majestic style. They were expected to meet in the St Leger, and the racing communities on either side of the Channel were loud in their assertions that victory for their own champion was a forgone conclusion. The outbreak of war led to the cancellation of the St Leger, and the question of supremacy was never solved. However, Blue Peter and Pharis would not have met at Doncaster even if the St Leger had been run, because Pharis went badly in his final gallop and would have been scratched. He never ran again.

No other horse bred by Boussac gave such breathtaking performances as those of Pharis II in the French Derby and the Grand Prix, and he has no serious rival to the title of Boussac's best horse. He spent the covering season of 1940 in France. But in August of that year Major Pulte, the German commissioner for the purchase and confiscation of French bloodstock, decreed his removal to Germany, where he was installed at the Altenfeld Stud until the end of the war. It was poetic justice that Pharis hated the high altitude and the harsh climate of the German stud. He never thrived and got only one top-class horse, the filly Asterblute, in his five seasons there. He was brought back to France in May 1945 and lived for another twelve years, proving himself a great sire in keeping with his brilliance on the racecourse.

By 1926 the process of accumulating the breeding stock deemed necessary for a first-class operation at Fresnay-le-Buffard was virtually complete. To the female strains collected from French,

American and English sources was added one stallion, Astérus, purchased for the equivalent of £2700 at the Deauville yearling sales in 1924. On pedigree Astérus had a great deal to recommend him. He was by Teddy, the best French racehorse during the First World War, and was a great grandson of the Triple Crown winner Flying Fox, who had been bought by Edmond Blanc, one of the leading French breeders at the turn of the century, with beneficial results for French Classic breeding. His granddam Astra won the French Oaks. In addition Astérus was a horse of faultless conformation and perfect quality. He lived up to his looks and breeding by winning the French 2000 Guineas and, although he did not stay well enough to finish closer than fourth in the French Derby, had a successful campaign as a four-year-old in which visits to England brought him victories in the Royal Hunt Cup and the Champion Stakes. At stud he fulfilled the role ascribed to him as a cross for the various strains represented by the mares at Fresnay-le-Buffard. He was leading sire of winners in 1934 and was in the top ten sires of winners on eight other occasions; and excelled as a sire of broodmares, holding first place in the list of sires of the dams of winners six years in succession from 1943 to 1948.

Boussac secured access to the Flying Fox–Teddy male line through the acquisition of Astérus. The other French male line for which he had great respect was that of Dollar, who had been second in the French Derby in 1863, begun the next season by landing a betting coup in the Great Northamptonshire Handicap, and then proved himself a fine stayer by winning the 2 miles 5 furlongs Goodwood Cup. By a happy chance, a first-class scion of the Dollar line was available during the formative period of the Boussac breeding operations. This was Ksar, who had signalled the recovery of French breeding from the devastation of the First World War by winning the Prix de l'Arc de Triomphe in 1921 and 1922. Ksar made a decisive contribution to the evolution of the Boussac breed.

During the 1920s and 1930s the growing influence of Lord Derby's stallion Phalaris could not be overlooked. As in the case of Ksar and the Dollar line, Boussac was lucky to find a first-class representative of this strain to hand, for Phalaris's son Pharos, like Astérus a winner of the Champion Stakes and a potent Classic sire, was stationed at the Haras d'Ouilly no more than a dozen miles from Fresnay-le-

Buffard. Pharos, too, made a decisive contribution to the Boussac breed as the sire of Pharis II.

The other two potent male influences of the twenty years between the two world wars, Gainsborough and Blandford, did not gain a foothold at Fresnay-le-Buffard. It seemed that Boussac had obtained a worthy representative of the 1918 Triple Crown winner when Goyescas was showing top-class form from two to five years of age, but his fatal accident at Saint Cloud robbed his owner of a potential Gainsborough stallion. He made little attempt to breed or buy a son of Blandford, the best Classic stallion in England or Ireland during the period between the wars, and did not introduce that invaluable element until many years later.

The Boussac racing and breeding enterprise was in full flow by the time the Second World War broke out. He had won his first five French Derbys with Ramus, Tourbillon, Thor, Cillas and Pharis II; his first Grand Prix de Paris with Pharis II; and his first French Oaks with Adargatis. British racegoers had a good inkling of the quality of his horses from successful raids by Astérus, Abjer, Goyescas, Goya II and Corrida. Although French racing was not then given the press coverage that it was to receive in Britain a quarter of a century later, reports of the prowess of Pharis II had made a deep impression on English minds. The expectation of a thrilling St Leger duel between the national champions Blue Peter and Pharis II, though ultimately disappointed, confirmed a growing fear that Boussac raiders posed a threat to traditional British supremacy in matters of the thoroughbred.

The foundations of the Fresnay-le-Buffard stud had been securely laid. Though deprived temporarily of the influence of its most gifted product Pharis II, the quality of the horses bred there continued to improve inevitably as the Boussac bloodlines and crosses began to reach maturity during the war years when contact between the racing systems of Britain and France was broken. This process was certainly aided by the German policy of encouraging French racing during the occupation.

When the war was over the full might of the Boussac stable quickly became apparent. The four-year-old Priam II, one of the first crop by Pharis II and a grandson of Heldifann, was sent on a fighting patrol to run in the Champion Stakes in October 1945. His chief opponent was Court Martial, who had beaten the hot favourite Dante by a neck in the 2000 Guineas that year. Court Martial had failed to stay and had been beaten into third place behind Dante in the Derby, but was believed to be invincible over the 1¼ miles of the Champion Stakes. Priam had a bad journey from his training quarters at Chantilly and had been delayed at the Channel ports for two days. Moreover, though a habitual front runner, he was bewildered by the open spaces of Newmarket Heath and looked about him continually instead of getting on with the job of putting Court Martial's stamina to the test. For this reason the race became a test of speed over the last 2 furlongs and, to the consternation of the crowd, Priam II battled it out with Court Martial every yard to the winning post and was beaten by no more than a short head.

Priam II was a very good horse in France, but he was not the best in Boussac's stable, and indeed had been sacrificed as pacemaker for Ardan in the Grand Prix de Saint Cloud in July of that year. Boussac also had two excellent three-year-olds, the French Derby winner Coaraze and the Grand Prix de Paris winner Caracalla II. Rarely has a scouting mission brought back more valuable information or pointed more clearly to the success of an impending general offensive. That offensive opened at Epsom the following June, when Ardan easily defeated his two opponents in the Coronation Cup. Two days later that most resolute of stayers, Marsyas II, then six years old, won the White Rose Stakes at Hurst Park. The main assault was delivered at the Royal Ascot meeting, where Caracalla II won the Gold Cup, Marsyas II won the Queen Alexandra Stakes and Priam II himself won the Hardwicke Stakes. Only the four-year-old Coaraze, who never showed his best form in England, was a failure. He was beaten by his English contemporary Hobo, to whom he was conceding 12 lb, in the Rous Memorial Stakes. In the autumn Boussac struck another blow when he sent over Djerba to win the Cheveley Park Stakes, the two-year-old fillies' championship race, at Newmarket.

From the British point of view, the ominous feature of these performances of Boussac horses in 1946 was not simply that they were successful, but that the victories were gained with almost casual ease. It really did seem that a superior breed of racehorse was emerging from post-war France, with the alarming inference that

British horses had been judged by false standards during the war years and that those acclaimed as genuine Classic horses had in truth been merely second-raters. Boussac raiders were, of course, by no means the only French horses to humble the British during the postwar era. Of nine individual French-bred horses who won British Classic races between 1947 and 1951, only four (Galcador, Asmena, Scratch II and Talma II) were bred and owned by Boussac. Nevertheless, the Boussac stud and stable was far the most powerful source of cross-Channel raiders, and it was customary to perceive the Boussac candidates as the principal threat to the home-bred contingent in the Classic races and other important races which, after the introduction of the Pattern race system, were to be classified Group 1.

At the same time these early postwar victories of some of the Boussac horses were exposing a great anomaly. Tourbillon was debarred from the *General Stud Book* because Durbar II was his maternal grandsire, and so were all his progeny and descendants. Of the successful raiders in 1946, Caracalla II and Djerba were classified as non-thoroughbreds or half-breds. Within the next three years other successful Boussac raiders like Arbar (Ascot Gold Cup), Coronation V (Queen Mary Stakes), Nirgal (Hardwicke Stakes and Princess of Wales's Stakes), Djeddah (Eclipse Stakes and Champion Stakes) and Corejada (Cheveley Park Stakes) were similarly classified. These horses were making the *General Stud Book* ridiculous, a kind of social register based on some notional purity of blood but divorced from any criterion of performance. The social-register principle was untenable for a breed whose justification for existence was ability to race. The authorities were compelled to take a fresh look at the *General Stud Book* rules and revise them in volume 31, published in 1949, so that Tourbillon and others were made eligible. The revision saved the *Stud Book* from a sublime absurdity because Boussac's two Epsom Classic winners in 1950, Galcador and Asmena, would have been excluded under the old rules.

The Boussac horses achieved a similar predominance in France during an extended period. For he won the French Derby five times (with Ardan, Coaraze, Sandjar, Scratch II and Auriban) in the nine years from 1944 to 1952. So high a striking rate testified to a degree of ascendancy seldom equalled by an owner–breeder in any important breeding country. Auriban, the last of that quintet, accomplished a feat worthy of his sire Pharis II in the French Derby. In the case of Auriban, however, it was temperament which was nearly his undoing. He whipped round at the start and set off 100 yards behind the rest of the field, yet was able to join the leaders as they turned into the straight and draw away to win by 3 lengths. He repeated his misdemeanour in the Grand Prix de Paris, and on that occasion gave away so much ground that even he was unable to make it all up, and had to be content with second place behind Orfeo.

The Boussac ascendancy was reflected clearly in the lists of the sires of winners in France. Astérus was the first of his stallions to head the list. Tourbillon was leading sire four times. Pharis, despite losing five of his prime seasons through his enforced absence in Germany, also was leading sire of winners four times. A Boussac stallion was the leading sire of winners eleven times during the sixteen years 1940 to 1955. As the Boussac stallions covered mostly Boussac mares, the lists of sires of winners provided incontrovertible evidence of the pre-eminence of Boussac breeding during the great age of Fresnay-le-Buffard.

Internal decay, as much as the pressure of external forces, brings about the collapse of empires. During the last twenty-five years of his life Boussac and his racing interests had to face stiffening opposition as other French studs improved their output, British breeding revived and the flow of high-class American horses into Europe steadily increased. But the decline of the Boussac empire in the mid-1950s could not have been so swift if it had not been precipitated by a disastrous deterioration in the quality of his horses. It was as if, say, the Roman Empire had been destroyed by a single onslaught of Goths and Huns. No such onslaught would have had the strength to succeed unless there were rottenness within. The extraordinary feature of the story of Boussac's breeding operations is that the very factors which had made them great were, through over-concentration, to be responsible for their later and fatal weakness.

The foundation strains of Boussac breeding were selected with immense skill for they were not, as we have seen, necessarily the most fashionable or the most obvious sources of top-class racing merit. They were a seeming hotchpotch of ingredients drawn from

the resources of France, England and North America and blended
with so much care and discernment that they created a distinctive
Boussac 'own brand' that stood out as a superior product on the
shelves of the world thoroughbred market. But an essential feature
of this 'own brand' was that it was intended to be permanent,
disdaining further additives and guaranteeing consistent quality by
using the same ingredients over and over again. All the quality
required was contained within the boundaries of Fresnay-le-Buffard,
and the only condition for perpetuation of the superiority of the
breed was endless crossing of the best elements that had created it.
There was to be no dilution. A brochure put out to accompany the
sale of forty-seven Boussac mares at Deauville in November 1975
summed it up in a passage which may be rendered in translation:

Monsieur Boussac has indeed created a breed within the breed of the
thoroughbred: a breed of homogeneous quality comprising horses with a
singular harmony of outline and marvellously spirited bearing. When one
of them appears in the parade ring at Longchamp people are often heard
to say: 'That's a Boussac'.

The stallions Astérus, Tourbillon, Djebel and Pharis II made the
most vital contributions to the 'own brand'. Their effectiveness
was realized not merely as individuals but through the exceptional
capacity of their transmitted characteristics to complement and
enhance each other. They were truly a team. Two or more of the
great stallions are found in various combinations in the pedigrees of
nearly all the top-class Boussac horses of the golden age after the
Second World War. Apollonia, the winner of the French Oaks in
1956, may be described as having the quintessential Boussac pedigree, as she was by Djebel (by Tourbillon), out of Corejada by
Pharis II, out of Tourzima by Tourbillon, out of Djezima by
Astérus. The influence of all the four great stallions had worked in
unison to produce a genuine Classic filly.

Tourbillon was duplicated in the second and third removes of
Apollonia's pedigree. The operation of the 'own brand' concept
leads inevitably to inbreeding, but in the case of Fresnay-le-Buffard
inbreeding did not occur adventitiously but as central to the whole
process. Réné Romanet showed himself uncompromising in his
espousal of this mating system when he wrote: 'Inbreeding is the

rule; the only problem to solve is how to employ it, how to direct it.' On another occasion he expatiated on the same theme:

When you succeed by inbreeding to good horses you have a purity and a quality not otherwise possible. Too much outcrossing results in a loss of quality, whereas inbreeding accentuates the good. The successes of inbreeding are the best, but they can be secured only by rigorous culling of substandard products.

The views expressed by Romanet on this subject were the antithesis of those formulated by Rhys Llewellyn in his idea of the international outcross.* Llewellyn argued that the Thoroughbred was founded and had been sustained by selection based on performance, not through breeding for purity. He claimed that outcrossing can give extra adaptability and efficiency, while inbreeding leads to the expression of unwanted recessive genes, together with increases of early mortality, sterility and general debility. The two theories could be partly reconciled only if inbreeding were associated with strict selection on performance and the systematic elimination of unsatisfactory individuals as recommended by Romanet. For a long time Boussac obeyed these simple rules and kept the increase of his mares under control by regular culling, but the numbers crept up relentlessly as the scope of his operations responded to the calls of the new era of international racing. There were 105 mares at the end of the Second World War, but an explosion of the broodmare population followed so that by the time Prince V. Wiazemski wrote an article 'Boussac English and Foreign Blood' in the *British Racehorse* in June 1953 the number had leapt to over 150. Since there had been no significant recruitment of bloodstock from outside, the 50 per cent increase could have happened only through relaxation of the standards of selection. The door had been opened to the baleful results of inbreeding postulated by Llewellyn.

Boussac, it is important to note, had some resounding successes through inbreeding. Apollonia was one example, though in her case the inbreeding to Tourbillon was balanced by the other potent factors of Pharis II and Astérus. Coronation V provided the most striking example of his practice of inbreeding, because she was by Tourbillon's son Djebel out of Tourbillon's daughter Esmeralda.

*British Racehorse, October 1967.

Although she was nervous and difficult to manage, Coronation V was sound, brilliant and remarkably consistent on the racecourse, since she had the Queen Mary Stakes at Royal Ascot, The French 1000 Guineas and the Prix de l'Arc de Triomphe among her six victories, and finished out of the first four in only one of her thirteen races during three seasons in training.

There was evidently no lack of vigour or efficiency in Coronation V as a racehorse; on the other hand she was infertile and, despite persistent matings, failed to produce a single foal. It is impossible to be sure whether her sterility was due to inbreeding or to another cause. Certainly inbreeding as intense as that of Coronation V does not lead automatically to sterility or even to the production of enfeebled offspring, for she had a full sister, Ormara, who had normal fertility and bred four winners including the high-class miler Locris.

The balance of probability is that the influence of inbreeding on the Boussac breed as a whole was debilitating. The Boussac horses showed a progressive loss of vigour, soundness, bone and physical substance. Of thirty-four mares bought from the liquidator of the Boussac estate and included in the Aga Khan's 1979 private stud book, eighteen had either not run or had failed to win a race, a deplorably high proportion of mares unequal to the racecourse test and indicating a drastic loss of efficiency in the produce of a stud once the envy of the racing world.

When the great stallions came to the end of their active stud life there were no stallions of equal merit to replace them. Horses like Auriban and Arbar, for all their excellence on the racecourse, were relative failures at stud. A vast and inward-looking breeding operation like that of Marcel Boussac could not survive at the top unless it could generate a supply of good stallions, and this it signally failed to do once what had seemed to be the magic formula involving Astérus, Tourbillon, Djebel and Pharis began to lose its force.

The need for outcrosses became apparent to Boussac himself, though the admission amounted to a denial of the principle on which the notion of the 'own brand' superior breed had been founded. A few female outcrosses had been introduced during the Second World War, though these arose rather from the chance availability of choice mares belonging to foreigners with breeding operations stranded in occupied France than from a planned expansion of the broodmare base. Thus he obtained Bouillabaise and Zulaikhaa from the Aga Khan and Lavendula from Lord Derby. Each of these three mares produced a top-class performer by a Boussac stallion. Lavendula bred Ambiorix, the best French two-year-old of 1948 and second in the French Derby the next year, by Tourbillon; Bouillabaise bred the Eclipse Stakes winner Argur, by Tourbillon's son Djebel; and Zulaikhaa bred the French Derby winner Sandjar, by Tourbillon's son Goya II.

After the war Boussac turned to the United States for stallion outcrosses and was responsible for importing Whirlaway, Fervent, Coaltown and Iron Liege. The American Triple Crown winner Whirlaway and the Kentucky Derby winner Fervent were representatives of the Blandford line which he had shunned before the war, for they were both by Blandford's Derby winning son Blenheim. Coaltown and Iron Liege also had top-class performance, though they had not won Classic races. They were both by Bull Lea, a scion of the Flying Fox–Teddy line which Astérus had represented at Fresnay-le-Buffard so well without ensuring the continuation of the dynasty. They were intended to fill the gap that Astérus had left. Not one of this quartet of American stallions was effective as an outcross. Only in the case of Whirlaway was bad luck involved. Boussac first leased him from Calumet Farm, then at the height of its fame as a leading American thoroughbred operation, and then bought him outright, but he died two years later. However, nothing achieved by his progeny left behind in North America suggested that his early death was a grievous loss, and of his progeny conceived in France only Kurun rose above mediocrity.

By a strange irony Boussac was more successful with representatives of the Blandford line located much nearer home. He patronized Blenheim's grandson Crepello, winner of the 1957 2000 Guineas and Derby, at stud at Newmarket and as a result bred Crepellana, who won the French Oaks in 1969 and was his last Classic winner apart from Acamas. As adverse economic forces closed in and the dissolution of his industrial and thoroughbred empire approached he could no longer afford many expensive outside nominations and was compelled to use home-bred horses of high-class pedigree but indifferent performance as stallions for his own mares. One such was Labus, whose only success in three outings had been gained in a maiden race, though he had finished second in the Group 2 Prix du Conseil de Paris. Labus was by Crepello's son Busted and proved a far better stallion than racehorse. His progeny included the brother and sister Akarad and Akiyda. But by the time Akarad won the Grand Prix de Saint Cloud and Akiyda the Prix de l'Arc de Triomphe the sky had fallen in on the Boussac empire, and they were carrying the colours of the Aga Khan.

Although the limitations of the 'own brand' concept were probably the decisive reason for the decline of Boussac's breeding, without doubt there were contributory causes. One of these was over-stocking. Boussac did add the Haras de Jardy, situated almost in the western suburbs of Paris on the way to Versailles, to his main stud base at Fresnay-le-Buffard in 1943. Jardy had formerly been the property of Edmond Blanc, the casino owner who had imported Flying Fox and owned Ksar when he gained his two victories in the Prix de l'Arc de Triomphe. Appropriately Boussac installed Ksar's most important son Tourbillon at Jardy. The land is not as good in the Ile de France as it is in Normandy, though Blanc claimed that he could have raised a winner of the Grand Prix de Paris on the Place de la Concorde by correct feeding. The quality of the pastures apart, the combined space of Jardy and Fresnay-le-Buffard was insufficient to accommodate the post-Second World War growth in the bloodstock population without the overcrowding which is inimical to the physical development and general welfare of thoroughbreds.

Although Tourbillon was the leading French sire of winners one time less than either Pharis II or Djebel, he was the greatest sire of them all in respect of the potency and the wide spread of his influence. Yet the influence of Tourbillon and the rest would surely have been all the greater if Boussac had not guarded their services so jealously. He believed that a visiting mare had once introduced a serious infection into his own broodmare band, and after that was always reluctant to admit outside mares to his studs. Naturally other stallion owners who sought reciprocal arrangements became equally reluctant to let him have nominations. This did not affect his plans to a serious extent while the 'own brand' concept held sway, but it certainly inhibited recovery when he switched, all too late, to a policy of outcrossing.

One practice which could have had grave implications for the selection criteria applied to the bloodstock was attributed to the Boussac stable by some critics during the years when it was dominating the European racing scene after the Second World War. Those critics alleged that some of the Boussac runners in big races were doped in a manner which gave them an unfair advantage. The allegations may have been, indeed probably were, inspired by envy and uncharitableness. However, the critics could point to certain damaging circumstantial evidence. The most discussed case was that of Talma II in the 1951 St Leger. Talma II had not run since he won the Prix Berteux over 15 furlongs at Longchamp in June. He was a tall, leggy colt, and his appearance and behaviour in the paddock at Doncaster were lamentable. Sweat poured off him, his eyes were starting from his head and he seemed to be in a state of extreme sexual arousal. However, some people were obviously not worried by his display as he was so heavily backed that his price shortened from 100–6 to 7–1. In the race his superiority was absolute. He took the lead with more than a mile to go and drew away steadily to win unchallenged by a distance recorded by the judge as 10 lengths, but which looked more like 15 lengths to experienced racegoers.

In later days when official vigilance was stricter and testing procedures more sophisticated Talma II would certainly have been subjected to a dope test. In the event no action was taken to clear the air. Instead, rumours were allowed to circulate unchecked, to the detriment of the reputation of racing in general and the Boussac stable in particular. Talma II visited England again a month later to run in the Cumberland Lodge Stakes at Ascot. This time he was in calmer mood but gave a much less impressive performance, as he only scraped home by a neck from Eastern Emperor, to whom he was conceding 3 lb. He visited England again twice the next year to run in the Ascot Gold Cup and the Doncaster Cup, but was soundly beaten in both races.

Boussac was a man unwilling to delegate more responsibility than he could help, in either his business or his racing and breeding operation. He had his private stables, and his trainers were allowed little freedom of choice or authority. After the death of Réné Romanet at the end of the Second World War he seldom sought advice on his breeding affairs, preferring his own counsel. The burden of work he took upon himself was prodigious. His businesses, his work as president of the Société d'Encouragement, the supervision of his horses in training and his studs – all these activities occupied him continuously. As his racing manager, the witty and charming Comte François de Brignac, once described it, '"Le Patron" now does everything himself, except cover the mares.' He would fly down from Paris to Fresnay-le-Buffard in his own light aircraft, landing precariously in a narrow field alongside the Falaise–Ecouche road and taxiing forward so that he could alight no more than fifty yards from the rear of the manor house. Time was precious. He became increasingly isolated from other breeders and breeding experts, and isolation leads to stubbornness and entrenched attitudes. This isolation inevitably hindered his ability to comprehend the changing fortunes of his horses and the threadbare condition of the once triumphant idea of his 'own brand'. His reactions had become too slow. And when he did move to take corrective action, his measures were too little, too late, and not well enough considered.

Because his twin empires collapsed finally, because a certain lack of resilience was discernible in his business ventures and his thorough-bred operations in the later years of his life, there had been a tendency to dismiss Boussac as an ultra-conservative who always lived in the past. The truth is altogether different. For most of his life Boussac was a pioneer, a man of vision, an innovator. In a somewhat turgid passage in his article in the *British Racehorse* Prince Wiazemski wrote of Boussac: 'His natural intelligence enabled him to devise methods never dreamed of by the traditional school of breeder. By the scope and grandeur of his proceedings he reminded me of Peter the Great's proceedings in ancient Russia.' Wiazemski was wise to specify the 'grandeur' of their proceedings, because in other respects a comparison of the two men would be grossly unjust to Boussac. For all the daemonic energy with which he dragged Russia out of the dark ages and propelled it into the mainstream of European material evolution, Peter the Great was in many ways a barbaric monster. Boussac, on the contrary, was essentially a civilized man. His attitude to his work force in his factories, his stables and his studs was enlightened and philanthropic. He instituted housing schemes and pension funds in days when compulsory social services on a national scale did not exist, and possessed a social conscience exceptional in the industrialists of the 1920s and 1930s.

Denigrated by the French social and Turf establishment as an upstart, Boussac was excluded for many years from the French Jockey Club. (In contrast to the British Jockey Club, which controls racing, the French Jockey Club is a purely social institution.) At the same time the establishment was glad enough to exploit his flair for organization and administration as president of the Société d'Encouragement. He and the director general, Jean Romanet, son and successor of Réné Romanet, were a formidable team. Men of first-rate intelligence and strong personality, they often disagreed vehemently over details of Société policy, but had such deep feelings of mutual respect that they always arrived at an amicable compromise in the end. Together they were much too powerful to be challenged by the other Stewards of the Société or by any factional racing interest. The benevolent despotism of Boussac and Romanet made French racing on the metropolitan circuit the most up to date and the best appointed in Europe. The modernization of Longchamp, involving the building of a new grandstand block beside the old and sliding it into place on rails, was an engineering miracle.

Boussac was a traditionalist in his attitude to the French racing programme, though he showed a disposition to promote the French Derby at the expense of the longer Grand Prix de Paris, which had been the premier French Classic race for a century; the prize money for the French Derby had overtaken the prize money for the Grand Prix before he resigned as president in 1974. He himself had made the French Derby the prime target for the best of his horses throughout his racing life.

He was, indeed, a shrewd and farsighted judge of racing programmes. In his speech as guest of honour at the York Gimcrack dinner in 1936 following the victory of his colt Goya II in the famous two-year-old race – he spoke in French and claimed it was the first speech he had ever made – he pleaded for a more international outlook in racing, and advocated the inclusion in the Ascot programmes of a weight-for-age race without penalties over 1½ miles, entries for which should be made not more than two or three months before running. He was anticipating exactly the conditions of the King George VI and Queen Elizabeth Stakes introduced fifteen years later and destined to become one of the foremost international races.

Boussac's breeding plan was inspired by a strikingly bold, original and imaginative approach to the problems of improving performance by selection. 'I believed from the first in the necessity of blending different bloodlines . . . This kind of "brew" has become commonplace today, but nobody else was practising it fifty years ago,' he stated in 1975. He went astray when he convinced himself that his original brew was strong enough to last for ever. The apostle of the international outcross became the arch-practitioner of interbreeding within a closed population.

Boussac was far ahead of his time in some of the practical arrangements for his horses. He was one of the first owners to make extensive use of air transport, discovering that the shorter time spent in travelling and the minimal disturbance of their normal routine enabled horses to show their best form with greater regularity than if they travelled by sea or road. This was one of the secrets of the high success rate enjoyed by his runners in England. At Fresnay-le-Buffard in the 1930s he anticipated the design of broodmare barns which was to be adopted generally after the war by building double rows of boxes facing each other across a central aisle under a single gabled roof. This economical and efficient design, later known as 'American style', should more properly have been called 'Boussac style'.

Marcel Boussac would not be described as a naturally sociable man, but he was well aware of the value of some sporting and social functions, especially if they were sustained by the provision of the best of food and drink in lavish quantities. His shooting parties in Normandy were preceded by a mid-morning collation of champagne and sweet cakes, and the morning shoot was followed by a magnificent luncheon; there was no afternoon drive. As president of the Société d'Encouragement he instituted an annual dinner on the eve of the Prix de l'Arc de Triomphe at that temple of gastronomy, Maxim's in the Rue Royale, to which French and foreign racing dignitaries were invited. It was intended as an occasion for making, renewing and extending friendly contacts within the racing establishments. In practice the combination of rich food, vintage claret served in magnums and prolix speeches was liable to be overpowering. One guest, whose experience was not untypical, insisted that he would make his way back to his hotel on foot after dinner because the fresh air and exercise would do him good. After going a few hundred yards he complained of a mysterious lameness until his companion pointed out that he was walking with one foot on the pavement and the other in the gutter.

Undoubtedly the Boussac textile businesses in later years were too slow to adjust to technological change. But, other things being equal, the decline would have been gradual and ultimately controllable. The crippling blow was delivered by the flood of cheap textile imports from the Far East with which businesses depending on a highly paid European labour force and obsolescent machinery had no chance of competing. Boussac's overall financial position was afflicted by a fatal weakness at precisely the same time as his thoroughbred empire was in desperate need of a substantial infusion of fresh capital and fresh blood. Circumstances conspired to undermine the textile and thoroughbred empires simultaneously, denying them the chance to be mutually supportive and dragging them down together in an ineluctable and irreversible decline.

5

The Aga Khan 1877–1957

The Aga Khan and Marcel Boussac laid the foundations of their racing and breeding empires almost simultaneously within a few years of the end of the First World War. They were both so successful that at times each threatened to sweep the board in the country in which he was directing the main thrust of the horses he had bred; and if the Aga Khan never quite equalled the dominance on the international scene achieved by Boussac in the decade following the Second World War, he bred consistently horses of such superb class that he headed the list of winning breeders in England seven times on his own and once in partnership with his son Aly Khan – a record surpassed in his time only by the seventeenth Earl of Derby.

Although the thoroughbred operations of the Aga Khan and Marcel Boussac began about the same time and ran concurrently, and often in competition, for nearly forty years, they were inspired by completely different philosophies. Whereas the Boussac philosophy, as we have seen, involved the creation of an 'own brand' separate from and superior to the rest of the racehorse population, and designed to endure for ever, the Aga Khan's philosophy envisaged a perpetual state of flux involving regular sales of individuals and even whole families, and their replacement by carefully selected fresh strains from whatever source they were available. The Aga Khan's approach to bloodstock was extremely commercial. He had a keen eye to the main chance, and it was said that anything he possessed was for sale if the price was right. Ben Clements, the editor of the *Sporting Life*, wrote in a letter to *The Times* in 1956 that 'the Aga Khan's interest in bloodstock is primarily that of the

143

dealer'. He had a penchant, shared to the full by his son Aly Khan, for a kind of package deal in which he would acquire all the blood-stock of another breeder and then sell off most of the mares and young stock, retaining the few he really wanted and making a quick profit on the whole transaction.

The Boussac philosophy seemed to be bearing the more abundant fruit for a time after the Second World War. But the decline of Boussac's fortunes and the devaluation of his 'own brand' had no parallel in the Aga Khan's studs. Although the latter died in 1957, the stud enterprises continued to flourish under his son Aly and his grandson Karim Aga Khan. The superiority of the commercial approach as a means of securing long-lasting success was symbolized by the events of 1978, when the Aga Khan's breeding empire swal-lowed the remnants of its old rival in yet another package deal, arranged this time with the liquidators of the bankrupt Boussac estate.

Some contrasting results of the Boussac inward-looking philos-ophy and the Aga Khan's outward-looking philosophy can be dem-onstrated from the pages of Karim Aga Khan's private stud book in 1979, the first year after the ingestion of the Boussac mares. Of the thirty-seven Boussac mares included in the book eighteen, or 49 per cent, had inbreeding within the first four removes of their pedigrees; while of the 104 non-Boussac mares only twenty, or 19 per cent, were so inbred. Moreover, inbreeding in every one of the inbred Boussac mares was attributable to Tourbillon, or to his son Djebel or grandson Arbar, all stallions bred by Boussac himself and retained for his own use. On the other hand, the inbreeding in the other mares was attributable to a variety of stallions, though Nearco was responsible for half the instances; and it is fair comment that the influence of Nearco had become so pervasive in the thoroughbred population that duplication of his name in pedigrees was inevitable for breeders seeking to produce high-class performers, in exactly the same way as inbreeding to St Simon became inevitable in the first quarter of the twentieth century.

Analysis of the origins of the two groups of mares (Boussac mares and the rest) in the Aga Khan's 1979 stud book underlines this contrast between the two philosophies in action. Of the Boussac mares, thirty-six, or 97 per cent, traced their descent from mares incorporated in the Fresnay-le-Buffard Stud in the formative period

Right: The Aga Khan at Epsom on Derby day in 1951. His runner on that occasion, the well fancied Fraise du Bois II, was left at the start

Below: Mahmoud, the winner of the Derby for the Aga Khan in 1936 in record time. He became a top class stallion in the United States

The great Italian breeder Federico Tesio with his faithful chauffeur and companion Battista Zibra, who carried the binoculars and acted as his eyes on the racecourse during the last years of his life

Donna Lydia Tesio, the wife of Federico Tesio. She kept the Dormello stud records and accounts throughout his career as breeder

Facing page:
Above: The Aga Khan leads in his first Derby winner Blenheim, ridden by Harry Wragg. The colt's breeder Lord Carnarvon is on the right

Below: Bahram, winner of the Triple Crown in 1935 and the best horse bred by the Aga Khan. His sale to the United States as a stallion in 1940 caused resentment among European breeders

Above: Ribot, the unbeaten winner of sixteen races and the second world-beater bred by Federico Tesio. Tesio died shortly before his first race as a two-year-old

Below: Nearco, the unbeaten winner of fourteen races and the first world-beater bred by Federico Tesio. He proved himself the best European three-year-old of 1938 by winning the Grand Prix de Paris and then became one of the greatest sires of the century during his stud career at Newmarket

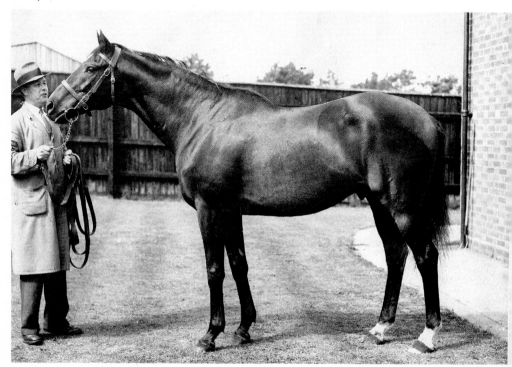

from 1919 to 1926; but only thirty, or 24 per cent, of the remainder traced from mares acquired during the first dozen years after the Aga Khan began to form his stud. Of those thirty, seventeen were direct descendants in the female line of Mumtaz Mahal, one of the most brilliant fillies ever to tread the British Turf and one of the most potent factors for top-class speed in the modern thoroughbred.

The Mumtaz Mahal family is the most constant thread running through the whole of the breeding operations initiated by the Aga Khan in the early 1920s, but even that thread, with support from other enduring strains derived from Teresina and Qurrat-Al-Ain, has been of secondary importance compared to the uninterrupted process of buying, improving and selling again which maintained a continuous flow of exchange and became the hallmark of the Aga Khan's breeding policy.

The Aga Khan was the hereditary chief and Imam of the Ismaili sect of the Shia Muslims. He was forty-ninth in line of descent from the Prophet Mohammed through his daughter Fatima and son-in-law Ali; he was also descended from the Fatimite caliphs of Egypt. The fact that he was a religious leader made him unique among the European owners and breeders of his time; indeed he was a phenomenon without precedent on the European Turf.

Although he was acknowledged as spiritual leader by millions of Ismailis, he was also a prominent secular figure and the grandson of a rich and powerful Persian nobleman, Mohammed Husain, the first holder of the title Aga Khan. Mohammed Husain became embroiled in a feud with the reigning shah in the 1860s and was forced to flee the country, making a new home in Bombay. The flight from his homeland involved little hardship in his adopted country, as he had been able to salvage most of his personal wealth. As W. Somerset Maugham wrote in his foreword to the Aga Khan's memoirs, *The Memoirs of Aga Khan – World Enough and Time* (1954). 'He acquired a vast estate upon which he built palaces, innumerable smaller houses for his dependants, and outbuildings, gardens and fountains. He lived in feudal state and never had less than a hundred horses in his stable.'

The first Aga Khan died when his grandson was a boy, and his son, the second Aga Khan, did not survive him long. Thus the third

Aga Khan, who was destined to have such a profound impact on thoroughbred racing and breeding, inherited his wealth, titles and responsibilities when he was only eight. He was brought up very strictly by his mother. He was taught English, French, Italian, Arabic and Persian. He was given intensive religious instruction and the widest possible education in world affairs. His development as a combination of religious leader and world statesman was greatly assisted by the fact that he was extremely intelligent and an avid reader.

The Aga Khan had a many-sided character. He was deeply religious, and took his duties as Imam very seriously. His broad education, his freedom from racial or religious prejudice, his gift of languages, his frequent travels to many different parts of the world and his sense of moderation enabled him to bridge the gulf between East and West more easily than the vast majority of men in his time. He believed in international understanding and reconciliation between peoples. He was appointed head of the Indian delegation to the Disarmament Conference at the League of Nations, and was elected president of the League in 1937.

He was sincerely religious, but he was certainly not saintly in his own way of life. He was truly a man of the world, and was also worldly; and he had, as Ben Clements suggested, many of the instincts of a horse-dealer. He was gluttonous, corpulent and concupiscent. The racing journalist Quintin Gilbey, who was invited to stay with him in his villa at Deauville two years running during the 1930s, testified to his earthy sense of humour in his autobiography *Fun Was My Living* (1970). Gilbey, having stated that lunch and dinner at the villa never took less than an hour and a half, described how the Aga loved to ply his guests with copious draughts of strong Normandy cider during the first course and gleefully observe their consequent discomfort during the later stages of the meal. He revelled in dirty jokes of the schoolboy variety, which he made a habit of repeating in several different languages so that none of his cosmopolitan guests should miss the point. In the 1930s he weighed more than 17 st and, in puritanical terms, had many of the characteristics of an ageing libertine. He was fortunate to be able to exert a charm which transcended most of his less endearing qualities.

It is obvious that racing was only one of many interests that had claims on his time and attention. Nevertheless, horses were an integral part of his family heritage. For the Persian nobles, horses and the chase had been more than a pastime. They were an essential ingredient of their way of life. Although his mother cut down the number of horses in the stables to about thirty after his father's death, he became a keen follower of jackal hunting in Bombay and kept numerous horses in training from an early age. He claimed that he and his cousin Aga Shamsuddin, with whom he was in partnership, dominated the Turf in western India for a time. He won the Nizam's Gold Cup, then the most coveted prize in the region, four years in succession, and also won the Governor's Cup in Poona with a horse called Yildiz. He won many races in Calcutta, Bombay and Poona with Beadsman.

Nor was his interest in racing as a boy and a young man confined to the subcontinent. He and other members of his family, including his mother, followed English racing form closely; and he recalled that one of his first equine heroes was Ormonde, winner of the Triple Crown in 1886.

The Aga Khan began to go racing regularly in the principal European thoroughbred countries about the turn of the century. Although he attended the races most frequently in England and France, he tried to see the big races in every country he visited, and accumulated considerable knowledge of the most successful performers and bloodlines on an international scale. He had the best of introductions to influential English racing circles, because he had become a close friend of Lord William Beresford, the military secretary to three successive viceroys and one of the leading racehorse owners in India; and Lord William was a brother of Lord Marcus Beresford, the racing manager to King Edward VII and later to King George V.

In 1904 the Aga Khan was invited to stay with William Hall-Walker (later Lord Wavertree), whose stud at Tully on the Curragh was one of the prime nurseries of high-class thoroughbreds in the British Isles, afterwards becoming the British National Stud and finally the Irish National Stud. Hall-Walker urged him to take up racing and breeding in Europe, but the Aga replied that he was too busy with political work and his religious responsibilities to spare the time required for a large-scale racing and breeding operation;

and he had no interest in acquiring a small stud. The proposal would have to be shelved until he had the time and the funds available to race as he would wish.

The decision to begin a serious European thoroughbred operation, when it came, was almost casually made. At a dinner party in the spring of 1921 he found himself sitting next to Mrs Asquith, a daughter-in-law of the former Prime Minister and sister of Cicely Lambton, the wife of Lord Derby's trainer. They talked about racing, and the Aga Khan confided his ideas about racing and breeding on a large scale. 'Why don't you send for my brother-in-law George Lambton and ask him to buy a few mares and yearlings for you?' she asked him.

He did not demur. As soon as he was back in his room at the Ritz he wrote to Lambton and asked him to call. And when he next went to Paris he sent for William Duke, the former trainer for an American friend, W. K. Vanderbilt, who had been one of the leading owners in France. As a result of those calls arrangements were completed for Lambton to buy yearlings and Dick Dawson to train for him in England, while Duke would both buy and train for him in France.

The Aga Khan was inclined to be selfconscious about his wealth. In his *Memoirs* he asserted that there were hundreds of people in both America and Europe who had more capital; and while he admitted that, thanks to his favourable tax situation, few people even in America had as large an income, he declared that the upkeep of all the Ismaili communal, social and religious institutions left only a small fraction for his own spending. That fraction, however, was enough for him to make an immediate sensational impact on the European yearling market and build up the scale of his operations so rapidly that within a few years he was not only one of the biggest European racehorse owners but had laid the foundations of a breeding empire in both Ireland and France.

Although George Lambton was commissioned to buy yearlings for the Aga Khan in 1921, he was not given unfettered freedom of choice. The Aga Khan himself studied the catalogue for the Doncaster St Leger sales, then the most important English yearling sales, picked out two by the St Leger winner Tracery, and instructed Lambton accordingly. They were a chestnut filly out of Blue Tit and a brown colt out of Miss Matty. Lambton duly bought the filly for

7700 guineas, the highest price of the sales. She was given the name of Teresina, and became not only a top-class stayer but also one of the few foundation mares whose family survived in the studs of the Aga Khan and his successors right down to the 1980s. On the other hand, Lambton did not like the look of the colt, whom he found too small and stocky, and declined to bid for him. This colt was none other than the future Derby winner Papyrus, and the fact that he had been denied possession of him by his agent undoubtedly rankled with the Aga Khan, who was sparing in his praise of Lambton's judgement and from that time on had a predilection for small horses.

Altogether Lambton bought eight yearlings for 24,520 guineas on behalf of the Aga Khan at the 1921 Doncaster sales, and the impact of his buying is indicated by their average cost of 3065 guineas in comparison with the average of 649 guineas for all the yearlings at the Doncaster sales that year. The highest price paid by Lambton on behalf of the Aga Khan, apart from that for Teresina, was 5000 guineas for another filly, a brown by Flying Orb (by Orby) out of Renaissance, by St Serf out of Rinovata. The reason for this choice is plain because the filly, who was given the name of Cos, was closely related to Lambton's favourite filly Diadem, who was by Orby out of Donnetta, by Donovan out of Rinovata. Lambton had won the 1000 Guineas for Lord D'Abernon with Diadem four years earlier and described her in his memoirs, *Men and Horses I have Known* (1924), as 'the sweetest and most gallant little mare that ever was seen on a racecourse'. Cos also proved well worth the money as both performer and broodmare, though her family did not persist in the same manner as that of Teresina.

Lambton had also been active in the Aga Khan's interests at the Newmarket July yearling sales, where he bought the fillies Paola (by The Tetrarch out of Pamfleta) for 2400 guineas and Bombay Duck (by Bridge of Earn out of Addenda) for 4000 guineas, these prices comparing with an average of 586 guineas for all yearlings at those sales. The following month William Duke spent the equivalent of £31,396, the highest aggregate for any owner, to buy fifteen yearlings on behalf of the Aga Khan at the Deauville sales. Those yearlings were so well chosen that they won him twenty-three races as two-year-olds and enabled him to gain seventeenth place in the overall list of winning owners in France in 1922. The Aga Khan was a heavy buyer again at the Deauville yearling sales in each of the next two years.

The Aga Khan's most significant invasion of the yearling market was at the Doncaster St Leger sales in 1922. In those days the appearance of the yearlings from the famous Yorkshire Sledmere Stud was the most eagerly awaited event of the sales and on that occasion the Sledmere batch included the individual that everyone seemed to know was going to top the sales. This was the filly by that paragon of speed The Tetrarch out of Lady Josephine, who was also exceptionally fast and had won four races, including the Acorn Stakes at Epsom and the Coventry Stakes at Ascot, over 5 furlongs as a two-year-old. She impressed onlookers as much by her strikingly spotted grey coat as by her quality, scope, air of athleticism and practically faultless conformation. Lambton thought her one of the best-looking thoroughbreds he had ever seen. There was an atmosphere of thrilled expectancy when she was led into the salering. The bidding opened at 2000 guineas, and a duel between Lambton and the Northumberland sportsman, Captain Percy Bewicke, quickly developed. Bewicke was not a rich man and was not normally a bidder for top-class yearlings, but he recognized something out of the ordinary in this The Tetrarch filly and was not to be easily brushed off. He made his final bid at 9000 guineas but Lambton, with the vast financial resources of the Aga Khan behind him, was bound to have the last word. He raised the bidding by 100 guineas, and Bewicke had to admit defeat. It was the highest price paid for a yearling filly since the record 10,000 guineas realized by Sceptre twenty-two-years earlier. Sceptre had won four Classic races, and although this The Tetrarch filly lacked the stamina to emulate that magnificent Classic record, she became, as Mumtaz Mahal, a byword for speed with the nickname of 'the Flying Filly'.

Lambton's purchases at the same sales also included colts who were to give the Aga Khan his first two Classic victories in England. One of these colts was by Orby's son Grand Parade out of Donnetta, and therefore closely related to Diadem and Cos. In view of this relationship, the price Lambton had to pay for him, 4000 guineas, was by no means excessive. Some people criticized the colt's forelegs as being too straight, but Lambton insisted that he was a well-made horse and was vindicated when Diophon, as the colt was named, raced with conspicuous success until he was four, and proved himself the male counterpart of Diadem by winning the 2000 Guineas.

The other colt was by The Tetrarch out of Salamandra, and cost 1000 guineas less than Diophon. Despite his own scintillating precocious speed and ability to pass on that attribute, The Tetrarch had been showing a capacity for siring horses of considerable staying power and was responsible for the St Leger winners of 1920 and 1921, Caligula and Polemarch. Salmon Trout, as the son of The Tetrarch and Salamandra was named, followed in their footsteps by winning the Doncaster Classic race in 1924.

These prices have to be set against an average of 653 guineas for the whole of the Doncaster St Leger sales, but the Aga Khan's purchases were not confined to the top end of the market in either 1921 or 1922. In the former year Lambton had to bid only 420 guineas to acquire Voleuse, a filly by Volta out of Sun Worship. This was a prescient intervention in the market, because Sun Worship later produced the St Leger winner and top-class stallion Solario. Voleuse was a wonderful bargain. She was very fast, and won three races as a two-year-old including the Great Kingston Plate at Sandown, in which she gave 12 lb and a beating to the subsequent Prix de l'Arc de Triomphe winner Parth; and she became the dam of nine winners. In 1922 Dick Dawson, also acting for the Aga Khan, bought Friar's Daughter for 250 guineas, a price well under half the average. The choice of Friar's Daughter was an inspired piece of judgement. She was a weedy-looking filly at the sales, but few of the potential buyers realized that this was due not to any congenital defect but to the fact that she had nearly died of pneumonia the previous winter and was badly retarded in her physical development. Her sire, Friar Marcus, had been a good sprinter during the First World War, but no one could then foresee that he was going to become an outstanding sire of broodmares. Nor could they foresee the eminence that the filly's family was to achieve during the next twenty years. Her dam Garron Lass was a half-sister of Plucky Liege, whose sons Admiral Drake and Bois Roussel were to win the Grand Prix de Paris and the Derby in 1934 and 1938. At the time of the purchase of Friar's Daughter the only evidence of the quality of Plucky Liege as a broodmare had been given by her son Sir Gallahad, who had been one of the leading two-year-olds, though overshadowed by the brilliance of Epinard, in France that year, and was to win the French 2000 Guineas the following season. One attractive aspect of her pedigree, however, was inbreeding to the prepotent St Simon, who appeared three times in the first four removes of her pedigree.

It was one of the ironies of thoroughbred history that these two inexpensive fillies were to have a much greater impact as broodmares than thousands of fillies who have cost many times more, in either real or relative terms. Friar's Daughter and Voleuse respectively bred the two enormously gifted contemporaries Bahram and Theft who, apart from other successful exploits, finished first and second for the Aga Khan in the 2000 Guineas in 1935.

Despite her good form, Voleuse was not the best of the Aga Khan's 1921 Doncaster purchases even in the specialized category of precocious speed. Cos was placed 9 lb above her in the Free Handicap and was the top-rated two-year-old filly of 1922. She was beaten only once, when she was second to the best colt Town Guard in the National Breeders' Produce Stakes at Sandown after being badly hampered at the start. She won her other six races, which included the Queen Mary Stakes at Royal Ascot and the Imperial Produce Stakes at Kempton, in effortless fashion.

Cos was big and strongly built and, unlike many less robust fillies who show fine speed as two-year-olds, she trained on well. She made a brave effort to give the Aga Khan his first Classic victory when she was second to Tranquil in the 1000 Guineas, and reverted to sprinting to give two distinguished performances over 5 furlongs at Royal Ascot, winning the Fern Hill Stakes and finishing third in the King's Stand Stakes. She concluded her racing career by winning the Oadby Breeders' Stakes over 1¼ miles at Leicester in July, when her two opponents were not good enough to test her stamina seriously, even after she had dwelt at the start.

Good as Cos was, as a three-year-old she was being overhauled in general esteem by two of the Aga Khan's other fillies, her contemporary Teresina and her junior Mumtaz Mahal. Teresina lacked the precocity of Cos. She did not run until the autumn as a two-year-old, when she was third in a big field over 5 furlongs at Newmarket on the second of her two appearances. As a three-year-old she developed into an immensely game and tenacious staying filly just lacking the ability to accelerate in the closing stages which is decisive in Classic races. She was third to Brownhylda and Shrove in the

Oaks and third to Tranquil and the Derby winner Papyrus in the St Leger. She was second in four other important races that season, including the Coronation Stakes at Royal Ascot in which she was beaten by the Aga Khan's other runner Paola, the Eclipse Stakes and that most stamina-testing of handicaps, the Cesarewitch. She needed all her courage and stamina to gain her only victory of the season by a neck from Light Jester in the Great Yorkshire Stakes over 1½ miles at York in August.

Teresina took time to find her form as a four-year-old and did not reach her best until midsummer. She then made up for her frustrations of the previous year by winning three races. Her dour stamina was what counted when she won the Goodwood Cup over 2 miles 5 furlongs in July, but she completed her racing programme with a top-class performance when she beat Papyrus and Parth in the Jockey Club Stakes over 1¾ miles at Newmarket two months later.

Fillies as brave and consistent as Teresina over long distances earn the respect and affection of racegoers, but they do not capture the imagination of the public to the same extent as a filly of Mumtaz Mahal's supreme brilliance. Mumtaz Mahal had revealed her prodigious speed as early as the beginning of May of her two-year-old season, 1923, when Dick Dawson subjected her to a formal trial at Whatcombe. The filly selected to try her with was Friar's Daughter, who had proved herself useful by gaining an easy victory at Alexandra Park, though she was never to win another race. Dawson set Mumtaz Mahal to give Friar's Daughter no less than 28 lb, but her superiority was so absolute that she took command from the first stride and proceeded to beat Friar's Daughter by half a furlong. 'I was so astounded,' Dick Dawson recalled years later, 'that I nearly fell off my hack.' Another trainer, Atty Persse, had experienced the same feeling of astonishment when he had witnessed the first trial of Mumtaz Mahal's sire The Tetrarch ten years earlier.

Brilliance on the home gallops is not always reproduced on the racecourse. But The Tetrarch and Mumtaz Mahal, who resembled each other closely in their grey colour, peculiar markings and lithe appearance, were also alike in their ability to dominate their rivals from the start of their races. Mumtaz Mahal was in front from the moment the tapes were raised in her first race, the Spring Stakes at Newmarket, and cantered in 3 lengths in front of her nearest rival, the subsequent Oaks winner Straitlace, in the record time for the 5 furlongs of 57.8 seconds. Mumtaz Mahal repeated this kind of performance in the Queen Mary Stakes at Royal Ascot, the National Breeders' Produce Stakes, the Molecomb Stakes at Goodwood and the Champagne Stakes at Doncaster, in which she attempted 6 furlongs for the first time.

Her only defeat that season was in the Imperial Produce Stakes, also over 6 furlongs. She had been off colour before the race, but it was confidently expected that her class would see her through. However, her problems were aggravated by the fact that the going was heavy, which chopped her speed and sapped her stamina. She was unable to set up her usual commanding lead, and although she was in front until close home, the colt Arcade finally wore her down and beat her by half a length.

The brilliance of Mumtaz Mahal nearly enabled her to win the 1000 Guineas the following May. She quickly opened up a lead of half a dozen lengths and was still clear in the Dip, but she began to falter in the last furlong of rising ground and, although she managed to hold off the challenge of her old rival Straitlace, she could not resist the late run of Plack, who swept past her to win by 1½ lengths.

Her efforts at Newmarket took a lot out of her, and she was not back at her best when she ran at Royal Ascot. She even made rather heavy weather of winning the King George Stakes at Goodwood at the end of July, but rounded off her racing career by one of her most scintillating performances in the Nunthorpe Stakes (later the Group 1 William Hill Sprint Championship) at York a month later, when she beat Drake by 6 lengths.

The victories of Teresina and Mumtaz Mahal, in addition to the Classic earnings of Diophon and Salmon Trout, took the Aga Khan to the top of the list of winning owners for the first time in 1924. He was also top of the list of winning owners in France the same year, thanks mainly to the victory of Pot-au-Feu, whom he bought at Deauville as a yearling, in the French Derby. At that stage his breeding operations were more advanced in France than they were in the British Isles. He bought his first French stud, La Coquenne, in 1923, and added two more, Marly-la-Ville and Saint Crespin, within the next four years. The first of his large-scale sales also took place in France. In 1925 he liquidated his French racing stable on the departure of William Duke to the United States, and among the yearlings he sold that year and two years later were the future French Oaks winners Fairy Legend and Ukrania, and Taj Mah, winner of the 1000 Guineas.

By the end of 1924 the Aga Khan had spent more than £100,000 on bloodstock in England, mostly through the agency of George Lambton. He remained a substantial buyer of yearlings for some years after that, but the volume of his purchases gradually declined as his own studs began to produce enough horses to fill his training stables. He had had a vital impact on the yearling market at a time when yearling prices were depressed.

Whereas the majority of the yearlings he bought in the early phase were bred in England, he directed his own breeding operations to Ireland. His first Irish stud, Sheshoon, was bought from Sir Henry Greer, one of the pioneers of high-class breeding in Ireland, the same year that he acquired La Coquenne. Sheshoon is situated at the Curragh, as is the Ballymany Stud, which he acquired three years later. Ballymany adjoins the racecourse. To this pair the Gill-town Stud at Kilcullen in County Kildare and the Ongar Stud in County Dublin were added later to complete the Aga Khan's quartet of Irish studs.

Sir Henry Greer stayed on as the Aga Khan's stud manager after he had sold Sheshoon. Cos, Voleuse and Friar's Daughter were among the first batch of mares to arrive there in the summer of 1924, and they were joined a few months later by Teresina and Mumtaz Mahal to form the nucleus of an extremely select band of young mares.

Every one of this quintet played an important part in founding the fortunes of the Aga Khan as a breeder. Friar's Daughter alone had not shown good or top-class racing form, and her serious illness may have accounted for her relative failure in this respect. Her genetic excellence was revealed by the fact that she bred eight winners in the British Isles and two more in France. The summit of her achievement was represented by her two Classic sons Dastur and Bahram. Dastur (by Solario), the older of this pair, was foaled in 1929. He began his racing career as a two-year-old by winning twice at Epsom, a programme which would not have been contem-

155

plated for potential Classic colts fifty years later. However, Dastur
was on the small side, compact and wonderfully sound, and came
to no harm running on the sharp downhill sections of the Epsom
course. Later he made a habit of finishing second in important races,
including the three British Classic races. However, his defeats were
certainly not due to lack of resolution, and his regular jockey,
Michael Beary, swore that he never rode a more genuine colt. His
limitations were of racing ability, and he had several compensating
victories in races afterwards classified Group 1, like the Irish Derby,
the Sussex Stakes, the Coronation Cup and the Champion Stakes,
in which he ran a deadheat with the year younger Oaks winner
Chatelaine.

Bahram was three years younger than Dastur. Like Blenheim,
who gave the Aga Khan his first Derby victory as owner in 1930,
Bahram was by Blandford, the best Classic stallion of the period
between the two world wars. Blenheim, whom the Aga Khan had
bought for 4100 guineas as a yearling, jarred himself badly soon
after the Derby and was retired to stud at Marly-La-Ville. Bahram
was taller and had more scope than Dastur, and that made all the
difference. Where Dastur had been beaten in the British Classic races
Bahram was uniformly successful, and became the eleventh horse
in Turf history to win the Triple Crown of the 2000 Guineas, the
Derby and the St Leger. Indeed, he was not beaten in any of the
nine races he contested at two and three years of age.

Like many great racehorses, Bahram was lazy and never exerted
himself much more than was necessary to win except in his last
race, the St Leger, in which he outpaced his rivals completely in the
straight and won by 5 lengths. His trainer Frank Butters, who took
over the Aga Khan's horses when the Aga fell out with Dick Dawson
in the autumn of 1931, had no doubt that Bahram was the best horse
he ever trained, and placed him above Lord Derby's exceptionally
talented Fairway.

Bahram's laziness at home had caused him to start unfancied at
20–1 when he made his debut in the National Breeders' Produce
Stakes, then one of the most valuable two-year-old races, at
Sandown in July. The Aga Khan's fancied runner was Voleuse's son
Theft (by Tetratema), who had already won the Windsor Castle
Stakes at Royal Ascot. Bahram was receiving 9 lb from Theft, and
did just enough to beat his stable companion cleverly by a neck.

Theft was a very fast colt and won his three subsequent races that season. However, there was no doubt that Bahram was his master and when they met again at level weights in the 2000 Guineas the following spring Bahram beat Theft decisively by 1½ lengths.

Voleuse produced a total of nine winners, whereas her contemporary Cos bred only four. However, the offspring of Cos included three high-class performers in Costaki Pasha, winner of the Middle Park Stakes, Mrs Rustom, winner of the Gimcrack Stakes, and Rustom Pasha, who won the Eclipse Stakes and the Champion Stakes and was third to Singapore and Parenthesis in the St Leger. Rustom Pasha was the Aga Khan's more fancied candidate for the 1930 Derby, for which he started second favourite at 9–2 while Blenheim was 18–1. Michael Beary made far too much use of Rustom Pasha, as he sent him to the front at the mile post and committed him to a desperate duel with the favourite Diolite in the straight. The result was that Rustom Pasha ran out of steam with 2 furlongs to go and dropped right out of the running.

Of the quintet of notable mares who were the foundation of the Aga Khan's breeding operations, Friar's Daughter, Voleuse and Cos were all prolific producers of high-class performers, but their influence on those operations did not extend much beyond their immediate progeny. Teresina and Mumtaz Mahal, on the other hand, established families whose influence was a persistent thread in the studs throughout the rest of the life of the Aga Khan and in the times of his successors.

Teresina and Mumtaz Mahal showed the very wide range of racing aptitudes from which successful broodmares may be drawn: on the one hand, Teresina, the slow-developing stayer; on the other hand, Mumtaz Mahal, the brilliantly precocious sprinter. The received wisdom is that staying mares tend to produce slow offspring and that mares who were themselves fast and precocious are more desirable as broodmares. It is true that Teresina produced offspring like the Irish Oaks winner Teresina and Shahpoor, who excelled as stayers, but she also produced Grand Terrace, Gino, Alishah and Tereson who all showed high-class form as two-year-olds. Nor did Teresina's stamina inhibit her as a broodmare, as she bred Turkhan, who won the St Leger and was second in the Derby, and the Derby third Ujiji, and it was due to her that the family took root permanently in the Aga Khan's studs.

Judged purely on the quality of their own offspring, Teresina was a better broodmare than Mumtaz Mahal, whose six winning offspring included only one really worthy of herself, the colt Mirza II (by Blenheim), who was third-rated in the Free Handicap of 1937 two-year-olds. Her daughters Mumtaz Begum, a full sister of Mirza II, and Mah Mahal (by Gainsborough) only managed to win small races, but became mares of such high quality that they ensured the continuity of the family in the same studs for generations to come.

Mah Mahal was the dam of Mahmoud, who won the Derby in 1936 and so enabled the Aga Khan to win the premier Classic race with a horse of his own breeding for the second year running. In this case the Aga Khan was saved from the dire consequences of his own willingness to sell, because Mahmoud was sent to the Deauville sales as a yearling, but the bidding did not reach his reserve price. Like Mirza II, Mahmoud was by Blenheim, and his two-year-old form showed that he had inherited a great deal of his granddam's precocious speed as well as her grey colour. His three victories included two important races, the Richmond Stakes at Goodwood and the Champagne Stakes at Doncaster, both over 6 furlongs. The question about his Classic prospects the next year clearly concerned his stamina. He gave a positive answer to the question as far as a mile was concerned by his running in the 2000 Guineas, in which he lost several lengths at the start through his reluctance to face the right way, but was beaten by only a short head by Pay Up. Obviously his ability to stay an extra half mile at Epsom was quite another matter. It was the opinion of the majority of racing experts, including his trainer Frank Butters, that one of the Aga Khan's other candidates, Taj Akbar, who had proved his stamina by winning the Chester Vase, would outstay him.

In the event, Mahmoud was greatly assisted by the state of the going, for the surface of the course was bare and hard and put a premium on a low skimming action such as his. Charlie Smirke cleverly nursed his stamina, and when he asked him for his effort 2 furlongs from home Mahmoud finished like a sprinter to win by 3 lengths from Taj Akbar in the record time of 2 minutes 33.8 seconds.

Mahmoud's display of stamina had surprised most onlookers, and when he was beaten into third place by Boswell and Fearless Fox in the St Leger he was again dismissed as a horse of limited staying power. However, Frank Butters had shed his doubts by that time, and afterwards declared that Mahmoud would surely have won the St Leger if his preparation had not been badly interrupted by an attack of heelbug. Nevertheless, he considered Mahmoud inferior to Bahram, and placed him only fifth or sixth among the best horses he had trained. Mahmoud did not run again after the St Leger, and retired to the Egerton House Stud at Newmarket.

Mah Mahal bred another top-class performer in Mah Iran, who was by Bahram and so very closely related to Mahmoud. She was rated the second best two-year-old filly of 1941 in the Free Handicap, after the future triple Classic winner Sun Chariot. In her case the influence of Mumtaz Mahal was too strong for her to stay further than sprinting distances. Yet at stud she demonstrated the faculty of her family for breeding middle-distance horses with powers of acceleration that raised them to the highest class. Mated with the Derby winner Bois Roussel, who transmitted a large measure of stamina to his progeny, she produced Migoli, who finished second in the 1947 Derby and went on to win the Eclipse Stakes, the Champion Stakes and the Prix de l'Arc de Triomphe.

The same ambivalence was found in the characteristics of the various offspring of Mumtaz Begum. She had a talented son and a talented if less versatile daughter, both by Nearco. The son was Nasrullah, who won the important Coventry Stakes as a two-year-old, and the Champion Stakes the next year, when he also finished third in the Derby. His record was that of a top-class middle-distance performer, but would surely have been better if the restrictions of the Second World War had not confined him to Newmarket for training and racing purposes; the monotony sometimes irked his mercurial temperament beyond endurance, and Butters had a hard job to ensure that he did himself anything like justice. The Aga Khan kept him for only one season as a stallion, and in 1944 sold him to the Irish owner – breeder Joe McGrath for £19,000. Six years later he was bought by Bull Hancock and shipped to the United States. He was leading sire once in the British Isles and five times in North America, where he proved one of the most influential stallions of all time.

The talented daughter of Nearco and Mumtaz Begum was Rivaz, who was three years younger than Nasrullah. She began her racing career with three stylish victories, showing electric speed to win the Bedford Stakes, the Queen Mary Stakes and the July Stakes, all run at Newmarket in 1945. However, she did not train on even as a two-year-old, and did not run again after that season. She became a wonderfully prolific mare with ten winning offspring. One of them was the blindingly fast Palariva, the granddam of the French 2000 Guineas winner and successful sire Kalamoun. So the Rivaz branch of the family continued to serve the stud well long after the death of the third Aga Khan.

Rivaz's half-sister Dodoma (by Dastur) lacked her great speed but founded an equally enduring branch of the family. Her daughter Diableretta, almost perfect in conformation and quality, was comparable to Palariva, even to Mumtaz Mahal herself, in terms of pure speed. As a two-year-old she won seven races in succession before she met her match finally in the Boussac filly Corejada, who beat her by a head in the Cheveley Park Stakes, the two-year-old fillies championship race over 6 furlongs at Newmarket. Diableretta was the fourth dam of Shergar, who in 1981 was one of the easiest of all Derby winners for the fourth Aga Khan but was the victim of a notorious kidnapping from the Ballymany Stud two years later.

The Aga Khan's reduced scale of yearling purchases after his first few years in the market still secured some notable acquisitions for his racing and breeding operations. None of these was more important than Qurrat-Al-Ain, whom he bought for 12,500 guineas, a price only 500 guineas less than the existing yearling filly record, at the Doncaster St Leger sales in 1928. Qurrat-Al-Ain was an obvious sales-topper because she was a half-sister of Royal Minstrel, who had been second in the 2000 Guineas and had won the St James's Palace Stakes at Royal Ascot that year. Qurrat-Al-Ain proved herself value for the money twice over: first on the racecourse, because visits to Royal Ascot brought her victories in the Queen Mary Stakes and the Coronation Stakes at two and three years of age; and later at stud, for she was the granddam of Masaka (by Nearco), who followed in her footsteps by winning the Queen Mary Stakes and went on to complete the double of the Oaks and the Irish Oaks the following year.

The Aga Khan's dissatisfaction with Lambton's refusal to buy Papyrus as a yearling was partly assuaged when he bought his relative Felicita as a foal for only 420 guineas at the December sales six months after Papyrus had won the Derby. Best Wishes, the dam of Felicita, and Miss Matty, the dam of Papyrus. were half-sisters. If this purchase was inspired at least partly by pique, it had a happy outcome when Felicita became the dam of the great stayer Felicitation, who left Thor and Hyperion, the winners respectively of the French Derby and the Derby the previous year, trailing far behind him in the Ascot Gold Cup in 1934. Felicitation was much better than a one-paced stayer, as he showed when finishing third in the Prix de l'Arc de Triomphe, and by his good form as a two-year-old. Frank Butters placed him among the best six horses he had trained.

The Aga Khan, it is evident, liked to take remedial measures when he was thwarted. The purchase of Felicita was one example of this trait. Another was the purchase of Brownhylda. In 1922 Dick Dawson was training the two-year-old filly Brownhylda for the French owner the Vicomte de Fontarce, and she shaped so well that Dick Dawson bought her full sister Valhalla for 1100 guineas at Doncaster on behalf of the Aga Khan. Brownhylda went on to win the Oaks, but Valhalla proved useless at both two and three years of age. To put matters right, the Aga Khan then bought Brownhylda privately as a stud prospect. She had only four foals, but one of them was Firdaussi (by Pharos), the winner of the St Leger of 1932 which brought the Aga Khan an amazing triumph as owner and breeder. For the Aga Khan's gallant little Dastur was second; then Silvermere intervened, to be followed by two other horses of the Aga Khan's, Udaipur and Taj Kasra, in fourth and fifth places.

The year 1927 was decisive in the evolution of the Aga Khan's racing and breeding interests, because it was the year in which the evidence emerged clearly that he had rejected the 'own brand' concept. In January Edouard Kann, one of the most successful French breeders, died, and the Aga Khan purchased from his executors his stud, Saint Crespin, situated between Caen and Lisieux in the heart of the Norman pasture lands, and most of his bloodstock in the first of his large package deals. He also bought Uganda, who had won the French Oaks for Kann in 1924, for one million francs in a separate transaction. In August the Aga Khan got 970,000 francs back by selling Uganda's daughter Ukrania at the Deauville sales, and although he lost the 1929 French Oaks winner by doing so he was able to retain Uganda and, by sending her to Blandford, to breed Udaipur who won the Oaks for him at Epsom in 1932. The series of transactions left all parties concerned with cause for rejoicing, and Uganda continued to serve the Aga Khan well as the granddam of the exceptionally fast Palestine, who won the 2000 Guineas for him in 1950.

The year of Palestine's Classic victory saw another of the Aga Khan's package deals when he bought the Phantom Stud at Newmarket and all the bloodstock, comprising twenty-five mares, fifteen yearlings and fourteen foals belonging to Wilfred Harvey, who had won the Ascot Gold Cup the same year with Supertello. The Aga Khan quickly disposed of the stud and most of the blood-stock, but those he retained included the two filly foals Kerkeb and Noorani. Kerkeb developed into a top-class staying filly and won the Yorkshire Oaks and the Park Hill Stakes; Noorani also showed good form, though her only victory was gained in the Duke of York handicap at Kempton, and gained fame as the dam of the Ascot Gold Cup winner Sheshoon and the French Derby and Grand Prix de Paris winner Charlottesville, who were bred by the Aga Khan although their important victories were gained after his death.

The Aga Khan had made two fruitful additions to his stud during the Second World War when he bought Eclair, carrying Khaled, in 1942 and Neocracy as a filly foal two years later in private deals. Neocracy was by Nearco out of Harina, who was by Blandford out of Athasi and therefore a full sister of the Derby and St Leger winner Trigo. Neocracy possessed good precocious speed and won the Princess Elizabeth Stakes at Ascot as a two-year-old. However, her major contribution to the Aga Khan's racing and breeding interests was as the dam of Tulyar, whose sire Tehran had been leased by the Aga Khan from his son Aly to win the St Leger in 1944. Tulyar, though slow to mature, became one of the best horses ever bred by the Aga Khan, going from strength to strength as a three-year-old to win seven races in succession including the Derby, the Eclipse Stakes, the King George VI and Queen Elizabeth Stakes and the St Leger. His owner's regard for him was enhanced by the fact that he was a smallish, compact horse, and conformed exactly to the Aga Khan's model of what a thoroughbred should look like.

The Aga Khan's purchases of valuable new potential broodmares like Neocracy, and larger-scale acquisitions through package deals, were balanced by frequent sales. In 1955 he sold nine yearlings, including the future Belmont Stakes winner Gallant Man, to the American Ralph Lowe; and followed that a year later by a much bigger deal in which he sold forty-one fillies and mares, including the Oaks winner Masaka and her dam Majideh, to the Californian breeder Rex Ellsworth.

The most publicized of his sales, however, were of stallions. The first of his important stallions to go was Blenheim, who was sold to the American studmaster Arthur Boyd Hancock for £45,000 after six covering seasons at Marly-la-Ville and syndicated to stand at Claiborne Farm in Kentucky. Blenheim was followed across the Atlantic in the autumn of 1940 by Bahram and Mahmoud, and his later stallion sales included Nasrullah and Tulyar, though the latter pair remained in Ireland for some years before being sold again to go to the United States.

Severe criticism was levelled at the Aga Khan for his sales of Blenheim, Bahram and Mahmoud on the grounds that his commercialism had deprived the European breeding industry, from which he had derived his own breeding stock and substantial profits, of essential means of maintaining the quality of its products. He made no defence in the case of Blenheim, admitting that he had sold him at a time he had no need to. The sales of Bahram and Mahmoud were in a different category. In the 1930s the Aga Khan had been duped by Hitler, accepting him as a man of peace. When the Second World War began he believed that Germany would win, but was surprised by the suddenness of the fall of France in the summer of 1940, and only managed to escape from France and go to ground in Switzerland at the last minute. He had no money in Switzerland, and found that the banks there would advance him enough Swiss francs to cover his living expenses only on condition that he introduced new dollars and invested them in England. He was forced to choose between disbanding his Irish studs altogether and selling the stallions, and decided that the latter alternative was less damaging to his breeding prospects in the long run. He obtained £40,000 for Bahram and £20,000 for Mahmoud, less than a third of their true value.

Blenheim and Mahmoud both became top-class stallions in

Kentucky, but Bahram never adapted himself properly to the environment of either the United States or Argentina, where he stood after failing in Kentucky. Mahmoud, on the other hand, achieved a degree of success in North America which was not foreshadowed by his early stud years in England. The loss of Blenheim and Bahram certainly prejudiced the quality of bloodstock in the principal European thoroughbred breeding countries.

The more sceptical of the critics were unconvinced by the defence of the sale of Bahram and Mahmoud. They were reluctant to believe that the Aga Khan, with his vast and far-flung sources of wealth, could not have found other securities for the borrowing he needed to support himself and his family in Switzerland for the duration of the war. They claimed to be able to detect an element of humbug in his pleas – an element of humbug which could be traced equally in his repudiation of a profit motive for his involvement on the Turf, which he included in his *Memoirs*:

Neither my grandfather, my father or I have ever looked on our racing simply as a money-making matter, but as a sport which by careful attention and thoughtful administration could become self-supporting and a permanent source of pleasure not only for ourselves as owners but for thousands, indeed for millions who follow our colours on the Turf; and we have considered our studs and our training stables as sources of wealth for the countries in which they are maintained, and practical usefulness from the point of view of preserving and raising the standard of bloodstock.

It is apparent that the Aga Khan's phenomenal success as an owner–breeder, exemplified by his dozen victories in British Classic races with horses of his own breeding, was due in the first place to his astuteness in employing the best man available to select and buy, regardless of expense, the fillies and mares who were to be the foundation of his stud; and, once the foundation had been well laid, to the skill with which the composition of his broodmare band was kept fresh and varied by opportunistic acquisitions of other high-class strains, sometimes through the medium of package deals which his great wealth placed him in a particularly favourable position to finance. Conversely, he was never inhibited by sentiment or false optimism from culling individuals and whole strains which were in excess of his requirements or showing signs of deterioration. He was a constant buyer and seller of thoroughbreds, and not of breeding stock only. It is significant that of his five Derby winners, a total equalled only by Lord Egremont in the early days of the race, no more than three (Bahram, Mahmoud and Tulyar) were home-bred, while Blenheim was bought as a yearling and My Love, in whom he bought a half share from his breeder Léon Volterra, was acquired only two weeks before his victory at Epsom in 1948.

The framework of his stud policy thus is clear. It is more difficult to discern the ideas, principles and theories of selection which inspired the conduct of his breeding operations and the matings of his mares. In spite of his family tradition of involvement with horses, his own understanding of horses as individual animals was rudimentary. He was said not to know one horse from another. Quintin Gilbey related the perhaps apocryphal story of the Aga Khan patting Blenheim on the neck as he led him in after winning the Derby and murmuring 'Good old Rustom Pasha', having mistaken him for his other runner. Sidney Galtrey (Hotspur of the *Daily Telegraph*) stated in *Memoirs of a Racing Journalist* that the Aga Khan shouted to him after the finish of the 1932 St Leger: 'Was it Dastur or Firdaussi?'

Galtrey, who had known him well in India in the early years of the century, praised his shrewdness in engaging the best brains available as his advisers, but added that he was very quick to learn and that the seeds of learning about the thoroughbred which he gained from his advisers put down deep roots. Lord Rosebery, who bred and owned the Derby winners Blue Peter and Ocean Swell, described him in his later years as the greatest living expert on the *General Stud Book*.

The Aga Khan himself was generous in acknowledging the debt he owed to Lord Wavertree, whom he consulted frequently after his initial visit to Tully in 1904. Wavertree himself was eccentric, opinionated and didactic. He was a firm believer in astrology and in the horoscopes of his mares as an indispensable aid to planning their matings, but otherwise was a pragmatist in his approach to the problems of breeding. He claimed that if the Aga Khan had laid out all the money he spent on bloodstock in strict accordance with his precepts there would have been no limit to his success. The Aga Khan did not deny it and wrote in his *Memoirs*: 'Looking back now

I see that was not mere optimism on his part, but it would have been proved to be true in practice year by year.'

Nevertheless, the Aga Khan did not say much about the advice he received from Lord Wavertree, nor did he explain how that advice would have changed the breeding policies he actually adopted. One reason why he admired Wavertree was that he achieved success without spending a great deal of money on bloodstock. But he gave only one example of Wavertree's doctrine and then expressed profound disagreement with it. Wavertree, he said, considered maternal much more potent than paternal influence, and even went so far as to say that as long as your mares are good it does not much matter what stallions you send them to. The Aga Khan flatly contradicted this doctrine, and stated in his *Memoirs*:

My own view is that you must try to secure the best and most suitable breeding through both sire and dam, bring it by both inbreeding and outcrossing as near perfect in the abstract as you can. Success will depend on whether any particular foal takes after his dam and the majority of his maternal ascendants or after his sire and the majority of his paternal ascendants.

Otherwise the Aga Khan was tantalizingly reticent about his breeding principles. He poured scorn on those who pooh-poohed science, study and knowledge in racing, but did not specify the directions which research into the problems of racing should take. After 1928 his matings were worked out theoretically by the French colonel, J. Vuillier, and by his widow after the colonel's death. Colonel Vuillier, who managed the stud at Marly-la-Ville, was the author of a book called *Les Croisements Rationnels dans la Race Pure* in which he analysed the pedigrees of 654 high-class racehorses and worked out the proportions in which certain notable ancestors, or *chefs-de-race*, appeared in them. The selection of a stallion for a mare, he argued, should be determined by his capacity for correcting any excesses or deficiences of past *chefs-de-race* in her pedigree and bringing the pedigree of the offspring closer to the normal dosage.

Vuillier and his wife had absolute faith in the infallibility of his theory of dosages, and it is certain that their calculations were one of the factors used in connection with the Aga Khan's matings. On the other hand the Aga Khan's successive stud managers in Ireland

(Sir Henry Greer, Colonel T. J. Peacocke, Nesbit Waddington and Cyril Hall) were experienced and practical men whose judgement of conformation and other relevant considerations counted for a great deal. It is significant that the Aga Khan refrained from mentioning the dosages or the name of Vuillier in his *Memoirs*.

H. E. Keylock made a critical examination of the dosage theory in his book, *The Mating of Thoroughbred Horses*, published in 1942. He discovered that the mating of Mah Mahal with Blenheim which produced the Aga Khan's masterpiece as breeder, the ~~Triple Crown~~ *Derby* winner ~~Bahram~~ *Mahmoud*, increased instead of reducing the deviation from the normal dosages of two of the most important *chefs-de-race*, St Simon and Bend Or, in the pedigree of Mah Mahal.

Probably the fact that the Aga Khan and his advisers latched on to Blandford, the best Classic stallion in the period between the two world wars, and Nearco, one of the two best Classic stallions based in England during and immediately after the Second World War, and used them intensively, was more effective in improving the quality of his horses than any amount of theory. He made more sparing use of the other great British-based Classic stallion of Nearco's era, Hyperion. The sole top-class progeny of Hyperion he bred was Khaled; and he was the breeder of Khaled only because he bought his dam Eclair when she was carrying him. This was surprising, as he had a predilection for small horses with concentrated vitality, a type of which Hyperion was a supreme example. He had been impressed by the opinion of Greer and Frank Butters that British breeders tended to select for size and bone at the expense of vitality and nervous energy. He would surely have been a great admirer of Northern Dancer if he had lived to witness the career of that brilliant little stallion of the 1970s and 1980s.

Vitality and speed – those were the qualities which, above all, the Aga Khan thought should be preserved and cultivated in the search for excellence in the thoroughbred. He expounded his ideas on the pre-eminence of speed in an article published in *The Times* on 15 July 1950 and written only days after the Boussac pair Galcador and Asmena had won the Derby and the Oaks and at a time when British horses were suffering regular defeats by French-bred horses in the most important races. After explaining that British and French horses had enjoyed alternate periods of superiority for a hundred years and that the current run of French success should not be regarded as tragic or signifying a permanent shift in the balance of thoroughbred power, he went on:

France produces a greater number of good stayers. England has gone in for speed, and continues to increase and improve the speed. Now, suddenly, there is a hue and cry that we must adopt French methods of breeding and racing. I, for one, consider that the remedies proposed are worse than the disease. We all know that there are certain treatments that will cure a disease but are certain to kill the patient in the process. The remedies proposed, such as the reduction of two-year-old and short-distance racing, if carried out, will kill the Turf in England, and though it may give us the satisfaction of holding our own with the French on equal terms, it will destroy the foundations on which the English thoroughbred has become the back parent of all thoroughbreds, including the French. Breeding for speed has made the English thoroughbred, and the ultimate remedy must be more and more speed.

And he concluded the article:

At this moment when so many who rule the Turf and so great a part of the press are obviously perplexed and on the lookout for ways and means to keep up the prestige of the English thoroughbred, I have only one piece of advice to offer – be careful when you throw out the water from the tub; do not let the baby fall as well. And that baby is speed.

He could afford to adopt this reassuring, even complacent, tone, because the same year he had won the 2000 Guineas with one of the most brilliant of his horses, Palestine. He took an optimistic view of the evolution of the thoroughbred provided that breeders adhered to sound principles, writing in his *Memoirs*:

I personally have not the slightest hesitation in saying that great progress has been made in the last fifty years. And why not? If it had not been, racing – with all its countless and elaborate methods of breeding and selection – would be senseless and time-wasting. The whole object of picking and choosing in mating is constantly to improve the breed by letting artificial selection assist natural selection.

Whether or not his faith in progress was justified, he was proved right in his confidence that the post-Second World War French supremacy was only temporary. That supremacy passed with the decline of the Boussac empire in the mid-1950s, and in the next decade the main threat to the British thoroughbred was to come not from across the English Channel but from across the Atlantic. The third Aga Khan did not live to witness the dramatic impact of American-bred horses in growing numbers. But the studs he had founded, continually refreshed by infusions of new high-class strains, proved capable of holding their own on the highly competitive international racing scene of the final quarter of the twentieth century.

6

Federico Tesio
1869–1954

The third Aga Khan strongly approved the training methods of Federico Tesio – methods which involved the most searching gallops, often repeated one or more times, over the full distance as part of the preparation of a candidate for a middle-distance Classic race. Tesio's methods inevitably broke down some horses, but he was adamant that it was better for an unsound horse to break down in training than in a race, and that, whatever the risks, it was imperative to present a horse on the day absolutely fit for the task in hand. The Aga Khan had high regard for Dick Dawson and Frank Butters, who trained most of his horses in England, because they adopted similar, if not perhaps equally severe methods. He believed that the majority of trainers in his time were much too inclined to keep their horses in cotton wool, and that was bad for the breed. The great difference was that Tesio's was a completely integrated operation in which he himself owned, bred and trained the horses, whereas Dawson and Butters were public trainers and the Aga Khan, a man of vast wealth drawn from non-racing sources, bred some and bought others of the horses he committed to their charge. For Tesio the operation was a continuous process of producing foals, training and testing them on the racecourse, and selecting the best of the females for the next cycle of production. It was this aspect which made Tesio unique among the great breeders of the twentieth century.

Tesio bred two world-beaters, Nearco and Ribot. This feat alone constituted a valid claim to greatness. The magnitude of his achievement stands out all the more clearly in the light of the facts that his studs were in Italy, a country producing only a few hundred thoroughbred foals a year and with very limited resources in high-class stallions, and that he himself was usually short of capital, at least until the 1930s. He never paid top prices for fillies and mares, and cheaply bought fillies and mares founded some of the most successful strains of his Dormello – Olgiata Stud. The scale of his stud operations was always small compared with some other contemporary operations, like that of Marcel Boussac. For most of his career he was breeding an average of no more than twelve foals a year. The Dormello – Olgiata private stud book for 1966–67, a dozen years after his death, announced with pride that the 1966 British *Statistical Abstract* showed that 62.5 per cent of the tabulated pedigrees of prominent winners in Great Britain and Ireland that year carried Dormello blood, and that the *Blood-Horse* supplement of Stakes winners of 1966 in North America showed that 36.99 per cent of the pedigrees carried Dormello blood. The influence of Dormello-bred horses continued to spread so fast that by 1982 95 per cent of the pedigrees of British and Irish Pattern race winners carried Dormello blood – the majority of them several strains of it; and the Nearco male line had become a dominant factor in Classic breeding in most parts of the world.

It is reasonable, but also facile, to describe Tesio as a genius. The word 'genius' conveys an idea of inspired and effortless mastery. Tesio certainly had flair; but any attempt to explain his unique kind of success would be misleading and inadequate if it did not take account of his courage, his perseverance, his unflagging energy and capacity for hard work. The glamour of the Turf meant little to him. The stud farm, the training stable and the racecourse were his places of work, involving a great deal of repetitive and unglamorous routine. What motivated him principally was the urge to prove, over and over again, that he could breed and train to perfection horses that were not only superior to those of his rivals, but equine prodigies.

Tesio was orphaned at an early age, and was educated at a boarding school. This was an experience shared by only a very small percentage of Italian boys and it was an important formative influence in his character, instilling in him a spirit of self-reliance and competitiveness that served him well in his chosen profession.

At the age of nineteen he received a patrimony of 500,000 lire (about £20,000), and was commissioned in the Italian cavalry. Already he was fascinated by thoroughbreds and racing, and became a competent amateur rider with a total of more than 500 rides in races over jumps. He also travelled widely, visiting China and Argentina, where he lived with the gauchos, learned to lasso and break wild horses, and took a mounted expedition into the steppes and semideserts of Patagonia.

By the late 1890s Tesio was back in Italy, determined to make a career in racing, and married to Lydia Flori, the daughter of a wealthy Dalmatian ship owner. He inherited a small estate in Brianza, a region of rolling hills and small lakes between Milan and Lake Como, from his grandmother, who had expressed the wish that he should breed horses there. Tesio considered Brianza a bad area for stud farming, promptly sold the estate and reinvested the proceeds in land at Dormello, close to the small town of Arona on the southwestern shores of Lake Maggiore. From then on Dormello, with his training stables 40 miles away in Milan, became the centre of his thoroughbred operations.

In stature Tesio and his wife were an oddly assorted pair. He was short, squat and somewhat sluglike; she was tall, upright in her bearing, plain and irresistibly reminiscent, in her posture but not in her colouring, of the Red Queen in Tenniel's illustrations for *Through the Looking-Glass*. But they complemented each other perfectly as a team to run an integrated thoroughbred operation. He was free to concentrate on training the horses and planning their running programmes, buying and selling bloodstock and thinking out the best matings for the mares; while she acted as secretary and accountant. Her accounts were simple but clear, kept in a notebook with the expenditures listed on one side and the receipts on the facing page. One of her chief secretarial duties was to maintain the Dormello register of mares, a duty she performed faithfully from the foundation of the stud until Tesio's death fifty-six years later. The register was a red leather-bound volume containing the pedigree of each mare, and terse comments on the mares and their offspring as dictated by Tesio himself. The entries were made in her own hand, firm and distinct in the early years, but increasingly shaky as she grew old. The comments collectively formed a record of the

Dormello broodmares and their produce of an accuracy and succinctness unparalleled in any stud of comparable importance.

The relationship of Tesio and his wife in respect of the thoroughbred operation was well summed up by Marco Luigi Poli in his introduction to the Dormello – Olgiata private stud book for 1961–62:

Throughout his lifetime Tesio remained the jealous custodian of his own thoughts, ideas and dreams. In his researches to breed a horse who could carry the heaviest weight in the shortest time over the longest distance, he consulted nobody. The greatest and only satisfaction was to succeed in his experiments without any assistance. Only when he was certain in his own mind that he had arrived at the right conclusion would he consult his lifetime collaborator, Donna Lydia Tesio. The conversation would be brief. A gentle smile from Donna Lydia would accompany her approval or dissent. The opinion of his wife and constant companion was all that was needed by Tesio. If it was one of approval, he knew that he could carry out his experiments to a happy conclusion.

Poli conveyed an enchantingly vivid impression of their mutual cooperation, but he was guilty of falsifying the aim of Tesio's researches which, as Tesio stated in the preface to his book *Breeding the Racehorse* (1958) was 'to breed and raise a racehorse which, over any distance, could carry the heaviest weight in the shortest time'. To write of the 'longest distance' was to misconstrue Tesio's aims entirely and to deny his belief that speed and acceleration were the attributes which distinguished the evolved thoroughbred from his ancestors.

The first mare entered in the Dormello register was Velika, a dark grey bought by Tesio as a three-year-old filly in Paris in 1897. Tesio rode her in steeplechases and won a few races with her before sending her to stud. In 1904, to a mating with Melanion, a moderate son of the great sire Hermit, standing in Italy, she produced Veronesa, the first high-class performer bred by Tesio. In her turn Veronesa bred Van Dyck, who in 1915 became Tesio's fourth winner of the Italian Derby.

However, Tesio had been forced to reappraise the whole basis of his breeding operation long before Van Dyck appeared on the scene. He had begun with the conceit that to breed the best horses was, in his own words, 'a difficult but not an impossible undertaking'. But, he admitted candidly, 'presumption was not long in changing to disappointment'. Chastened by the discovery that his recipes for success were to no avail against the products of rival breeders, he was forced to realize that the breeding of champions was not so easy after all. 'The truth', he wrote in the preface to *Breeding the Racehorse*, 'was that in spite of all I had seen and read I had not yet learned to reflect – to reflect, that is, on the whys and the wherefores.' As far as breeding at Dormello was concerned, he had to go back to the beginning and start all over again.

Whether Federico Tesio was paying his first visit to the Newmarket December sales in 1904 cannot be confirmed. What is sure is that this visit was the occasion of his first significant broodmare purchase in England when he bought the six-year-old Jenny Hampton for 200 guineas. Jenny Hampton set the pattern for most of Tesio's subsequent purchases of fillies and mares in England, because she was very well related, but had been an inferior performer and could therefore be bought at a price within his means. Jenny Hampton came from the same family as the Oaks winners Jenny Howlet and Musa (incidentally she was a half-sister of Cassis, the great granddam of Marcel Boussac's most brilliant product Pharis II, though the exploits of Pharis were far in the future), but she had raced for three seasons before she gained her solitary victory in the Arden All-Aged Plate over 5 furlongs at Warwick on her last appearance on a racecourse. Tesio had another reason for choosing Jenny Hampton. His observations had led him to suppose that there was an affinity between the two stallions Isonomy and Hermit. Jenny Hampton was by Royal Hampton out of Isonomy's daughter Domiduca, and when he got her back to Italy he mated her with Hermit's son Melanion. Tesio was proved right, for this mating produced Guido Reni, who gave him his first Italian Derby victory in 1911.

Tesio was at Newmarket again in 1905, when he bought the ten-year-old Jiffy II, by the American stallion The Sailor Prince, for 600 guineas in foal to Bay Ronald. This purchase also turned out extremely well, for the foal she was carrying was Fidia, who gave him his first victory in another of Italy's most important races, the Premio del Commerico, afterwards renamed the Gran Premio di Milano.

His next important purchase at Newmarket was made in 1911, when he bought a three-year-old filly by the Triple Crown winner Isinglass for 1650 guineas at the second spring sales. She had run unnamed and unsuccessfully five times as a two-year-old and once already that year, when she was unplaced in the 1000 Guineas. She was, however, a daughter of Sceptre, who had won all the Classic races except the Derby, so she had parents who had won seven Classic races between them. Given the name of Coronation (Coronation IV in England), she founded a family of lasting importance at Dormello, which eventually produced the 1944 Italian Derby winner Torbido. Having had three good fillies from her, Tesio sent her to the Newmarket December Sales in 1920 and sold her to the British National Stud for 3800 guineas, but she bred only one more winner.

Although the majority of the fillies and mares who made vital contributions to the evolution of the Dormello Stud were bought in England, he did not confine himself entirely to the English market. In 1912 he bought the yearling filly Fausta from another Italian breeder, Count Schleiber, and she proved herself the best of her age at two and three, winning both the Italian Derby and the Italian Oaks. She was equally successful at stud. Tesio mated her regularly with Signorino, a half-brother of the Derby winner Signorinetta, who was champion sire in Italy ten times, and bred the Italian Derby winners Meissonier, Michelangelo and Melozzo da Forli besides three influential daughters Michelozza, Maratta Faustina and Anne d'Alençon. Michelango also did well at stud and sired Navarro, one of the half dozen best horses bred by Tesio and an outstanding broodmare sire, though he was killed during an air raid during the Second World War at the age of thirteen.

Fausta had a superb pedigree. She was by the Derby winner Spearmint out of Madree, the winner of the first race for the Italian 1000 Guineas (Premio Regina Elena), by the Triple Crown winner Flying Fox. Tesio's respect, amounting almost to an obsession, for the Derby as the most important race in the world and the fundamental criterion of selection, and his constant later practice of patronizing Derby winners as stallions, may perhaps be traced to reflection on the excellence of Fausta and her offspring.

More specifically, the racecourse deeds of Fausta inspired him with a liking for the progeny of Spearmint; and in 1915 he went to the December sales and bought his five-year-old daughter Catnip, the most famous of all his inexpensive purchases. Catnip had been a moderate performer, gaining her only victory in a mile nursery at Newcastle. But besides being by Spearmint she had the recommendation of being a daughter of Sibola, who had won the 1000 Guineas and finished second in the Oaks in 1899. Moreover, Sibola was by The Sailor Prince, who had done Tesio a good turn as the sire of Jiffy II.

Tesio paid 75 guineas for Catnip. That was indeed a very low price for a winner of illustrious pedigree, but to appraise it realistically account must be taken of more than half a century of subsequent inflation of bloodstock values. The 1915 December sales were held against a background of a bleak war situation, and the average price realized at the whole sales was only 169 guineas. Tesio was paying well over the average price when he bought Spring Chicken, covered by Spearmint, for 610 guineas when she was submitted four lots after Catnip. Catnip and Spring Chicken were both submitted by the executors of the late Major Eustace Loder, the owner of Spearmint.

The purchases of Catnip and Spring Chicken revealed in Tesio a moving and almost heroic dedication to his vocation of improving bloodstock. He was prepared to face the difficulties and personal discomforts of wartime winter travel from Lombardy to East Anglia with the object, always liable to be frustrated by bidders with longer pockets, of obtaining the mares of his choice; though even he was circumspect enough to wait until the end of the war before committing his precious acquisitions to the long railway journey across France to their destination on the shores of Lake Maggiore. While other breeders in the British Isles and on the continent of Europe were daunted by the uncertainties of war and virtually suspended the development of their breeding interests for the duration, Tesio singlemindedly and systematically continued the process of building up the resources he considered necessary to produce champions. He had his reward, for both his December 1915 purchases came up trumps. Spring Chicken became the dam of Scopas, the first horse to project his reputation as a breeder into the international arena; and Catnip was the great granddam of Navarro and the granddam of an even better horse, Tesio's first world-beater Nearco.

The end of the First World War heralded an era of relatively lavish spending by Tesio at Newmarket. He bought the three-year-old

above: Jim Joel with trainer Henry Cecil and jockey Lester Piggott in the paddock at Ascot in 1980

right: Jack Joel with the Prince of Wales at Epsom on Humorist's Derby day in 1921. His son Jim is pictured between them

*: High Hat, ridden by Duncan
, leaving the paddock before
ng the Paradise Stakes at Hurst Park
1. High Hat was the first of the
stallions installed by Tim Rogers at
rlie Stud

Tim Rogers. He played a decisive
n raising the standard of Irish
ing by installing top class stallions at
rlie and associated studs

page:
Hancock with Buckpasser at
orne Farm

: The brilliant but temperamental
Illah, ridden by Sir Gordon
rds, in obstinate mood before the
Guineas at Newmarket in 1943. He
e a champion sire in both the
h Isles and the United States, where
od at Bull Hancock's Claiborne

Above: Habitat, the champion European miler of 1969. He was outstandingly successful as a sire of fast horses at Tim Rogers's Grangewilliam Stud

Below: Petingo, one of the most successful Rogers stallions and sire of the Derby winner Troy. He died of a heart attack at Rogers's Simmonstown Stud at the age of only eleven

filly Vice Versa for 3000 guineas at the December sales in 1919, the four-year-old filly Chuette for 5000 guineas at the same sales a year later, and the eight-year-old mare Angelina for 3400 guineas at the July sales in 1921. Of this trio Chuette alone had won a race, although Angelina had been second in the Houghton Stakes at Newmarket as a two-year-old. Chuette, whose price was the fourth highest realized at the 1920 December sales, had won two nurseries over the Newmarket Ditch Mile as a two-year-old, and four races including the North Derby at Newmarket and the Breeders' St Leger at Derby the next year; and had finished second to Orpheus in a high-class field for the Duke of York Handicap at Kempton as a four-year-old. Tesio's 1921 purchases also included a yearling filly by Bridge of Earn out of Dutch Mary, a daughter of the triple Classic winner Pretty Polly, for 210 guineas at the Newmarket July sales. She proved a·marvellous bargain, for she was a top-class racehorse, winning the Gran Premio d'Italia and the Italian 1000 Guineas, and became the granddam of one of Tesio's best horses, Donatello II. Vice Versa, Chuette and Angelina also fitted well into the Dormello broodmare band. Many other purchases made by Tesio periodically during the next quarter of a century were much cheaper than this trio, especially when allowance has been made for the progressive inflation of bloodstock values. The purchases included Bunworry, bought as a six-year-old for 2600 guineas at the Newmarket December sales in 1927; Tofanella, bought as a yearling for 140 guineas at the Doncaster St Leger sales in 1932, and her dam Try Try Again, bought for 800 guineas as a ten-year-old at the Newmarket December sales the same year; Bella Minna, bought for 1200 guineas as an eleven-year-old at the December sales in 1934; Barbara Burrini, bought for 350 guineas as a foal at the December sales in 1937; Windsor Park, bought for 6000 guneas as a five-year-old at the December sales in 1946; and Veto, bought for 4800 guineas at the December sales a year later. All these became the dams or ancestresses of top-class performers bred at Dormello.

The Italian thoroughbred was virtually unrecognized in international racing until Tesio began to launch some of his horses at carefully chosen objectives abroad during the 1920s. Tesio saw his raids on foreign races as a yardstick for measuring the progress of his breeding plans and the only way to increase the value of his own bloodstock. He had to show that the products of Dormello were worthy of being judged by the best European standards. His first winner abroad was Scopas (by the Derby winner Sunstar), who won La Coupe at Maisons Laffitte in Paris in 1923 and the Grosser Preis von Baden, at Baden-Baden in Germany, the next year. Scopas was accompanied to Baden-Baden by the filly Rosalba Carriera, who won another important race, the Fürstenburg Rennen. Rosalba Carriera was by the Derby winner Lemberg out of Venture, whom he had bought for 1300 guineas at the Newmarket December sales in 1916.

The victories of Scopas and Rosalba Carriera evoked a rare burst of confidence from Tesio on the train journey back to Italy, when he remarked to his companions that trekking in Patagonia had taught him to 'listen to the stars and speak to the horse'.

The next horse to carry the message of Dormello's growing might abroad was Apelle two years later. Apelle, by Sardanapale out of Angelina, won the Italian Derby from another colt belonging to Tesio, Vice Versa's son Cranach, and was then sent to Paris to run in the Grand Prix, a race he would probably have won but for a thoroughly injudicious piece of riding by his jockey Regoli. Regoli set a breakneck pace from the start and, although Apelle kept up the gallop with great courage, he came to the end of his tether in the last furlong of the 1-mile 7-furlong race and was beaten into fifth place behind Take My Tip.

Apelle may have been beaten, but the merit of his performance in adverse circumstances had not been lost on discriminating observers. An offer for him was made by a French syndicate headed by the Duc Decazes immediately after the race, and when the transaction was not completed the American Richard McCreery stepped in and bought him, and sent him to England to be trained by Atty Persse. Two years later Apelle gave the ultimate proof of his high class as a middle-distance performer by winning the Coronation Cup over the Derby course. Subsequently he was sold to a syndicate of English breeders, insured for £31,000 and installed at the Littleton Stud in Hampshire.

Before leaving Italy Apelle had added the Gran Premio di Milano to his Italian Derby victory, and his Derby victim Cranach went on to win that race in each of the next two years. In 1930 Tesio won the Gran Premio di Milano again with Cavaliere d'Arpino, a half-brother of Cranach. Cavaliere d'Arpino was a brilliant but unsound horse who could outclass any other horse of his time in Italy. Twenty years later Tesio remarked to the English breeder Clifford Nicholson, who bought the stallions Torbido and Niccolo dell'Arca from him after the Second World War to stand at his Limestone Stud in Lincolnshire, that Cavaliere d'Arpino was the best horse he ever bred. 'Surely you mean Nearco,' replied the astonished Nicholson. 'No, Cavaliere d'Arpino,' Tesio repeated firmly.

Cavaliere d'Arpino was to have a potent influence on the development of Tesio's breeding, for he established a dynasty of stallions comprising Bellini, Tenerani and his second world-beater Ribot, whom he bred but did not live to see run. The supreme intrinsic class of Cavaliere d'Arpino may have impressed his owner – breeder – trainer, but it is true that Nearco and Ribot proved themselves in international races whereas Cavaliere d'Arpino, due to his doubtful legs, was denied the opportunity to do so.

In 1932 Tesio was represented by one of the most talented of his fillies, Jacopa del Sellaio, a daughter of the Derby winner Coronach and Vice Versa. Jacopa del Sellaio proved herself the best of her age in Italy by winning the Italian Derby and the Italian Oaks. Nevertheless, despite her resounding victories following those of Cavaliere d'Arpino, the development of the Dormello breeding and racing enterprise had reached a critical point in the early 1930s. Other Italian breeders had followed Tesio's example and had established high-class breeding operations. Giuseppe de Montel, of the Gornate Stud, had introduced the French-bred Havresac II, who became the most successful stallion ever to spend his whole stud career in Italy and headed the list of sires of winners eleven times. Montel bred Ortello, who won the Prix de l'Arc de Triomphe in 1929, a finer feat in international racing than anything yet achieved by Tesio himself. Tesio made extensive use of the services of Havresac II, who was the sire of Cavaliere d'Arpino and the maternal grandsire of Nearco. The Crespi brothers, owners of the Bellotta Stud, also bred on the best lines and gave Italy a second Prix de l'Arc de Triomphe victory with Crapom in 1933.

It was clear to Tesio that his operations were undercapitalized, and that if he were to renew the momentum of Dormello's evolution and reassert his dominance of Italian racing and breeding he must

obtain access to fresh capital. He found the right source in the wealthy Marchese Mario Incisa della Rochetta, who had been hovering on the fringes of the racing scene and often visited the Tesios in the Hôtel Nettuno at Pisa, where they stayed regularly for the early spring racing and training. At the beginning of 1932 Tesio invited Incisa to become a partner in his stud and racing stable, and Incisa quickly agreed. Incisa wrote of the deal in his memoir of the Tesios: 'The price was, for the time, colossal, but the situation was unique so could not be discussed on the basis of any precedent.'*
In addition to the injection of capital, the partnership had the advantage of adding Incisa's stud at Olgiata to the facilities at Dormello. Olgiata, near Rome, was 300 miles south of Lake Maggiore and enjoyed a much milder winter climate. As a result of the agreement, the horses began to run as the property of Tesio – Incisa from the spring of 1932, and the stud operation gained the name of Dormello – Olgiata.

The effects of the easier financial conditions were not seen in greatly increased spending on fillies and mares. In this respect Tesio remained as selective and as cautious as ever. On the other hand, the former financial stringency affecting the day-to-day business of running the whole operation was removed; in particular Tesio was able to pursue his cherished policy of sending mares to be covered by high-class stallions, especially Derby winners, in England and France – a policy which involved heavy expenditure on transport costs and nomination fees. The benefits of the partnership began to manifest themselves in the later 1930s, when Donatello II and Nearco proved themselves performers of the highest international class and finally established the reputation of Tesio as one of the foremost thoroughbred breeders in the world.

Donatello II and Nearco were both grandsons of fillies of whom Noble Johnson, the manager of the Eyrefield Lodge Stud in Ireland where they were bred, thought nothing. Johnson described Duccia di Buoninsegna, the granddam of Donatello II, as a 'very moderate looking yearling, with very straight fore joints, and as bad a mover as ever I saw'. Even Tesio could not bring himself to enthuse over her appearance despite her excellent racing form, describing her in the Dormello register as 'very straight in front, with a broad chest

*The Tesios as I knew Them (J. A. Allen, 1979).

180

and a slightly dipped back'. Johnson saw Catnip as a 'light, narrow filly that carried very little flesh. She ran about nine times without being placed, and was very moderate, hardly good enough to have won a good seller.' He was not even accurate about her racing career, because she did win a mile nursery. Tesio on the other hand, noted her as 'small, sound and well made'. There was a world of difference between the two descriptions, the one indicating a filly to cull and the other a mare to cherish. Tesio added the observation that her offspring invariably followed the physical type of the stallion and not her own.

Tesio's description of Donatello's dam Delleana demonstrated his painstaking search for precise definition of racing aptitude: 'Not very fast, nor a true stayer, but at 1¼ miles very hard to beat.' Coming from anyone less dedicated to truthful and realistic comment, that would have seemed a patently absurd gloss on the form of a filly who had won the Italian 2000 and 1000 Guineas over a mile and the Gran Premio d'Italia over 1½ miles. It was a mating with the 1930 Derby winner Blenheim, stationed at the Aga Khan's Marly-la-Ville stud near Paris, that enabled her to produce Donatello II.

Donatello was unbeaten in Italy. His four races as a two-year-old included the Gran Criterium, and the next year he won the Italian Derby, the Gran Premio dell'Impero and the Gran Premio di Milano. He was then sent to Paris on the mission which it was hoped would crown his career with a victory in the Grand Prix de Paris. Tesio was an extremely superstitious man, and when at lunch at Maxim's before the race the waiter spilt the salt all over the tablecloth, he went white as a sheet and exclaimed, 'We're beaten.' That was a true prediction, because Donatello was beaten by three-quarters of a length by the French Derby winner Clairvoyant. However, Tesio himself was mainly responsible for the defeat through his orders to his jockey Gubellini to counter Donatello's tendency to hang to the left by keeping him on the inside rail until they were in the straight. As a result Donatello was badly shut in, and his strong challenge in the last furlong came just too late.

Tesio's orders invited disaster in view of his own comment on Donatello in the Dormello register, 'A bit long, with a very long stride. Did not go from one pace to another very quickly, but when he did so he was formidable.' No wonder Gubellini said after the

Grand Prix that he would never pay any attention to Tesio's orders again.

The comment on Nogara, the daughter of Catnip who produced Nearco, in the Dormello register was glowing: 'Small, elegant, light, magnificent hocks, magnificent action. Top class from 6 furlongs to a mile.' As a two-year-old she won the Criterium Nazionale over the lower and as a three-year-old the Italian 2000 Guineas and 1000 Guineas over the upper limit of her distance range. So good-looking and talented a filly deserved special consideration as a broodmare. Tesio, after lengthy cogitation, decided that Fairway, the tall, rangy horse who had won the St Leger for Lord Derby in 1928 and had proved himself a brilliant middle-distance horse as a four-year-old, was the ideal mate for her. Derby's former stud manager Walter Alston had been a good friend to Tesio, and would have granted his request for a nomination to Fairway without hesitation. But Alston had retired and had been succeeded by the ignorant and arrogant Captain Paine, who regarded Tesio as a contemptible little foreigner and turned him down point blank. In dismay Tesio booked a nomination to Fairway's brother Pharos, who was standing at the Haras d'Ouilly in Normandy. He did not have much hope of the union because Pharos was compact and much smaller than his brother and, in his opinion, too similar to Nogara to be a suitable mate for her. He was astonished when the produce proved a world-beater.

Nearco was small as a foal, but soon showed that he had the strength and character to dominate the other colt foals in the paddocks. From the moment he went into training he showed blinding speed and, after he had won all his seven races as a two-year-old over distances from 5 to 7½ furlongs including the Gran Criterium and the Premio Chiusura, Tesio thought that a horse with so much speed could not possibly stay as well. Believing that he would be found wanting in stamina in the Classic races, Tesio tried to sell him in England soon after he had reached the official age of three, but failed to find a buyer. It was as fortunate a let-off for him as that for the Aga Khan when the bidding for Mahmoud as a yearling did not reach his reserve price.

Nearco had seven more races as a three-year-old, and outclassed the opposition in all of them. His races in Italy included the Italian Derby over 1½ miles and the Gran Premio di Milano over 1 mile 7 furlongs. After his victory in the Italian Derby Tesio was still in doubt whether he could stay the distance of the Gran Premio and the Grand Prix de Paris, so he arranged the most searching of trials for him over the 15 furlongs at Milan's San Siro racecourse. The other two horses in the trial were the three-year-olds Ursone, a high-class stayer who went on to win the Italian St Leger, and Bistolfi, the best specialist miler in Italy. Ursone, receiving 11 lb from Nearco, was to go the full distance, and Bistolfi, at level weights with Nearco, was to jump in after the first 7 furlongs. The result was that Nearco beat Bistolfi readily, with Ursone far behind. The result satisfied Tesio that Nearco had enough stamina, but events were to show that Nearco's performance was one of the most brilliant ever recorded. When Bistolfi won the Prix d'Ispahan, now a Group 1 Pattern race, earlier on the afternoon of the Grand Prix, it was evident that it would need a miracle to stop Nearco winning. Nearco made no mistake. As soon as Gubellini asked him for his effort he accelerated and put the issue beyond doubt, drawing away to win effortlessly by 1½ lengths from Canot, with the Derby winner Bois Roussel a further length behind in third place, and the French Derby winner Cillas unplaced. As Nearco sailed past the winning post Tesio thumped Mario Incisa on the back and let out a cry of triumph. Incisa commented in his memoir, 'Tesio's great dream' (to produce a thoroughbred prodigy) 'had come true and, thank God, he lived to see it.'

The entry for Nearco was the most laudatory in the whole of the Dormello register. Tesio described him as *'proportionatissimo'*, a superlative which loses some of its impact in its literal English translation of 'perfectly proportioned'. Tesio amplified this impression of absolute thoroughbred perfection by adding: 'Just the right size and of great quality. He had speed and stamina at the same time. He won all his races as soon as he was asked to do so.' But even in his hour of triumph Tesio did not allow himself to be carried away, nor did he abandon his conviction that even the best colts should be sold if the right price was obtainable. To keep them involved tying up funds that should be reinvested, and fostered the temptation to use them as stallions on too many of his own mares. The production of a champion marked the end of a process; the correct sequel was to go back to the drawing board, take out a fresh sheet and begin planning the production of the next.

Four days after he had won the Grand Prix Nearco was sold to the English bookmaker Martin Benson for the then record price of £60,000, and was retired to the Beech House Stud at Newmarket. He became a great sire and the most potent of all influences on the modern thoroughbred. A year earlier Donatello II had been sold to Edward Esmond for £47,500 after his honourable defeat in the Grand Prix and had been retired to the Brickfields Stud at Newmarket. He was not prepotent like Nearco, but had two sons, Alycidon and Crepello, who were leading sires in England and helped to spread the influence of Dormello far and wide. But once he had sold them Tesio washed his hands of them, and developed other strains in his attempt to breed another prodigy.

Tesio adhered to his policy of not keeping stallions at Dormello until the Second World War, when the impossibility of sending mares to England and the growing difficulties of transporting them anywhere on the Continent compelled him to modify his prejudices. One by one, Bellini, Niccolo dell'Arca and Torbido were installed as stallions at Dormello.

All these three horses won wartime Italian Derbys. Niccolo dell'Arca was the best of them on the racecourse. A half brother by Coronach to Nearco, Niccolo dell'Arca had most of the attributes of an outstanding racehorse except the spark of acceleration that made Nearco exceptional. Tesio wrote of him: 'He was a free-goer, and, although he could not pull out anything extra in a close finish, he was a top-class horse. It was his habit, after covering a mile in a longer race, to get his second wind and then go on again with renewed energy.' He was unbeaten as a three-year-old, when his successes included the Italian Derby and the Gran Premio di Milano, and the Grosser Preis der Reichshauptstadt in Berlin.

Bellini was the best son of Cavaliere d'Arpino and was out of Bella Minna, who had been bought as an eleven-year-old at the December sales and was also the dam of Bistolfi. Bellini was a very different kind of horse from Niccolo dell'Arca, as Tesio's description makes clear:

Bellini was certainly not a stayer, but he had a terrific burst of speed. If the pace were not too stiff and his jockey waited until the last 50 yards before demanding an all-out effort, Bellini was sure to win, such was his

184

drive in those last 50 yards. But one more yard and he would have been beaten.

Bellini won the Italian St Leger and, like Niccolo dell'Arca, had an important success in Germany when he won the Braune Band at Munich.

Torbido lacked the outstanding quality of either Niccolo dell'Arca or Bellini, though he added the Gran Premio d'Italia to his victory in the Italian Derby in 1944. He retired to stud at Dormello the following year, but after only two seasons there was transferred to Clifford Nicholson's Limestone Stud, where he was joined by Niccolo dell'Arca a year later.

Bellini made a vital contribution to the progress of Dormello as the sire of Tenerani. Foaled in 1944, Tenerani was out of Tofanella, whom Tesio had bought as a yearling at Doncaster in 1932 for 140 guineas. It may be surmised that the principal reason for the purchase was that she was by Apelle, whose blood he was anxious to recover for the stud. Tofanella herself had shown good form and won the Braune Band at Munich. Tenerani was one of the toughest and most resolute of all Tesio's horses, and won sixteen races in an active career which spanned his two-year-old and his four-year-old seasons. His victories in his native country included the Italian Derby, the Italian St Leger and the Gran Premio d'Italia. As a four-year-old he made Dormello history by becoming the first of Tesio's horses to run and win in England. His first venture in England was in the Queen Elizabeth Stakes over 1½ miles at Ascot in July, when he proved his high class as a middle-distance performer by winning from the subsequent St Leger winner Black Tarquin.

Tesio then decided to leave Tenerani with Norman Bertie at Newmarket for the next two weeks and run him in the Goodwood Cup, one of the greatest tests of stamina, over an additional distance of 9 furlongs. When Tesio travelled to Newmarket to see Tenerani at the weekend before the Goodwood meeting he considered that the horse had been allowed to put on weight and needed a really strong gallop to put him right. Accordingly he arranged for Tenerani to work over the full distance of 2 miles 5 furlongs, with two sprinters to make the pace for the first 5 furlongs and the high-class stayer Whiteway to jump in for the last 2 miles. The result was that Tenerani beat Whiteway by 2 lengths. The Newmarket trainer Cecil

Boyd-Rochfort, who had an enviable reputation for the development of stamina, described the gallop as the hardest he had ever seen.

At Goodwood Tenerani was confronted by the Boussac four-year-old Arbar, who had won the Ascot Gold Cup and the corresponding French race, the Prix du Cadran, and was regarded as much the best stayer in Europe. Tenerani put him in his place by beating him by 1½ lengths. After the race the excuse came from the Boussac camp that Arbar had broken down, but Tesio and Incisa claimed to have seen Arbar walk away sound and were convinced that the lameness was only in the excuse.

Tenerani stood for the three seasons 1949–51 at Dormello before he was sent on lease to the British National Stud at West Grinstead. Subsequently he was bought by the National Stud. Ribot was conceived in his last season in Italy as a result of a mating with Romanella, whose dam Barbara Burrini Tesio had bought as a foal at the Newmarket December sales for 350 guineas. Romanella had been a good two-year-old, winning the Criterium Nazionale, but developed ringbones at the beginning of her three-year-old season and never ran again. Tesio was very disappointed with her; nor did he regard Tenerani as a horse that he should be proud of having bred. 'Tesio disliked Romanella and despised Tenerani,' wrote Incisa in his memoir, implying that Tesio expected little of the mating and that the breeding of Ribot was a fluke. However, one circumstance casts doubt on this dismissive notion, and it is that Ribot was born at the National Stud, where Romanella had been sent to be covered by Tenerani a second time. It would have been out of character for Tesio to incur the expense of sending a mare to England for a repeat mating with a stallion he despised unless he thought that something special could be expected of the offspring.

Incisa put forward Tesio's contempt for the colt's parents as the reason for omitting Ribot from the entries for the early closing Classic races. He may have been right. But it is a fact that Ribot was small and insignificant in appearance in his early days and Tesio may have considered that he lacked the scope to become a Classic horse. It is tantalizing that the birth of Ribot was simply recorded in the Dormello register, without a note of any kind.

Ribot was never a big horse, but he was strongly made and beautifully balanced, with fine, clean legs. Of his world-beating quality there is no doubt. Tesio died on 1 May 1954, just two months before Ribot made his victorious debut in the Premio Tramuschio over 5 furlongs at Milan. Incisa was emphatic that Tesio could have obtained no impression of Ribot's potential greatness one he went into training, because by then Tesio was frail and ill and almost blind, and seldom visited the stables. The running of the stable had been virtually handed over to Ugo Penco, Tesio's faithful head lad for many years.

Thus Tesio died without the satisfaction of knowing that he had produced a second masterpiece. Ribot had two more races than Nearco and, like Tesio's first world-beater, never knew defeat. Most of Ribot's victories in Italy were in minor races, though he did win the most important Italian two-year-old race the Gran Criterium and the Gran Premio del Jockey Club, a race afterwards classified Group 1, as a three-year-old. On the other hand, he remained in training longer and had more opportunities to assert his supremacy in international races than Nearco. He was victorious by emphatic margins in the two principal European races in which three-year-olds meet older horses; he won the Prix de l'Arc de Triomphe at both three and four years of age, and the King George VI and Queen Elizabeth Stakes as a four-year-old.

Tesio would not have disapproved of the fact that Ribot, having gone to stud at first in Italy, spent most of his career in the United States. His location in Kentucky gave him far better opportunities of covering mares of quality than he could ever have had on his native soil. He seized those opportunities to become a Classic sire of undeniable excellence; and if it seems unlikely that his influence will ever be as profound or as widespread as that of Nearco, then that is to compare him with the stallion of the century.

The approach to Dormello was directly from the main road south of Arona. There was an inconspicuous white gate which would not have suggested the entrance to a stud, let alone one of the most famous thoroughbred nurseries in the world, but for the Dormello symbol, a red circle and cross on a white ground, attached to it. A gloomy avenue of evergreens led to the stud house, a plain building with ochre walls, green shutters and a red-tiled roof. Beyond the house lay paddocks stretching to the lakeside, with a view of the hilltop castle of Rocca on the far shore.

Tesio did not believe in showmanship. For all the beauty and the uniqueness of its situation, Dormello, in its owner's conception, was nothing more than a factory for producing racehorses. The stud house was cold and damp, having been erected on the bare earth without foundations, and unpretentious in its furnishing. As for the stud, it was not compact or centralized like most of the great studs of the British Isles, France and Kentucky. Instead, it was a loosely connected group of small farms, some on the flat ground beside the lake and others at various altitudes in the hills on the west side of the main road. This had come about because Dormello lies in a region of smallholdings, and as Tesio sought to expand his breeding operations he had been compelled to buy individual small farms as they came on the market.

Tesio made a virtue of necessity. He was sure that horses thrive on paddocks that are virgin land for stud farming, and pointed out that Apelle and Cavaliere d'Arpino as foals and yearlings had run on pastures that had never been grazed before, but had previously been devoted to the cultivation of maize and potatoes. Moreover, he argued that the division of the stud into small units with widely separated stable blocks helped to control the spread of diseases; while the different altitudes of the units meant that horses could spend the hot summer months on hill pastures and descend to the lakeside for the winter.

The partnership with Mario Incisa brought another great advantage in addition to the injection of much needed capital. Tesio considered that the horse is by nature a migratory animal moving south in search of warmth in winter and north in search of lusher grazing in summer. The location of Incisa's Olgiata Stud in the Roman Campagna enabled Tesio to satisfy this migratory instinct, and he introduced the practice of sending his weaned foals to Olgiata for the winter months and bringing them back to Dormello in the spring. He was fond of explaining that Donatello II and Nearco had been raised in this way.

Partly by design, partly through circumstance and partly through good fortune, Tesio had gathered together a patchwork of studs that provided an ideal environment for the breeding and physical maturing of thoroughbred prodigies.

Federico Tesio was a man of high intelligence and many talents. He was a competent architect and furniture maker, an expert on Chinese ceramics, and a gifted and imaginative painter in oils; and he had a well-developed sense of artistic appreciation which was expressed in his choice of the names of painters and sculptors for most of his horses. He had no taste for, or patience with, the gossip, the stories of betting coups and other trivia which delight the racing community at large.

In spite of his intelligence and his wide knowledge of many subjects, he was prone to harbour fanciful ideas which sprang incongruously from the mind of a hard and dedicated breeder. His book *Breeding the Racehorse* was a hotch-potch of the wise, the banal, the incisive and the trivial, all sprinkled with scraps of information so commonplace that they were not worth recording. Some of the ideas he expressed were demonstrably nonsense. He claimed to have proved that jumping ability is not heritable because the large majority of sires of chasers are horses that have not succeeded as chasers themselves but have made their names as performers on the flat; ignoring the fact that the vast majority of chasers are geldings and unable to reproduce their kind. And he argued that by 1958 no Classic or semi-Classic winner in any country had been bred by artificial insemination because if a single product of AI had achieved even a resonable degree of success those in favour of AI 'would have proclaimed it through loudspeakers'. He was absolutely wrong. If a top-class horse had been bred by AI those responsible would have bent their utmost endeavours to suppressing the fact, because the products of AI are outlawed by every stud book and racing authority.

Many of the contradictions may be explained by the supposition that he was an intuitive genius, and intuitive geniuses are not disposed to rationalizing their methods or codifying their thoughts. Mario Incisa embarked on their partnership with no illusions, having realized that Tesio was not only unwilling but incapable of communicating the whys and wherefores of his breeding and training policies, and that nothing could change him. The portrait he drew of Tesio in his memoir was candid, but affectionate and understanding. Tesio was essentially a loner. When one of his horses was running in an important race, he liked to station himself at the farthest point in the cheap enclosure, distant from friends and rivals, where he could study at close hand the reactions of the horse when pressure was first applied. And he set himself apart from other breeders and trainers whom he despised either as men bound by traditional methods which they copied from each other or as fools who indulged in intellectual dalliance with half-baked breeding theories. He was sure that he alone was an innovator and a creator of great racehorses, unfettered by preconceived notions about the thorough-bred. In his heroic dedication, his isolation and his creativeness he was the Cézanne of breeders.

Although he became an Italian Senator, he was not honoured by the Italian Turf establishment in his own lifetime. The members of the establishment never sought his advice about race programming or any of a hundred other matters of which he should have had expert knowledge. They may have been right, because Tesio's single-minded pursuit of his own aims left no room for disinterested application to the problems of the racing industry as a whole.

It followed that he was determined not to give his secrets away. Indeed, he was compulsively reticent and would resort to frivolous prevarication and even to downright lying to put questioners off the scent. To an inquiry about the type of horse the breeder should aim at he replied 'Why, very long ones.' And when the questioner pleaded for an explanation he added, 'It stands to reason. If you could breed a horse a kilometre long he would have won a 1000 metre race before he had even started.' On one occasion the French breeder Elisabeth Couturié and Adrian Scrope, Lord Derby's stud manager, visited him at Dormello. While they were touring the stud Elisabeth Couturié asked whether he dressed the paddocks with artificial fertilizers. 'Never,' answered Tesio abruptly. A few minutes later he was called away to the telephone. Couturié and Scrope were left waiting for his return near a barn. The door was ajar, and peering inside they found that it was stacked to the roof with sacks of artifical fertilizer which, to add piquancy to the discovery, bore the label of a factory at her home city Le Mans.

Some sceptics even expressed doubts whether he ever set foot in Patagonia, and invented his accounts of mounted expeditions through the desert and communing with his horses under the stars. To be fair, it is necessary to admit that nothing he wrote about Patagonia is incompatible with the contemporary descriptions of the country in the naturalist W. H. Hudson's *Idle Days in Patagonia*. He could have lifted his own description from Hudson's pages, but to assume that he did so would be to carry scepticism to lengths impossible to justify.

Incisa recorded that Tesio did once say to him at Dormello, 'Come with me and I will show you how to do the matings.' But when Tesio was seated with his split-pedigree book open on his knees, his explanations of mating were so garbled and so complicated that they were incomprehensible. Incisa, like everyone else, could only put two and two together, seizing on bits of information that Tesio let fall from time to time, noting the composition of individual Dormello pedigrees and trying to arrive at his general principles by a process of inductive reasoning.

It is indeed possible to assemble a picture of much of Tesio's thinking on the subject of matings in this way. His most explicit statement of his beliefs was made in *Breeding the Racehorse*, when he postulated three main factors, apart from those which are purely environmental, which contribute to the development of a good racehorse: inbreeding, 'nicks' or the almost constantly successful matching of certain bloodlines, and selection of the best quality of stock. Of inbreeding he wrote: '. . . although we cannot reduce the number of a horse's ancestors, we can select his parents in such a way that one particular ancestor will occupy more than one place in his pedigree, thus ensuring a greater probability that certain desired characteristics will be inherited.'

During a conversation on one of his visits to Newmarket he told Cecil Boyd-Rochfort that it was impossible to have too much of the incomparable St Simon, who headed the British list of sires of winners nine times, in a pedigree; and it is a striking fact that both his world-beaters were inbred to him. In the case of Nearco, his sire Pharos was inbred to St Simon in the third and fourth removes, and his maternal grandsire Havresac II was inbred to St Simon in the second and third removes; and Ribot, whose pedigree contained thirteen crosses of St Simon altogether, had a horse inbred to St Simon in each of the four quarters of his pedigree represented by his grandparents – these inbred horses being Havresac II, Apelle, Pharos and Papyrus. However, his recommendation of inbreeding was qualified by the caveat that inbreeding to excess could lead to loss of fertility.

Tesio himself gave an instance of his exploitation of nicks in his

191

account of the breeding of Guido Reni. He used a striking metaphor to describe the beneficial results of some and the baleful results of other mating patterns: 'Certain combinations are always pleasant: a mixture of oil, salt and vinegar is pleasant in any salad. Coffee, salt and vinegar invariably form a repulsive mixture.'

His faith in selection was based on the conviction that the thoroughbred had improved immeasurably, and that progress had come about because breeders always used the winning post in important races, particularly the Derby, as the criterion for the selection of breeding stock.

He was consistent in his allegiance to the Derby as the supreme test of the thoroughbred. He made a practice of sending mares to be covered by Derby winners, even those rated substandard in the entire canon of the race and those that had already proved disappointing at stud. He patronized more than twenty different Derby winners standing in England, and it is a remarkable tribute to the shrewdness of his selection that he bred high-class horses from several whose overall stud performance was below par. From Coronach he bred Jacopa del Sellaio and Niccolo dell'Arca; from Airborne, Surdi; from Blue Peter, Botticelli, winner of the Italian Derby and the Gran Premio di Milano in the year of Tesio's death and the Ascot Gold Cup a year later; and from Dante, Toulouse Lautrec, winner of the Gran Premio di Milano.

Tesio did not keep his own stallions when he could avoid it because that would have tended to inhibit what he considered to be his essential freedom of choice of stallions. He mated Nogara eleven times while she was in his possession, and Ortello was the only stallion he mated her with more than once; the first time she was barren and the second time she produced her only daughter, the Italian Oaks winner Nervesa.

The same principle of retaining the broadest possible base of selection was expressed in his refusal to become too attached to individual female lines. Although he cultivated assiduously certain families, like the 'T' family derived from Tofanella and the 'D' family derived from Duccia di Buoninsegna, he was prepared to cull fillies and mares ruthlessly and was always seeking to acquire members of fresh high-class strains, even if he had to be content with inferior representatives of the familes of great racemares like Sceptre, Pretty Polly and Sibola. He never allowed his judgement to be obscurred by sentimentality. Even his favourite Nogara was sold when he considered – rightly as it turned out – that her useful stud life was over. For Clifford Nicholson, who bought her when she was eighteen, it seemed a reasonable proposition because she would have proved a priceless asset if she had produced one filly for him. He was disappointed in that hope, and the Irish vet Maxie Cosgrove wrote this account of her end:

It fell to my lot to humanely destroy this most famous of mares when she sustained a broken leg at the Tara Stud in County Meath when she was twenty-two. She had a reputation of fighting with other mares and despite her small size usually came off best except for this last occasion.

I have a recollection of her as very young for her age – sharp, quality head, exceptionally deep of girth, light-framed and short-coupled. I made her not more than 15.1 hands and distinctly remember her exceptionally high withers. Were she of average conformation at this point of her anatomy I doubt very much whether she would have stood 15 hands.

These are all aspects of Tesio's breeding policy which can be discovered from his own statements and from observation and analysis of his practices. The aspect which cannot be pinned down and dissected like a biological specimen concerns his intuitive genius, whose working, as Incisa found, was incommunicable. In most respects his approach to the problems of breeding was severely practical and unsentimental, but tempered by an almost mystical element described as a faculty of listening to the stars and speaking to the horse. He depended to a great extent on his 'impressions' of stallions and mares and the way their individual characteristics could be blended to produce an improved racehorse. He insisted that these 'impressions' must be refreshed continually, and for that purpose he made an annual tour of inspection of the stallions he proposed using. He would gaze at a stallion for minutes on end, so that its conformation, physique and character were imprinted indelibly on his memory, and then turn away without a word. The 'impressions' of a score or more of stallions were stored away, invisibly and inscrutably, and so formed the true fountainhead of his genius – a genius whose fruits included not only two world-beaters, but twenty-two winners of the Italian Derby in the space of less than half a century and a revolutionary impact on Classic breeding throughout the world.

7

Jack Joel 1868–1940
Jim Joel 1894–

In the early 1980s the Childwick Bury Stud of Mr Jim Joel was one of the longest running top-class private breeding enterprises in Britain. Indeed, only the royal studs could claim a longer history of operation by a single family. The first Classic winner bred by Jim's father Jack, the founder of the enterprise, was Our Lassie, victorious in the 1000 Guineas in 1903; the last was Fairy Footsteps, who won the same fillies Classic race in 1981. In between times the black, scarlet cap colours of the Joels were carried to victory in fourteen other Classic races, including the most coveted of all, the Derby, by Sunstar, Humorist and Royal Palace.

On the other hand, this record of success at the highest level of racing, though exceptional in its time span, had not been continuous. The whole history of the Jack and Jim Joel breeding operation may be divided into three distinct and contrasting periods. The first, comprising the first two decades of the twentieth century, brought a degree of success for which there are few parallels in thoroughbred history, and a total of eleven Classic victories; the second, from 1922 to the death of Jack Joel in 1940, was a period of recession unrelieved by even a single Classic victory; the third saw the renaissance of the fortunes of the Childwick Bury Stud under the direction of Jim Joel, the Classic victories of Picture Palace, Royal Palace, Light Cavalry and Fairy Footsteps and seven other Classic placings, and a return to the former glory of Childwick Bury as one of the foremost nurseries of top-class thoroughbreds.

These extreme fluctuations give strong dramatic point to the story of Jack and Jim Joel as breeders, and make their stud operations a richly promising subject for study.

The wealth which enabled Jack Joel to enter racing and breeding on a large scale came from the vast mining and financial empire founded by his uncle Barney Barnato in South Africa. The son of a small Whitechapel shopkeeper, Barnato had the kind of genius that would have enabled him to succeed in almost any profession he had cared to adopt. He certainly had rare talents for politics, for sport and for the stage, as either a serious actor or a light entertainer. He chose to exploit those talents merely as peripheral activities. Like many other hungry but ambitious young men of his generation, he decided to seek his fortune in South Africa, whence tantalizing stories of the huge sums to be made from mining and selling diamonds at Kimberley were emanating. In 1873, at the age of twenty, he landed in Cape Town with a few pounds in his pocket, made his way to Kimberley and, within ten years, had formed the De Beers Consolidated Mines in partnership with Cecil Rhodes and achieved a dominant interest in the businesses of mining and trading in diamonds.

Even control of the diamond market, and the riches which it brought, was not enough to satisfy Barnato's ambition. In 1888 he moved to the Witwatersrand of the Transvaal, where the discovery of gold offered literally glittering prospects. Within a few months of his arrival on the Rand he had founded six mining and three real-estate companies, built a stock exchange in Johannesburg and obtained control of the town's water supply. In due course all these diverse Transvaal interests were brought under the sway of the company he set up for the purpose, the Johannesburg Consolidated Investment Company.

Barnato helped to start and encourage horse racing as early as his days in Kimberley, even though the horses available were an ill-assorted lot and the meetings were rudimentary in their organization. He extended his racing interests to England in 1895, when he had a few horses in training at Newmarket under the management of Lord Marcus Beresford. At the end of that year he bought the good-class five-year-old entire horse Worcester for £2000, and the following season Worcester gave him his first taste of real success on the Turf by winning four races including the City and Suburban Handicap, the Trial Stakes at Ascot – a race the horse had also won the previous year – and the July Cup.

Barnato's achievement in obtaining a large measure of control of the production and marketing of gold and diamonds before he had reached the age of forty, while also taking an active part in the politics of the Cape Parliament as Member for Kimberley, bordered on the incredible. He had accomplished so much through the driving force of his ambition, his inexhaustible vitality, his skill in assessing commercial risks, his flair for finance and business organization, and his amazingly retentive memory which enabled him to grasp and understand every detail of all his enterprises. But his success demanded constant vigilance and expenditure of intense nervous energy, and no man could have stood the strain indefinitely. In the early 1890s a business associate wrote of him: 'You know how quick and lively he always is, just like a parched pea in a frying pan, as the saying is. Well, he has always been like that, just a bundle of quivering nerves, and some day that marvellous vitality will cease. Either life or brain will go.' The words were prophetic. He had a nervous breakdown in early 1897, but made a partial recovery and decided to return to England. On 14 June 1897 he committed suicide by jumping overboard from the liner *Scot*. He was forty-four years old.

Barney Barnato had three children – Leah, Isaac Henry and Woolf – but the eldest of them was only four when Barnato died. Much earlier he had felt the need of family support in his growing South African enterprises and had sent for his three nephews, Woolf, Solly and Jack Joel, to assist him. There was more than a hint of a wild-frontier element in the South African mining community of the time, and the Joel brothers did not escape unscathed. Woolf was shot dead in his Johannesburg office by a trigger-happy German. Solly was implicated in the notorious Jameson Raid and sentenced to two years' imprisonment, though this was commuted to a fine of £2000 after Barnato had intervened with President Paul Kruger. Then the mining businesses were disrupted temporarily by the outbreak of the second Boer War. By 1900 Jack Joel was back in England, never to return to South Africa, though he was chairman of the Johannesburg Consolidated Investment Company for many years and immersed himself in the management of Barnato Brothers, the company controlling the family business interests.

Jack Joel was first and foremost a man of business who worked at the interests of his companies with much of the same dedication as his uncle Barney Barnato. Unlike his flamboyant brother Solly, he shunned the limelight as much as possible and preferred to be unobtrusive in both business and recreational matters. Although the affairs of Barnato Brothers necessitated their cooperaton, Jack and Solly did not get on well together and communicated through an intermediary whenever possible. Solly was obsessively jealous of his superior rights as the elder brother. Once, at a family party, Jack informed his brother that he had sold 20,000 De Beers shares on behalf of the firm that day because he thought their price had risen too high. Solly scratched his voluminous beard, as was his habit, and did not utter a word in reply. The next day he bought all the shares back again. Nor did they have any joint ventures in racing and breeding, though they often sent mares to each other's stallions, once with calamitous results. They loved to pit their horses against each other in races, and often bet furiously on the result.

Horses provided Jack Joel with most of his leisure interests. He was an expert driver. An early riser, he liked to drive or ride for an hour every morning, whether in London or the country, before setting off for his office in Austin Friars. One morning in Hyde Park his very strong lead pair got completely out of control. To his horror he saw Queen Alexandra's carriage approaching in the opposite direction, but managed to take one hand from the reins for a moment and raise his hat as he dashed past.

Jack Joel's major recreational interest was in racing and breeding, and as he was a horseman in the truest sense of the word he was able to develop that interest much more fruitfully than many of the wealthy men who have tried to take the Turf by storm. As Charles Morton, his trainer for a quarter of a century, wrote in his autobiography *My Sixty Years of the Turf*: 'There are very few trainers who have remained with the one master over such a long period, and it came about because Mr Joel not only thoroughly understands the breeding and training of thoroughbred horses, but also knows human nature.'

Morton went on to say that Jack Joel did not fall into the trap of imagining that money constitutes the royal road to success on the Turf. Joel began his breeding operation quietly when he bought the seven-year-old mare Emita in 1897. Emita had failed to win a race, but she had the recommendation of being by the excellent Derby winner and stallion Galopin, the sire of St Simon. He registered his colours in 1900 when Kilcheran, the Kilwarlin colt foal Emita had been carrying when he bought her, was a two-year-old. In July of that year Kilcheran gave him his first victory in the Great Lancashire Breeders' Produce Stakes at Liverpool, and went on to win seven more races during the next four years. In the year Kilcheran was born, Emita was sent to the Derby winner Ayrshire, and was shown to have been even more of a judicious purchase when His Lordship, the produce of that mating, became a good sprinter and won the Wokingham Stakes at Ascot.

Jack Joel owed the acquisition of his first great broodmare, Yours, to the murder of his brother Woolf. Yours was sired by Melton during the temporary stay of the 1885 Derby and St Leger winner in Italy. She was brought to England as a three-year-old and ran unplaced in four races before being submitted at Tattersalls Albert Gate December sales, where she was bought by Woolf Joel for 750 guineas. She passed into the ownership of Jack Joel after Woolf's death.

In 1898, her first season at stud, Yours was covered by Worcester, a mating no doubt dictated by family piety. The produce, the filly Our Girl, never ran. For her second mating Yours was upgraded to Ayrshire, and the resulting produce was the top-class filly Our Lassie, who gave Jack Joel his first Classic victory by winning the Oaks. Yours bred only three more foals, but demonstrated her ability to produce top-class offspring again when Your Majesty, her son by the Derby and St Leger winner and four times champion sire Persimmon, won the St Leger in 1908.

A few years later Your Majesty was exported to Argentina, where he became a successful stallion. As Yours had only two daughters and Our Lassie was a failure at stud, the family did not make much of an enduring contribution to the development of the Joel breeding interests, Jack Joel owed the acquisition of his second great broodmare, Doris, to his other brother, Solly. Doris, who was named after their sister, was owned by Solly when she raced as a two-year-old in 1900, showing fair precocious speed to win races over 5 furlongs at Leicester and Epsom. The latter race, the race immediately before Diamond Jubilee's Derby, had selling conditions, and Solly bought her back after it for 300 guineas. He regretted it later in the season when she broke down, and announced his intention to sell her. Jack protested that it was unthinkable to sell a filly named after their sister, so Solly responded by giving her to him. Jack was landed with her, and this time his family piety was rewarded, because Doris became not only a great dam of winners but a lasting beneficial influence on Jack Joel's breeding.

Doris was no bigger than a pony: too small, it was said, to make a broodmare. But in the world of the thoroughbred such criticisms are made only to be refuted, and Doris confounded her detractors by producing a total of ten individual winners including the 2000 Guineas and Derby winner Sunstar and the 1000 Guineas and Oaks winner Princess Dorrie, and three other top-class performers in White Star, Radiant and Bright. Princess Dorrie could not win as a two-year-old, but was clearly the best of her age and sex the following year. She was sired by Your Majesty before he was exported, and proved a disappointing broodmare, breeding only three moderate winners. Sunstar, White Star, Radiant and Bright were all by Sundridge.

White Star was the best two-year-old of 1911, but the hard effort involved in winning five races including the July Stakes, the Champagne Stakes and the Dewhurst Plate took its toll of his enthusiasm for racing. He started a hot favourite for the 2000 Guineas, but finished unplaced and never recovered his two-year-old form. Radiant won the Imperial Produce Stakes, then one of the most important two-year-old races, and Bright, though winning only once, demonstrated her class by finishing third in the 1000 Guineas and second in the Oaks in 1915.

Sunstar, the eldest of this quartet, did not convince Morton that he was a potential Classic colt when he went into training as a yearling in 1909 or during his two-year-old season, when his successes were confined to the International Plate at Kempton and the Hopeful Stakes at Newmarket, in which he deadheated with Borrow, the subsequent winner of the Middle Park Plate. However, he developed remarkably well during the winter and when he began to work again in March it was obvious that he had become a grand horse. 'He gave me the impression of smothering everything else in the stable, and I don't mind saying that I had some very useful animals at that time,' wrote Morton.

Morton's impression was confirmed when Sunstar easily beat another Classic colt, Lycaon, and the three high-class older horses, Dean Swift, The Story and Spanish Prince, in a formal trial at

Wantage on Good Friday. Shortly afterwards The Story won the Prince of Wales Stakes at Epsom and Spanish Prince the Victoria Cup at Hurst Park, and Morton was moved to state that victory for Sunstar in the Derby was 'practically a foregone conclusion'.

Morton was proved right, but adverse circumstances made it a desperate affair. The 2000 Guineas presented no problem, and Sunstar won comfortably from Lord Derby's good colt Stedfast and the Joel second string Lycaon. Two weeks later Sunstar won the Newmarket Stakes over 1¼ miles cleverly. Then, with only nine days left before the Derby, disaster struck, for Sunstar pulled up lame at the end of a gallop. He had sprained a ligament, an injury which should have terminated any hopes of running in the Derby. It needed something like a miracle, plus infinite skill on the part of his trainer, to get him to Epsom, where, beautifully ridden by George Stern, he lasted just long enough to win by 2 lengths from Stedfast. In the event he was probably lucky to win, because Stedfast whipped round at the start and lost 100 yards. On the other hand, the fact that Sunstar was able to win the Derby on three sound legs was incontrovertible proof of his class and courage. He was never sound enough to run again, and the St. Leger, which should have been at his mercy, was won by Prince Palatine from Lycaon.

Sundridge, who mated so fruitfully with Doris, was Jack Joel's own stallion. He raced for his breeder, Sir Samuel Scott, until the end of his four-year-old season, by which time he had won the July Cup and proved himself the best sprinter in England. Scott, believing that he was showing signs of being touched in the wind, then sent him to the Newmarket December sales where Jack Joel bought him for 1450 guineas, a ridiculously low price, even in those days, for a top-class horse. When Morton began to train him in the spring of 1903 he found that he was perfectly sound in wind and limb, and he raced for two more seasons, winning two more July Cups and also the King's Stand Stakes. It was not until the end of his six-year-old season that he became seriously ill and, on recovery, developed a whistle which thwarted plans to keep him in training for another season and run in races longer than the sprints in which he had been supreme.

Sundridge went to stud at a fee of 9 guineas, but it had been raised by stages to 200 guineas by 1911, when he was sold for £16,000 and exported to France. Although he was a specialist sprinter himself he had not a sprinter's pedigree, as his sire Amphion was a high-class middle-distance horse and his dam Sierra was a sister of the Derby winner Sainfoin. As a stallion he showed the characteristics of his pedigree rather than the characteristics of his own performance, and was able to sire top-class middle-distance horses.

Absurdity, who followed Yours and Doris to become the third great broodmare for Jack Joel, also passed through the hands of another member of the family. Like Yours, she was by Melton, and was bought by Joel's uncle Harry Barnato for 310 guineas as a yearling in 1904. She was a moderate racehorse, as she ran only once unplaced as a two-year-old and won two small races, the Vyner Handicap over 7 furlongs at Hurst Park and the Alfriston Plate over a mile at Brighton the following year. Barnato did not own a stud, and she became the property of Joel as a broodmare.

The immediate fame of Absurdity rested on the fact that she equalled the achievements of Yours and Doris by breeding two individual Classic winners. These were Jest, winner of the 1000 Guineas and the Oaks in 1913, and Black Jester, who won the St Leger a year later. She bred three other winners, of whom much the best was Absurd, who showed excellent form as a two-year-old, winning the Middle Park Plate, and became an extremely successful stallion in New Zealand.

Morton considered Jest, who was by Sundridge, easily the best of the fillies he trained for Joel. She was very hot-tempered and after her two-year-old season, which she concluded by winning two races at Newmarket, she was sent back to the stud to be mated in the hope that pregnancy would make her more amenable. Unfortunately she did not get in foal, but Morton found a good companion for her when she went back into training and she calmed down enough to do herself justice at home and on the racecourse. She had to survive an objection for bumping after she had beaten Taslett by a head in the 1000 Guineas but was a decisive winner of the Oaks, although three other fillies were preferred to her in the betting. She made brave attempts to give large amounts of weight to the winners when she was third and second respectively in her last two races, the Coronation Stakes at Ascot and the Nassau Stakes at Goodwood.

Black Jester was by Polymelus, who was owned by Solly Joel and stood at his Maiden Erlegh Stud near Reading. He was a moody and stubborn horse who sometimes refused to display his undoubtedly great ability. He ran a satisfactory race to be third to Kenny-more and Corcyra in the 2000 Guineas, but threw away a winning chance in the Derby by refusing to race in the last 2 furlongs. He was caught in the right mood on St Leger day and gave a smashing performance to win by 5 lengths from Kennymore in record time.

Joel kept Black Jester as a stallion, but he was disappointing at stud. He sired no horses of his own class, and the most influential of his progeny was the celebrated broodmare Black Ray, a grand-daughter of Our Lassie. However, it was not the Childwick Bury Stud that enjoyed the benefits of Black Ray's excellence. When she was six she was sold to the American Marshall Field and became the foundation mare of his breeding operations in Ireland.

Jack Joel's first stud was at his home Northaw House near Potter's Bar in Middlesex. Our Lassie and Your Majesty were bred there, and so was Glass Doll, by the Triple Crown winner Isinglass, who won the Oaks for him in 1907. Sundridge spent his first three covering seasons there.

The same year that Glass Doll won the Oaks, Childwick Bury, 10 miles to the northwest of Northaw and close to the city of St Albans, came on the market as a result of the death of its owner Sir J. Blundell Maple. Maple had established a thriving stud there, and won Classic races with Kirkconnel, Siffleuse and Nun Nicer. Jack Joel drove over to inspect the vacant house and estate, and was not much impressed. He found the solid Georgian mansion, with a huge wrought-iron-framed conservatory clapped to the west side, too big, and the grounds and gardens, which required seventeen gard-eners for their upkeep, too extensive and uneconomic to run. But the agent was determined that he should have the place. 'Surely there must be a price at which you would want to buy?' he demanded. 'Only if it is very cheap,' Joel replied tersely.

One evening two weeks later when he was changing for dinner Joel was brought a message that the agent had called and wished to see him urgently. Joel gave instructions that he should be shown up. 'Well, what is it that is so urgent?' he asked as the agent came in. 'I bought Childwick Bury for you this morning,' was the reply. 'I was so astonished that I nearly fell over backwards into the bath,' Jack Joel told his son Jim some time later.

A dozen years earlier the periodical *Racing Illustrated* had described the Childwick Bury Stud as 'one of the most complete and beautifully arranged of its kind'. It was not complete enough to satisfy Joel, who soon put in hand plans to enlarge and improve the stud amenities. One of the principal improvements concerned the old cattle yard adjacent to the stud manager's house. The cattle stalls were pulled down and replaced by an L-shaped range of modern boxes; and the yard itself was filled in and planted with clumps of trees and shrubs set in the midst of spacious lawns. Childwick Bury became a show place among the English studs.

The departure of Sundridge from Childwick Bury was followed by the advent of Sunstar, whose breakdown meant that he began stud duty as a four-year-old. Two years later he was joined by Prince Palatine, who had profited from his absence to win the St Leger. Prince Palatine went on to win the Ascot Gold Cup twice and prove himself the best stayer in the country. After the second of the Gold Cup victories, Joel negotiated the purchase of Prince Palatine for £45,000, with a contingency that the price would be reduced by £5000 if he should be beaten in the Goodwood Cup. At that time he had not even examined the horse, and when he and Morton went to have a look at him in the paddock at Goodwood they did not like what they saw. Their forebodings proved correct because Prince Palatine, having started at 5–2 on, finished unplaced behind the 100–8 chance Catmint and pulled up lame. Nor did Prince Palatine give Joel any cause to congratulate himself on the purchase by his deeds at Childwick Bury. After four seasons there, during which a high proportion of his mares were barren, he was sold to go to France for £18,000. There he partly redeemed himself by founding a male line which has produced such top-class racehorses and sires like Prince Chevalier, Sicambre and Princequillo.

Sunstar was far more successful than Prince Palatine at Childwick Bury. He was never leading sire of winners, but was second twice and third twice. However, the best of his progeny were bred by mare owners other than Jack Joel, particularly Lord Astor, for whom he sired the top-class horses Sunny Jane, Buchan, Craig-An-Eran and Saltash. The best of the progeny of Sunstar bred by Joel were Star Hawk, who won two races at Newmarket as a two-year-old in 1915 and was then exported to the United States, where he was second in the Kentucky Derby; and North Star, who won the

Middle Park Plate in 1916 and was also exported to the United States, but broke down on the eve of the Kentucky Derby.

Star Hawk and North Star were only two of many horses sold by Joel to America during the First World War when racing in England was severely restricted. The breeding stock were preserved intact, and when the war was over the racing activities were resumed in full. The way ahead was to the climactic year 1921 and its season of triumphs and tragedies for the Childwick Bury Stud. The protagonists in the 1921 dramas were Jest and her son Humorist.

The stud career of Jest began inauspiciously. She had failed to get in foal to a cover while in training, and was barren in each of her first three seasons at stud. In 1916 she was covered by Sunstar and became pregnant for the first time, but the foal was born dead. She was then sent to Polymelus and at last produced a live foal, the chestnut colt Humorist.

Twenty-five yearlings entered Morton's stable from Childwick Bury in the autumn of 1919, and it did not take the trainer long to discover that Humorist was easily the best of them. Moreover, he had none of the moody nature of his close relation Black Jester, who was by the same sire out of Jest's dam. He was one of the most charming and even-tempered horses that Morton had ever trained, and the stable staff found him a joy to handle. His failings were not of temperament, but of constitution. Morton prepared him to make his debut in the Woodcote Stakes at the Epsom Summer Meeting, and considered him a certainty on the way he had been working. But shortly before the race he went off his feed and became dull in his coat. He ran in and won the Woodcote Stakes, but started to cough before the Royal Ascot meeting and could not run there. He took a long time to recover, and Morton wrote uneasily of his general state of health: 'I knew him to be at least a stone in front of the other two-year-olds, but all the time I felt there was something wrong with him. It continually puzzled me why he would be perfectly well one day and listless the next.'

Although he won two minor races during the autumn, he ran far below his proper form in the Champagne Stakes and was unluckily beaten by Monarch in the Middle Park Plate. His performance in the latter race inspired Brownie Carslake, who rode him, to remark that with ordinary luck he would win the Derby. Carslake added that he was a dead stayer, and it is a remarkable example of the different impressions that experienced jockeys can obtain of the same horse that Steve Donoghue, having been beaten on him in the 2000 Guineas the following spring, told Morton that Humorist did not stay. There seemed to be good reason for Donoghue's opinion, because Humorist was cantering in front a furlong from the finish, but then collapsed and was overtaken by Craig-An-Eran and Lemonora. On the other hand, Morton was not deceived by appearances and replied to Donoghue, 'All the same, I think he will win the Derby.'

At that time Donoghue was in a class of his own as a jockey over the Derby course. He liked to get away well from the start and hold a position close to the leaders the whole way. He adopted those tactics on Humorist, sent him to the front 2 furlongs from the finish and, although Craig-An-Eran put in a strong challenge, kept him going to win by a neck.

The result vindicated Morton's judgement completely, but his and Joel's sense of triumph was shortlived. It was intended that Humorist should run in the Hardwicke Stakes on the Friday of the Royal Ascot meeting, and he was sent to Ascot at the beginning of the week so that he could have a gallop on the course on the Tuesday morning. But he was unable to have the gallop, let alone run in the Hardwicke Stakes, because he was found to be bleeding profusely from the nose when he pulled up at the end of the preliminary canter.

Humorist was sent home to Wantage. The next weekend A. J. Munnings went down to Wantage to make some sketches for a portrait of Humorist he had been commissioned to paint. Humorist was led out onto the lawn in front of Morton's house to be sketched on the Saturday and Sunday mornings, and each time Munnings remarked how well he looked. But on Sunday afternoon one of the stable lads noticed a stream of blood flowing under the door of Humorist's box, and when he opened the door he found the Derby winner lying dead. He must have been standing by the manger when the bleeding started, because a trail of blood round the walls showed how he had reeled round the box in search of air and finally collapsed with his nose close to the gap under the door. The postmortem revealed that he had been suffering from tuberculosis and had died of a severe haemorrhage of the lungs.

The death of Humorist had been preceded by that of his dam Jest in the spring. She had been covered by Polymelus the previous year and returned to Maiden Erlegh in 1921 to have her foal and be mated once more with the sire of Humorist. But the foal was born dead, and when she was washed out some disinfectant was left inside her, and septicaemia set in with fatal results. Jack Joel was absolutely furious at the manner of her death, and swore that he would have sued for negligence were it not for the fact that his brother's stud was involved. He worked off some of his anger by writing against the name of Jest in his stud notes: 'Murdered at Reading!'

Success in Classic races is the criterion by which a stud aiming to produce high-class thoroughbreds is judged. Furthermore, Classic winners, once produced, are the base upon which the future operations of the stud must stand either through their use as breeding stock or their sale to generate funds for investment in fresh stock. The loss in a single season of a Derby winner within three weeks of his Epsom victory and his dam, herself a dual Classic winner, after producing only three foals is a double blow which is bound to prejudice gravely any stud's chances of breeding further top-class performers. In the case of Jest, her two offspring besides Humorist were the colt Chief Ruler, who never ran and was exported to New Zealand, and the filly Laughter, by Polymelus's son Pommern, who ran three times without winning a race.

The fortunes of Childwick Bury could not be expected to recover easily from the reverses of 1921. The stud produced no more Classic winners for Jack Joel, and only one Classic-placed horse. That was Sunstar's son Green Fire, who was beaten by a head and a neck by Diophon and Bright Knight in the 2000 Guineas in 1924 after winning the Greenham Plate at Newbury. The extent to which the Childwick Bury standards slipped from the golden days of the first two decades of the century is indicated by the fact that Priory Park, the biggest stakes earner owned by Jack Joel between the racing career of Humorist and his own death, was not even bred at Childwick Bury. Joel bought Priory Park as a three-year-old for £3000 and had to wait nearly two years before winning a race with him. Priory Park then became a highly lucrative performer in big handicaps, winning the Lincolnshire Handicap and the Stewards' Cup in 1927, and the City and Suburban and the Royal Hunt Cup the next year.

The deaths of Humorist and Jest could be held responsible for a temporary slump in the quality of the Childwick Bury bloodstock. They could even account for a failure ever to recover the marvellous Classic striking rate of the first phase of the stud's evolution. It would be stretching credulity to breaking point to suggest that the complete collapse of Childwick Bury as a source of Classic winners in the 1920s and 1930s should be attributed to this cause alone. Jim Joel was convinced that Childwick Bury was condemned to a long spell in the wilderness by his father's policy of installing second-class stallions there and using them on his own high-class mares. There was Black Jester, admittedly a performer of great talent on his day, but a horse of doubtful temperament; his progeny won more than 200 races altogether, but they all had limitations. There was Thunderer, a contemporary of Humorist and, according to Morton, at least a stone inferior to him; and there was Othello, the most surprising choice of all for a breeder aiming to produce the best, since the summit of his achievement was to win the unimportant Wharncliffe Handicap over 7 furlongs at Doncaster.

Jim Joel was acutely aware of his father's fundamental errors of selection. The Joels' box at Doncaster was next door to that of Lord Derby. On St Leger day in 1933 Derby invited Jim to his box for the race in which his great little horse Hyperion was a hot favourite to supplement his Derby victory. Derby was too nervous to watch and, as there was no broadcast commentary in those days, asked Jim to read the race for him. Derby sat with his eyes tight shut, his bushy moustache and red cheeks quivering with excitement, while Hyperion jumped off briskly and took the lead after going half a mile. When they were 2 furlongs from the finish and Hyperion was still cantering in front, Jim turned to Derby and told him, 'It's all right. You can open your eyes now.'

Afterwards Derby confided to Jim Joel that he had a recurrent nightmare in which the quality of his bloodstock had sunk so low that he could not produce a winner of any kind. Jim quickly reassured him. 'You have nothing to worry about. You are doing all the right things. But we are committing suicide.'

For a long time Jim Joel was unable to persuade his father to change his disastrous policy. In the last few years before the Second World War Jack Joel began to realize the gravity of his mistake, and made bids for the two outstanding Italian horses, Donatello II and

207

Nearco, after they had travelled to France to run in the Grand Prix de Paris. (Donatello was second in 1937 and Nearco won the following year.) In each case he was forestalled, though by English breeders with the result that the two horses spent their stud careers at Newmarket, to the inestimable advantage of the British thoroughbred.

It was Donatello, indeed, who was the agent of the revival of Childwick Bury as a source of Classic winners after the death of Jack Joel in 1940. Jim, who inherited the stud and the bloodstock, promptly sent the mare Amuse to Donatello. The produce of this mating was the bay filly Picture Play, who won two of her four races, and was third in the Queen Mary Stakes, as a two-year-old in 1943 and proved herself a top-class miler by winning the 1000 Guineas by 4 lengths the following year. She started favourite for the Oaks, but broke down during the race and finished sixth behind Hycilla.

The Classic victory of Picture Play was not only a dramatic revival of the fortunes of Childwick Bury but also of its best family, that of Absurdity. However, the genealogical thread ran not through Jest and her only daughter Laughter but through Absurdity's far less talented daughter Gesture, who was by Sunstar and therefore extremely closely related to Jest (by Sunstar's sire Sundridge).

Morton did not consider Gesture worth even a mention in his memoirs, though he expressed the opinion that Laughter would one day do justice to her breeding and produce a great horse. Laughter showed first-rate speed on the home gallops but always disappointed on the racecourse, though she ran the subsequent Oaks winner Pogrom to a head in the Great Sapling Stakes at Sandown as a two-year-old. Morton's hopes of her as a broodmare were not fulfilled, but her relative failure may have been due to the fact that most of her matings were with stallions whom it is charitable to call undistinguished – Othello, Thunderer, Oojah and Lay Lord. However, her branch of the family did survive tenuously for several generations and produced Gallant Knight, the winner of the Dante Stakes at York in 1961.

In spite of being ignored in print by her trainer, Gesture was endowed with respectable ability. First time out she beat her solitary opponent in the Ham Stakes at Goodwood in a canter, and she was second to the top-class colt Monarch, who went on to win the

Middle Park Plate, in the Boscawen Stakes at Newmarket. She did not win any of her three races as a three-year-old, but finished about halfway down a big field in the Oaks.

The stud career of Gesture, like that of Laughter, was blighted by too many matings with bad stallions, and she bred only three winners. On the other hand, she was sent to better horses on a few occasions. To the wartime Triple Crown winner Pommern she bred Love Dream, a fast filly who won the Acorn Plate at Epsom; and to the great Classic sire Phalaris she bred Picture Palace's dam Amuse.

Amuse had an extraordinary career. She ran only twice, finishing second in a race over 5 furlongs at Newmarket in the autumn of her three-year-old season and unplaced in the King's Stand Stakes at Royal Ascot the next year. She was fourteen when she produced Picture Play and had not bred a single winner up to that time. She had one more foal after Picture Play and then died, so the opportunity to profit from the lesson and send her back to Donatello did not arise. Picture Play was her only winning offspring, and she had seven foals by other stallions.

The responsibility for continuing the revival of the fortunes of Childwick Bury thus lay squarely with Picture Play, and was safe with her. She bred seven winners and three of them, Red Shoes, Queen of Light and Promulgation, were high-class performers. Queen of Light (by Borealis) had excellent speed. She won races at Goodwood and Newmarket as a two-year-old, and won the important Falmouth Stakes over a mile at Newmarket the next year. In her turn Queen of Light bred the equally talented Crystal Palace, who followed in her footsteps by winning the Falmouth Stakes and went on to win the still more important Nassau Stakes over 1¼ miles. Mated with Ballymoss, a horse who had proved his excellence in the best international company at three and four years of age, Crystal Palace completed the final stage of the renaissance of Childwick Bury by producing Royal Palace, who became the stud's third Derby winner when he triumphed at Epsom in 1967.

Most of Jim Joel's horses were with Noel Murless, the leading Classic trainer of the day, by the time Royal Palace went into training. Murless was noted for the patience with which he developed high-class horses, but Royal Palace was so outstanding from an early age that Murless was able to tell Jim Joel that this colt

209

would be a Classic horse in the spring of his two-year-old season. By the end of that season the trainer's opinion was held generally, because Royal Palace had won the Group 2 Royal Lodge Stakes, one of the most reliable guides to future middle-distance excellence, at Ascot in September and was officially rated the second best of his age.

As a three-year-old Royal Palace did not have a preliminary race before the 2000 Guineas. He looked rather uneasy, sweating and on his toes, in the paddock before the race. But he was fit enough and, thanks to a consummately artistic ride by George Moore, the Australian jockey who was retained by Murless that season, he won by a short head from the French colt Taj Dewan. He was much more composed on Derby day, and did not sweat at all. He was more impressive in the race, too, and he was able to dominate his opponents in the straight and win by 2½ lengths from Ribocco.

At that stage of the season Royal Palace seemed so superior to his contemporaries as a middle-distance performer that he needed only to stay sound and healthy to win the St Leger, and so the Triple Crown. However, that condition was not fulfilled, for Royal Palace rapped himself at exercise in the middle of August and had to miss the St Leger, in which the Derby form worked out well with the victory of Ribocco. Nor was Royal Palace restored to his best form when he reappeared in the Champion Stakes, and he was beaten into third place by Reform and Taj Dewan. It was a different story when he returned to racing as a four-year-old, as he reinstated himself completely as a middle-distance horse of true excellence. He won all his five races that season, including the Group 1 races the Coronation Cup, the Eclipse Stakes and the King George VI and Queen Elizabeth Stakes. His performance in the last-named race was reminiscent of Sunstar's in the Derby, because he broke down and finished on three legs with nothing but his class and courage to sustain him.

Royal Palace did not retire to Childwick Bury, where Jim Joel had terminated the practice of keeping stallions. Instead he went to the Egerton Stud at Newmarket as the joint property of Jim Joel, Lady Macdonald-Buchanan and Lord Howard de Walden. He did not sire a single high-class horse for Jim Joel, and his breeding record generally was disappointing. The only Classic winner among his progeny was Dunfermline, who won the Oaks and the St Leger for the Queen.

If Royal Palace failed to come up to expectations as a stallion, that did not mean that the usefulness of his family at Childwick Bury was at an end. He had a half-sister called Glass Slipper by the Derby winner Relko. Glass Slipper won one race, a maiden race over 1 mile 5 furlongs at Newbury, but she was better than that bare fact suggests because she also finished second in the Group 3 Musidora Stakes. She was only a fair racehorse, but a great brood-mare, equalling the feats of Yours, Doris and Absurdity by breeding two Classic winners – the St Leger winner Light Cavalry and the 1000 Guineas winner Fairy Footsteps.

The success of the Childwick Bury Stud after the Second World War did not depend wholly on the strong and lasting revival of the Absurdity family. That family alone could not have provided a broad enough base of operation for a large private stud aiming to maintain a constant flow of high-class performers of various types. It was clear that the Childwick Bury stock as a whole needed an injection of top-class speed.

In the summer of 1945 the antique dealer Frank Partridge, who had sold a number of articles to Jack Joel and become a friend of the family, called at Childwick Bury for tea. It was his habit to decry the Joel preoccupation with thoroughbreds. 'I can buy you a beautiful piece of furniture which will be a delight for ever, but a horse does not last long,' he used to lecture them. So Jim Joel was astonished when on this occasion Partridge asked him whether he would like to buy a horse. 'What horse?' Joel asked. 'Court Martial,' Patridge replied.

Court Martial was a horse of brilliant speed who had won the 2000 Guineas that year. He had no pretensions to stay 1½ miles properly, but his class had enabled him to finish third to Dante in the Derby. The prospect of acquiring him as a stallion was alluring, and Joel asked the price. '£60,000.' 'I'll give you a cheque for that amount now,' replied Joel, eager to conclude the deal.

Partridge said that the matter could not be settled there and then, but that he would see what could be done. Soon afterwards he left the house, and Joel did not hear from him again for weeks; for so long, indeed, that he thought that Partridge must have forgotten all about it. But Partridge returned at last, and confirmed that Court Martial could be bought, but that the price was £65,000. Joel did not hesitate to agree. Partridge knew nothing about horses, but he had done a good deal of business in antiques with Lord Astor, the owner of Court Martial, and knew that he did not keep stallions. He realized, therefore, that Court Martial must be for sale at the end of his racing career.

Court Martial took up stud duties at Childwick Bury for the covering season of 1946 and remained there until 1958, when he was sold to the United States for £60,000. In purely financial terms, therefore, his acquisition had turned out an unqualified success. That was not all. Court Martial also was a sire of exceptional merit. He was leading sire of winners in the British Isles twice, and his influence on the Childwick Bury bloodstock was profound and wholly beneficial.

The best horse that Court Martial sired for Jim Joel was Major Portion, who was second to the Queen's Pall Mall in the 2000 Guineas in 1958 and went on to prove himself an outstanding miler by winning the St James's Palace Stakes, the Sussex Stakes and the Queen Elizabeth II Stakes. He also assisted in the later evolution of the Absurdity family when he sired Picture Light as a result of a mating with Picture Play's daughter Queen of Light. Picture Light was more than useful on the racecourse and became an excellent broodmare, producing nine individual winners including two of Classic calibre; Photo Flash, who was second in the 1000 Guineas, and Welsh Pageant, who was third in the 2000 Guineas. Welsh Pageant was a durable performer who raced with distinction until he was five and then became a successful stallion.

Jim Joel owned and bred three other horses who were placed in Classic races during the 1960s and 1970s. They were West Side Story, who was third in the 1000 Guineas and second in the Oaks; Maina, who was second in the Oaks; and Connaught, who was second to Sir Ivor in the Derby in 1968. Connaught was one of the great characters among thoroughbreds, and had a racing career fraught with incident. He was a chestnut colt by the Derby and St Leger winner St Paddy out of Nagaika, a mare purchased from the Jockey Club Senior Steward Sir Randle Feilden and representing a new strain in the Childwick Bury Stud. He was an enormous horse, standing 16.3 and broad in proportion. His bulk was the root cause of his problems, because when he was in the starting stalls he was touching both ends and both sides. Not surprisingly he was a prey to qualms about entering the stalls and became notorious for recalcitrance at the start.

Connaught refused to enter the stalls for what should have been his first race, the Acomb Stakes at York in August of his two-year-old season, and again for what should have been his first race as a three-year-old, the Greenham Stakes at Newbury in April. He had to be withdrawn on both occasions. After the Greenham Stakes Noel Murless took him home and gave him an intensive course of starting stalls practice on Newmarket Heath. He was put through the stalls repeatedly, allowed to gallop for a couple of furlongs, and was then brought back to do it again. Connaught began to overcome his fear of confinement in the stalls. But horses are creatures of habit, and when Connaught ran in the 2000 Guineas he jumped off well, galloped for a couple of furlongs and then tried to pull himself up, finishing last but one behind Sir Ivor. The aberration exasperated Murless, who was beginning to think that Connaught was incorrigible. He thought of advising Jim Joel to have the horse gelded and then send him to Bob Turnell, the Wiltshire trainer who had charge of Joel's hurdlers and chasers. However, he relented and decided to give Connaught one more chance. It was a wise decision, as Connaught quickly indicated when he ran in the Chester Vase early in May and finished a close second to Remand. He had rehabilitated himself to such an extent that he was then trained for the Derby, and very nearly won it. He was in a clear lead a furlong and a half from home, but weakened in the last 100 yards and was caught and beaten by Sir Ivor.

Connaught would have won many Derbys, but the 1968 Derby winner Sir Ivor was an exceptional colt, capable of exposing his inability to stay the last furlong of the 1½ miles. He emerged as a superbly talented specialist over 1¼ miles during the next two years, and won both the Group 2 Prince of Wales Stakes and the Group 1 Eclipse Stakes in record time as a five-year-old.

Although the purchase of Nagaika and other mares was evidence of Jim Joel's willingness to diversify and introduce new strains into the Childwick Bury Stud, the Absurdity family, so vigorously restored by Picture Play, remained its mainstay right through to the

1980s. In 1983, when Jim Joel was one of a handful of large-scale owner – breeders of high-quality thoroughbreds left in England, eleven of the nineteen mares listed on the Childwick Bury Stud card traced their descent from Absurdity through Picture Play. The future of the family seemed to be assured by mares like Fairy Footsteps, one of the most attractive and promising young mares in the stud and a Classic winner herself.

Thus the story of the Childwick Bury Stud under the Joels was indissolubly linked with the rise and fall and resuscitation of the Absurdity family. By comparison the role played by Doris, despite her pre-eminence among the three great broodmares of the first phase as an actual dam of winners, was ancillary in terms of the long-term evolution of the stud; and the influence of Yours was transitory. When the reasons for the abundant success of the Joel horses at the highest level of competition during the first phase are sought, the conclusion that much of the stud's greatness was due to an unusually generous measure of luck becomes inescapable; unless it is argued that family piety had its just reward, since it is true that each of the three mares who produced two Classic winners each for Jack Joel was obtained from a close relative for one reason or another distinct from a cool assessment of probable breeding value. They certainly were not selected on performance, for Absurdity, the best of the three, was no better than a moderate handicapper.

If Yours, Doris and Absurdity were the foundation mares who made the fortunes of the Childwick Bury Stud on the female side, then Sundridge deserves equal credit as the maker of the stud on the male side. The acquisition of Sundridge probably owed a good deal more to shrewd prediction of breeding value. Morton wrote that Joel bought Sundrige when 'he was looking for horses to establish his stud', and a horse with brilliant speed, Classic middle-distance pedigree, tremendous courage and the soundness to stand much hard racing was an excellent stallion prospect.

On this analysis the selection of Sundridge to be an intensively used resident stallion may be regarded as astute and farsighted. Yet the very success of the cheaply bought Sundridge and his son Sunstar in helping to raise Childwick Bury to a pinnacle of achievement as a source of Classic horses may have had an insidious influence on Jack Joel's judgement of stallions in later days. Yours, the first of the great mares, had been sent to leading outside stallions, Derby winners like Ayrshire and Persimmon. But the advent of stallions first to Northaw and then to Childwick Bury changed all that, and led to the adoption of mating policies that were increasingly inward-looking. For example, Doris, during her twelve seasons at stud, was not covered by a single stallion that did not stand either at Childwick Bury or at Solly Joel's Maiden Erlegh Stud. The effects of such a policy when the cheap stallions used were not supremely gifted horses like Sundridge, but third-raters like Othello, were correctly perceived and condemned as suicidal by Jim Joel.

The part played by Morton in the first phase of the evolution of Jack Joel's breeding operations would be hard to overestimate. The kind of relationship between owner – breeder and trainer, based on mutual confidence and respect for each other's interests, such as existed between Jack Joel and Morton, can exercise nothing but a beneficial influence on the bloodstock. Joel never interfered in the training; and Morton had a deep understanding of successive genera-tions of Childwick Bury stock to guide him in developing their individual talents, and a constant awareness of the importance of fillies in securing the future of the stud. He made forbearance in handling fillies a matter of principle, believing that too much hard racing could prejudice their stud prospects. He was also a perfec-tionist and intensely conscientious in the practice of his profession. On one occasion in the early 1920s Jim Joel invited him to dine with him in the Adelphi Hotel, where they were both staying for a Liverpool meeting. Morton accepted on the condition that they should dine punctually at seven. After dinner he took a taxi for the 5 mile drive to Aintree racecourse to give his horses their final feed and make sure they were settled for the night.

Jack Joel was the son of an East End publican, and learned to do business in the hard school of the pioneering days of diamond and gold mining in South Africa. He returned to England with an addiction to work which persisted through the rest of his life. Few days passed without him spending at least a few hours at his desk in Austin Friars. Only his habit of very early rising gave him the time to indulge in recreations of driving, racing and supervising his stud.

His son Jim was brought up in England and educated at a well-known public school, Malvern College. He was commissioned in the 15th/19th Hussars during the First World War, and served in France and afterwards in the army of occupation in Germany. Although he has played a full part in the management of the businesses in which the family has large interests, serving for a time as chairman of the Johannesburg Consolidated Investment Company, and kept up the habit of regular visits to his Austin Friars office when he was in his late eighties, his attitudes have always been far removed from those of the South African mining pioneers. In younger days he was an eager follower of the English field sports of hunting and shooting. Above all, he has always been a gentle man, whose shyness has been tempered by a lively sense of humour and a love of entertaining his friends, particularly at Childwick Bury and at his house at Newmarket, which he occupied regularly for the race meetings. He enjoys a glass of vintage champagne, but is invariably sparing in his consumption of food and drink; at the same time nothing gives him more pleasure than to ensure that his guests are sumptuously fed and plied liberally with fine wines.

Jim Joel was born in 1894 and has never married. In the late 1970s he found that the house at Childwick Bury was too big and the upkeep too costly for his personal needs. Accordingly he sold the house and grounds while retaining the adjoining stud, and moved into the small and convenient stud house. The front door of the stud house gives on to a short drive, with parking space for a few cars. Beyond the car park lies the yard with lawns and spinneys so carefully laid out by Jack Joel in the first decade of the century. In summer the open spaces of the yard are ablaze with colour. There are borders massed with scarlet salvias, urns trailing geraniums, standard roses. The lawns are dotted with headstones commemorating the famous horses bred by the Joels at Childwick Bury. The largest and most ornate of the stones honours Doris, and the names of all her winning offspring are inscribed on it. It is flanked now by stones commemorating Crystal Palace and Picture Play, two of the famous mares of the third phase of the history of Childwick Bury. There are stones for Sunstar, Humorist and Royal Palace, the three Derby winners bred there. That for Royal Palace has been erected in his lifetime because Jim Joel was afraid that the horse might outlive him and then be denied a proper memorial. If one of Britain's traditional private studs is to produce a Derby winner in the near future, Childwick Bury is one of the two or three most likely to achieve that feat, and so provide occasion for a fourth commemorative stone for an Epsom hero in the shadow of the spinneys.

8

Bull Hancock
1910–72

The term 'international outcross' as the description of a distinctive breeding policy or an identifiable factor in thoroughbred evolution originated, it seems, in an article by Rhys Llewellyn in the 1967 October Sales issue of the *British Racehorse*. Llewellyn argued that the thoroughbred was founded and has been sustained as a breed by selection based on performance, not through breeding for purity, and that there is no justification for assuming that purity and performance are to be achieved by the same selective process. Outcrossing, in his opinion, led to greater adaptability and efficiency, whereas inbreeding led to the expression of unwanted recessive genes, together with an increased early mortality rate and sterility. The most beneficial kind of outcrossing involved bringing together unrelated, or only distantly related bloodlines from widely differing environments – in other words, the 'international outcross'.

Of course, many prominent breeders had practised the international outcross long before Llewellyn formulated it and coined the phrase. Indeed, the source of the thoroughbred was an international outcross between mares of 'running strains' which had evolved in Britain for centuries and imported Eastern stallions like the Darley Arabian, the Godolphin Arabian, the Byerley Turk and the Curwen Bay Barb. Marcel Boussac's thoroughbred empire sprang from crosses between choice strains derived from England, France and North America; and Federico Tesio never wavered in his consistent adherence to the custom of sending mares from his Italian stud to the best stallions in England and France. However, in the context of the immense leap forward of the American thoroughbred after the Second World War, an advance which took it to a position of commanding superiority on the global racing scene, one man stood out as the personification of the determined, even agressive, and highly selective buying of the choicest strains wherever they were available, which provided the dynamic impulse for the most dramatic of all manifestations of the international outcross. That man was Arthur Boyd ('Bull') Hancock Junior of Claiborne Farm, Paris, Kentucky.

Although he had, appropriately for a man who was to excel in this profession, read genetics at Princeton University, Bull Hancock was essentially a practical breeder whose general approach to the problems of selection was pragmatic. He attributed his success to a combination of common sense, judgement and luck. But there is ample evidence of his conscious adoption of the idea of the international outcross. In an interview with William Robertson (*Thoroughbred Record*, 30 October 1965) he uttered the most concise possible statement of his preference: 'I like hybrid vigour'; and in reply to a newspaper reader's query (*A Treasury of Questions and Answers*, compiled by Joe Hirsch in 1969) he was marginally more expansive when he gave his opinion, 'It is the infusion of different blood which invigorates the thoroughbred.'

His belief in the international outcross was emphatically not purely formal. The twenty-seven stallions standing at Claiborne in 1970, two years before he died, included Ambiorix and Herbager from France; Forli and Pronto from Argentina; Pago Pago and Sky High from Australia; Hawaii from South Africa; and Tulyar from Ireland. He was without doubt one of the greatest modern exponents of the international outcross. His example was followed enthusiastically by scores of American breeders with the will and the means to invest on a huge scale, and it fuelled revolutionary change in the distribution of high-class thoroughbred stock between the Old World and the New.

Bull Hancock had a correct pedigree for a master thoroughbred breeder. His grandfather, Captain Richard Hancock, fought in the Civil War and then returned to his Ellerslie Farm at Charlottesville in Virginia to breed thoroughbreds in earnest. He bred such good horses as the Suburban winners Eurus and Elkwood and the Brooklyn winners Russell and Diavolo in the days when the

Suburban and Brooklyn Handicaps, now Grade 1 Stakes, were among the most important races in New York. He made Ellerslie the leading stud farm in Virginia. Bull's father, the first Arthur Boyd Hancock, built extensively on the secure foundations that Richard Hancock had laid.

After studying at Chicago University, the first Arthur Hancock became assistant to his father at Ellerslie until 1909 when, at the age of thirty-four, he took over sole control of the breeding operation. American racing was entering a period of crisis in which anti-betting legislation forced the New York tracks to close down, and in consequence bloodstock values slumped. At one time thoroughbreds were fetching little more than draught horses on the open market. At this time Arthur Hancock displayed vision and courage in deciding to swim against the tide and first lease and then buy outright the stallion Celt to stand at Ellerslie. Although he was overshadowed by his stable companion, the invincible Colin, Celt was the second-best performer of his day and won three of his four races including the Brooklyn Handicap. Colin and Celt were both scions of the powerful Domino male line. By realistic pricing Hancock ensured that Celt always had a full book of mares and plenty of runners on the track. Celt became a leading stallion and headed the North American list of sires of winners in 1921, making Hancock's name as a stallion promoter.

A turning point in Arthur Hancock's life had come in 1910 when his wife, the former Nancy Clay, inherited 1300 acres of rolling limestone land in Bourbon County, Kentucky. The Clays were one of the most influential Kentucky families and one member of the family, Henry Clay, who coined the phrase 'I'd rather be right than President', was one of the leading American statesmen in the middle of the nineteenth century. It was appropriate that Nancy Hancock's inheritance should have the name of Claiborne.

Arthur Hancock lost no time in extending his breeding operations to the newly acquired land west of the Appalachians. As Ellerslie was a going concern and the development of the virgin stud farming land at Claiborne required constant supervision, he decided to move with his family to Kentucky. The Kentucky 'Bluegrass', with its unsurpassable pastures and benign climate, enjoyed a steadily growing reputation as the heartland of the American thoroughbred, and inevitably the weight of the Hancock breeding operations was transferred from Ellerslie to Claiborne.

Although Arthur Hancock's first important venture in stallion promotion had involved the thoroughly American Celt, his conversion to the faith of the international outcross did not take long to manifest itself. In 1915 he imported the first of his foreign-bred stallions Wrack, who had been bred and raced in England by Lord Rosebery. Wrack had been an exceptionally tough horse, running forty-three times on the flat and also showing good form over hurdles, but he was no more than a useful mile handicapper and gained his two principal victories in the Newbury Spring Cup. On the other hand, he was a member of one of the best Mentmore families, that of Illuminata, the dam of the Classic winners Ladas and Chelandry. He provided a singular example of Bull Hancock's dictum that different blood can invigorate the thoroughbred strains; for, mated with American mares, Wrack became a far better stallion than he had been racehorse and finished second once and third three times in the North American list of sires of winners.

The increasing renown of Claiborne soon attracted some of the leading owner – breeders, men like William Woodward and Marshall Field, who began to board mares there and to lean increasingly on Hancock in respect of stallions. In 1924 Hancock became interested in the four-year-old Sir Gallahad III, who had won the French 2000 Guineas and finished third in the French Derby the previous year, and had that year landed a gamble in the Lincolnshire Handicap and beaten Epinard, the most brilliant horse in Europe, by a neck when in receipt of 11 lb in a match over 6½ furlongs at Saint Cloud. Sir Gallahad was by Teddy, the best horse in France during the First World War, out of Plucky Liege, who had won four races including two Newmarket nurseries as a two-year-old in 1914 and was to gain lasting fame as the dam also of the Grand Prix de Paris winner Admiral Drake and the Derby winner Bois Roussel. After lengthy negotiations Hancock bought Sir Gallahad for $125,000 and immediately formed a syndicate to own him consisting of Woodward, Field and Robert Fairbairn besides himself. Although this was not the first stallion syndicate ever formed it certainly represented a new factor in the international stallion market. Its significance lay in the fact that it ensured solid support for the stallion from the owners of some of the best mares in the United States. One of the first mares covered by Sir Gallahad at Claiborne was Woodward's Marguerite, by Celt, and the produce of the mating was Gallant Fox, winner of the American Triple Crown in 1930. Sir Gallahad, like Wrack, was better as a stallion than he had been on the racecourse; he was leading North American sire of winners four times, and was even better as a broodmare sire, heading the list of sires of dams of winners twelve times.

Twelve years after the Sir Gallahad deal, Arthur Hancock organized another syndicate which was to have momentous consequences for American breeding. The horse involved was the Derby winner Blenheim, whose son Mahmoud had won the Derby that year in record time. Hancock arranged the purchase of Blenheim from the Aga Khan for $250,000, and at Claiborne Blenheim sired the Kentucky Derby winners Whirlaway and Jet Pilot and became the maternal grandsire of two more winners of the premier American Classic race, Ponder and Hill Gail. He was the leading sire of winners in 1941, the year of Whirlaway's victories in the Kentucky Derby and the Belmont Stakes.

The evolution of Claiborne as a commercial producer of yearlings proceeded simultaneously with its development as the foremost stallion station in Kentucky. He persuaded other Kentucky breeders to follow his example and begin to sell yearlings at Saratoga, in New York State, as early as 1917, and was one of the founders of the Keeneland Association which began to conduct bloodstock sales near Lexington in the midst of the Bluegrass during the Second World War. The combined Ellerslie and Claiborne operations put him at the top of the list of breeders in respect of the number of races won nine times and in respect of prize money earnings five times between 1935 and 1946. The Newmarket trainer Sir Cecil Boyd-Rochfort, who had as good a reason to appreciate his expertise as any Englishman or Irishman through training many of the best horses bred by William Woodward and Marshall Field, paid him the warmest of tributes when he remarked many years after the death of the creator of the Claiborne empire, 'Arthur Hancock was the ablest bloodstock man I ever knew.'

Arthur Boyd Junior was born at Marchmont Farm, the family home in Kentucky, on 24 January 1910. He was educated at St Mark's

School in Massachusetts, Woodberry Forest in Virginia and Princeton University. It was as a football player at Woodberry Forest that he was given the nickname of 'Bull' by which he was to be generally known for the rest of his life.

Bull never had any doubt that his career would be in bloodstock. He had worked on the farms during school holidays from an early age, learning all the essential tasks from cleaning out boxes upwards. He learned to handle all the farm stock, including mares and stallions. He was a big man, standing 6 foot 2 inches – his father was even taller at 6 foot 6 inches – and powerfully built in proportion; he was also a brave man. At a much later stage of his life when he had overall responsibility for the Claiborne operation, the strong-willed stallion Nasrullah showed signs of getting out of control in the covering barn; Bull himself picked up a broom that was lying handy, set about him and tamed him. Although Nasrullah mistrusted him and laid his ears back whenever he saw Bull after that beating, he gave no further serious trouble.

Bull became assistant manager at Claiborne when he left Princeton. In 1937 his father sent him to Virginia to manage Ellerslie Farm. He made a profit the first year and congratulated himself on his management skill. After the second year he had to make a rueful confession that the Ellerslie accounts had plunged into the red to the extent of $15,000, but his father took the loss calmly, saying that he had been trying for thirty years and had never managed to make a go of it at Ellerslie.

Bull served in the Army Air Corps during the Second World War. He rose to the rank of captain, and his promotion to major had already been approved when his father suffered the first of a series of heart attacks in 1945 and he left the army to return to Kentucky. Three years later he took charge of the whole Hancock breeding operations when his father had an incapacitating stroke. Arthur Hancock did not die until 1957, when he was eighty-one, but was never fit enough to resume his responsibilities at Claiborne.

Wise men do not rush in to make sweeping changes in a successful business, and Bull Hancock avoided that mistake when he took charge at Claiborne. On the other hand, he was aware that some of the female strains that had served Claiborne well were beginning to lose their vigour, and he embarked on a patient and unobtrusive process of selling some of the old strains and replenishing the Claiborne bloodstock. He went to the Newmarket December sales in 1951 and in pursuance of this policy bought four mares and two filly foals for 21,700 guineas. Those purchases included one of the most remarkable double coups in thoroughbred history, for in the space of twenty-four hours he bought the seven-year-old mare Rough Shod, in foal to the 2000 Guineas winner My Babu, for 3500 guineas, and the ten-year-old mare Knight's Daughter, in foal to the Derby winner Watling Street, for 2500 guineas. Each of those mares was to have a dramatically beneficial impact on the fortunes of Claiborne as a producer of top-class performers.

Rough Shod, to whose name the Roman numerals II were added when she arrived in the United States, was by the great sprinter and sire of sprinters Gold Bridge, but had inherited only a small measure of her sire's ability. Her sole victory was gained in the Gailes Handicap over 6 furlongs at Bogside, a Scottish course attracting only the lowest grade of horse. However, her attractiveness as a stud prospect was enhanced by the fact that she was a daughter of the Yorkshire Oaks winner Dalmary and came from the same family as the Second World War Classic stars Godiva, winner of the 1000 Guineas and the Oaks, and Windsor Slipper, winner of the Irish Triple Crown. Bull's judgement in buying her was totally vindicated when the filly she was carrying turned out to be Gambetta, a good racemare and better broodmare who founded a flourishing branch of the family; and Rough Shod herself went on to the breed Moccasin, a brilliant filly who was voted Horse of the Year in one of the American polls as a two-year-old, and two top-class colts in Ridan and Lt Stevens. The family went from strength to strength in the next thirty years, producing a legion of talented performers including Thatch, Apalachee, Cellini, King Pellinore, Lisadell and Nureyev.

Knight's Daughter had shown a good deal more racing ability than Rough Shod. Bred and owned by King George VI, she was so unruly in her early days that her trainer, Cecil Boyd-Rochfort, feared the worst the first time he produced her on a racecourse at Newmarket as a two-year-old. 'Try and jump her off at the start, and whatever you do avoid finishing last,' he told her jockey Doug Smith. To the amazement of her trainer and jockey, Knight's Daughter was as quiet as a lamb at the start, and raced like an old hand to win easily. She won three of her four races that year, her only season to race.

Like Rough Shod, Knight's Daughter was very well related. Her dam Feola was second in the 1000 Guineas and third in the Oaks. By the time Bull bought her, her half-sisters Hypericum had won the 1000 Guineas and her half-sister Angelola and Above Board had won the Yorkshire Oaks. The family continued to do good service for the royal studs, and its later representatives included the King George VI and Queen Elizabeth Stakes winner Aureole, and High-clere, who won the 1000 Guineas and the French Oaks for Queen Elizabeth II. For Claiborne Knight's Daughter bred Round Table, one of the best and toughest American horses of modern times. Knight's Daughter was honoured as Broodmare of the Year by the Kentucky Thoroughbred Breeders' Association in 1959, and her commemorative plaque hangs with those of four other Claiborne mares so honoured (Miss Disco, Misty Morn, Pocahontas and Delta) in the hall of the stud office.

The first Arthur Boyd Hancock had been primarily a producer for the yearling market, apart from his activities in stallion promotion. He had a flair for salesmanship. Bull did not enjoy selling yearlings, and modestly declared that he did not possess his father's skill in that respect. Whereas Arthur loved to go to Saratoga and show his yearlings, Bull greatly preferred to work on the farm. Accordingly, Bull decided to switch the weight of his breeding operation from selling yearlings to racing the horses he bred. In 1953 Claiborne discontinued selling yearlings at public auction altogether.

The first crop that Bull put into training included the fillies Delta and Courtesy. Delta was exceptionally fast and won the Arlington Lassie Stakes, later classified as a Grade 1 Stakes, as a two-year-old, and became a broodmare of the year. Courtesy was not a top-class racemare, but won three races and became the dam of the top-class performer Knightly Manner. Both fillies were by Claiborne's great stallion Nasrullah. The second crop included Doubledogdare, one of the best of her age and sex at both two and three years of age.

Later Bull introduced the practice of selling a half interest in all his yearlings before they went into training. His first idea was to sell a half interest in the colts and lease half the fillies to various people, but nobody would come in with him on that basis. So he decided to offer a half share in all the yearlings, and this attracted a willing associate in Howard Keck. The yearlings were divided into pairs, and the partners then tossed a coin for first choice. Each partner took one yearling from every pair, and raced it in his name, but had a half interest in every horse. The valuations were based on the average prices of all yearlings at the Keeneland and Saratoga sales the same year, less 10 per cent. The racecourse earnings were divided between the partners, who owned the horses in equal shares when they were sold out of training or returned to the stud for breeding. The first crop which was subject to this arrangement included Nas-Mahal, a filly by Nasrullah and from the same family as Knight's Daughter. Nas-Mahal won five races and became the dam of two top-class horses, the Hollywood Derby winner Tell and the Hollywood Oaks winner Turkish Trousers. Howard Keck was unable to continue the partnership owing to business commitments, but William Haggin Perry took his place and the new partnership continued indefinitely.

The business of boarding the mares and managing the breeding operations of some of the wealthiest American owner – breeders assumed increasing importance in the economics of Claiborne in Bull's time. James Cox Brady, Charles Engelhard and Bunker Hunt were among the large-scale breeders who kept mares there. Another of the owner – breeders was Gladys Mills Phipps, who for decades before her death at the age of eighty-seven in 1970 was regarded as the grande dame of the American Turf. Indeed, the Phippses were one of the most prominent families in American racing, and the Phipps connection with Claiborne was preserved by her son Ogden and her grandson Ogden Mills Phipps, who became president of the New York Jockey Club. Gladys Phipps was a matriarch and an eccentric whose frugal expenditure on clothes meant that she was often turned out looking more like the owner of a corner store than a woman owning some of the finest property on Rhode Island and in Palm Beach, besides racehorses and breeding stock of the highest class.

One of Bull's transactions with Gladys Phipps had epoch-making repercussions for the thoroughbred not only in North America but round the world. In the early 1950s he had his eye on Miss Disco, a young mare by the excellent broodmare sire Discovery. Miss Disco had been sound, tough, courageous and talented on the racetrack; she raced until she was five, ran in fifty-four races and won ten of them including the Test Stakes, a race over 7 furlongs at Saratoga which was afterwards classified Grade 2. He thought she would be an ideal mate for the impetuous Nasrullah. Eventually he succeeded in buying her for $27,500. However, at the same time negotiations concerning a mare he had been trying to buy for Gladys Phipps fell through, so he offered her Miss Disco and she accepted. 'So Mrs Phipps got Bold Ruler and I didn't,' Bull observed wistfully in later years, for Bold Ruler was the produce of the Nasrullah and Miss Disco mating.

Bold Ruler was born at Claiborne on 6 April 1954. By an extraordinary coincidence, just half an hour earlier Bull had witnessed the birth of his own colt foal by Princequillo out of Knight's Daughter, who was to be called Round Table. It is doubtful whether two thoroughbreds destined for such singular greatness had ever before been born on the same stud within an hour. Each became a Horse of the Year on his racing performances, and a champion sire.

Round Table was a colt of striking good looks from the day he was born, but Bold Ruler was a wretched, skinny foal with a double hernia and a rheumatic condition which was to plague him at intervals throughout his life. At one time he was running with Miss Disco in a paddock facing the Claiborne Farm office, and Bull gave orders that he should be moved on the grounds that he was a bad advertisement for the place. However, Bold Ruler soon gave a taste of his quality when he was sent to the veteran trainer 'Sunny Jim' Fitzsimmons. He was very quick into his stride and had brilliant speed. When he was at the height of his fame on the racetrack Fitzsimmons reported, 'Bold Ruler could beat any horse in the world at any distance from 6 furlongs to a mile and an eighth.' Although he was leggy and immature, he won seven of his ten races as a two-year-old, and would no doubt have done better still if he had not been kept inactive for weeks in the middle of the season by sprained back muscles.

Bold Ruler grew and filled out during the winter, and his record of eleven wins from sixteen races as a three-year-old brought him the title of Horse of the Year. His most resounding victory was gained in the 9½ furlongs Preakness Stakes, the middle leg of the American Triple Crown, and he was third to Gallant Man in the third leg, the Belmont Stakes over the distance of 1½ miles which was patently beyond his best. He won five more races as a four-year-old, including the Suburban and Monmouth Handicaps which were afterwards classified Grade 1 Stakes and finished with a career score of twenty-three victories from thirty-three starts.

Bold Ruler retired to stud at his birthplace Claiborne, where he was to achieve even greater fame than he had on the racetrack. He rose to the top of the list of sires of winners in 1963, when his first crop were three years old, and remained there for seven consecutive seasons. He dropped to second place behind Hail to Reason in 1970, the same year in which he became seriously ill with an inoperable cancer in the upper nasal passage. Although cobalt treatment at Auburn University arrested the course of the disease temporarily, the cancer spread into his head, neck and chest, and he had to be humanely destroyed at Claiborne on 12 July 1971, just fourteen months before the death of Bull Hancock himself.

Bold Ruler returned to the top of the list of sires of winners in 1973, his eight being the largest number of sires championships since the sixteen of Lexington in the nineteenth century, when the North American thoroughbred population was much smaller and the competition between stallions less keen. For most of his stud career he was recognized as an exceptional sire of fast, precocious horses, and he was leading sire of two-year-olds a record six times. On the other hand, none of his progeny won any of the American Triple Crown races during his lifetime, when his only true Classic winner was the filly Lamb Chop, winner of the Coaching Club American Oaks in 1963. His reputation as a Classic stallion was enhanced posthumously when his son Secretariat won the American Triple Crown in 1973 and was hailed as one of the best racehorses of the century. Indeed, his male line dominated the Kentucky Derby during the 1970s, supplying the winner of the premier American Classic race seven times.

Round Table so impressed Bull as a foal and yearling that he wanted to keep him and put him into training. He had two other colts by the same sire, Princequillo, that year. He priced Round Table at $40,000 and the other two at $20,000. Many people went to have a look at him, but nobody bought him, so Bull's wish was fulfilled. Round Table raced for his breeder as a two-year-old, when he won five of his ten races including the Grade 2 Breeders' Futurity at Keennland. When his father died in 1957, Bull found it necessary to raise cash to pay estate duties and keep the Claiborne Farm and breeding operations intact. Accordingly he sold Round Table to Travis M. Kerr for $175,000, but retained a quarter share in the horse as a potential stallion. As a three-year-old, and during the next two seasons, Round Table proved himself not only a horse of the highest racing class but also the possessor of a marvellous constitution and limbs of steel. He was voted Champion Grass Horse in each of the three seasons. He was given only a pound less than the leader Bold Ruler in the *Blood-Horse* handicap of 1957 three-year-olds. By the time he retired as a five-year-old he had the splendid career record of forty-three wins from sixty-six races, with eight victories in races afterwards classified as Grade 1 Stakes.

Round Table followed Bold Ruler home to Claiborne as a stallion a year later than his famous contemporary. Though superior in toughness, he lacked the brilliance of Bold Ruler as a racehorse. Nor did he achieve the same greatness as a stallion, though he gained high distinction in this role; he was consistently in the upper ranks of sires of winners and headed the list in 1972. Many of the best of his progeny, including Baldric II, Artaius, Targowice, Apalachee and Flirting Around, raced in Europe, while the best of his progeny to race in North America included the brilliant mare Drumtop, and the colts Tell and Royal Glint.

Round Table and Bold Ruler were both by foreign-bred sires that Bull Hancock had integrated with great skill into high-class North American breeding operations. Princequillo, the sire of Round Table, had raced in the United States, but had been foaled in England and reared in Ireland, and had a wholly European pedigree. Nasrullah had been bred in Ireland and raced in England, and had been at stud in both those countries before he went to Claiborne.

Princequillo had a pedigree which did not seem conducive to either racing or stud success in the United States. He was by Prince Rose, who traced his descent from St Simon in the male line through Prince Palatine, a stayer who won the Ascot Gold Cup over 2½ miles twice; and his dam was by Papyrus, a rather ordinary Derby winner not noted for transmitting much speed or precocity to his progeny. The racing career of Princequillo began in humble circumstances in Louisiana, where the eagle eye of Horatio Luro noticed him running in a claiming race at the New Orleans track Fair Grounds. Luro, a great trainer who later had charge of the epoch-making Northern Dancer, claimed the colt for $12,000, and Princequillo developed into the best American stayer of his day, winning the Saratoga Cup over 1¾ miles and the Jockey Club Gold Cup over 2 miles, then the most important American tests of stamina. Bull liked him as a prospective stallion because he had won over 6 furlongs in the same year that he won the Saratoga Cup, proving that he had speed and resilience. He bought a quarter share in the horse and sent him to stud at Ellerslie. He was the first stallion that Bull had recruited since his return from the war, and the first foreign-bred horse to join the Hancock stallion ranks since Blenheim. Princequillo's fee for his first covering season was $250, and he attracted only seventeen mares. However, his second crop of foals included Hill Prince, who won the Preakness Stakes, and Prince Simon, who was second in the 2000 Guineas and the Derby, and his name was made. Bull was able to move him to Claiborne, where his fee was immediately increased to $1000 and he became one of the leading stallions in the country, heading the list of sires of winners in 1957 and 1958. Round Table came from his ninth crop of foals. Princequillo excelled as a sire of broodmares, and headed the list of sires of the dams of winners eight times.

Bull had to look further afield and show greater perseverance to obtain Nasrullah in his first important venture in the international stallion market. He had been looking around the world thorough-bred scene, searching for top-class representatives of strains that were successful in other countries but absent or thin on the ground in the United States. His eye lighted on Nasrullah because his sire Nearco was one of the best horses ever bred in Italy, proved himself internationally by winning the Grand Prix de Paris and become an instant success as a Classic sire in England; while Nasrullah had been the best two-year-old colt of his year and, despite quirks of temperament, had been third in the Derby and proved himself an excellent performer over 1¼ miles by winning the Champion Stakes. Moreover, the only stallion by Nearco then at stud in the United States was the moderate Rustom Sirdar, whose sole victory had been gained in a maiden race at Salisbury as a two-year-old.

Bull made his first bid for Nasrullah in the autumn of 1944, after the horse had stood for one season at the Barton Stud in Suffolk, but he was forestalled by the leading Irish owner – breeder Joe McGrath. The second negotiation stalled on account of an unexpected devaluation of the pound sterling. But in 1950 the purchase of Nasrullah was finally completed for $340,000 plus one nomination a year for McGrath.

An insight into the rapid escalation of the value of Nasrullah during the time when Bull was trying to buy him was given by the late Bert Kerr, one of the shrewdest Irish bloodstock agents. Kerr first heard that Nasrullah was for sale by his owner – breeder the Aga Khan on the Saturday following the Dublin Horse Show of 1944, when Nasrullah had completed his first stud season in England. He was approached in the hall of the Dolphin Hotel by Gerald McElligott, a director of the British Bloodstock Agency and an old friend. McElligott invited him to take part in a deal over Nasrullah; and asked him what he thought the horse was worth. Kerr suggested £25,000, and McElligott replied that his office valued the horse at £20,000. McElligott then showed Kerr a telegram from the Aga Khan's son Aly Khan, then serving with the army in the Middle East. The message ran: 'Nasrullah fifteen thousand Umidwar ten thousand Winterhalter eight thousand.' Naturally Kerr agreed to go in with McElligott and, after negotiations with various possible buyers, Nasrullah was sold to Joe McGrath for £19,000.

Kerr wrote:

We had Nasrullah for three weeks and the nett profit was around £3600. Joe McGrath had the horse for six seasons and did not want to sell, but to get rid of an inquirer he asked a figure which he calculated the particular party would not give, i.e. £150,000. Unknown to him the agent was acting for A. B. Hancock.

Incidentally Clifford Nicholson, the owner of the Limestone Stud in Lincolnshire, was one of the people to whom Kerr offered Nasrullah, but he replied that he thought he was too dear. Instead Nicholson bought Umidwar, who never achieved a small fraction of the success of Nasrullah as a stallion.

Nasrullah had been represented by his first Classic-winning progeny, the 1000 Guineas and Oaks winner Musidora, the year before Bull bought him. But his best days as a stallion, even as far as his progeny sired in Ireland were concerned, were still to come. The next year, 1951, his daughter Belle of All won the 1000 Guineas and he was leading sire of winners in the British Isles. Two years later his son Nearula won the 2000 Guineas, and in 1954 his son

Never Say Die won the Derby and the St Leger. Thus his reputation began to grow almost from the day he arrived at Claiborne, and before he had had a single American-bred runner. Indeed, he had caused a stir in American racing circles as early as the year of his purchase when his Irish-bred son Noor gained a series of sensational victories over the American Triple Crown winner Citation in important races in California.

Nasrullah headed the list of North American sires of winners when his first crop of foals sired at Claiborne were three-year-olds. They included Nashua, a horse of brilliant gifts who won two of the American Triple Crown races, the Preakness Stakes and the Belmont Stakes, and was second to Swaps, a horse he afterwards beat out of sight in a much publicized match, in the Kentucky Derby. He headed the list four more times, the last three after his death at the age of nineteen. The best of his progeny included Bold Ruler, who was to excel even his own splendid achievements at stud, the dual Washington D.C. International winner Bald Eagle and Bull's admirable filly Delta. Many of his progeny inherited his highly strung character, but their speed and class often compensated for their flaws of temperament.

An invaluable bonus from the simultaneous presence of Nasrullah and Princequillo at Claiborne was that strains derived from them blended with an extraordinary degree of success and regularity. Two of the best racehorses of the third quarter of the twentieth century, Mill Reef and Secretariat, sprang from this cross. Mill Reef won the Derby and six other Group 1 races, including the Prix de l'Arc de Triomphe in record time; and Secretariat won the American Triple Crown, beating the track record in each of the three races. Mill Reef was by Nasrullah's son Never Bend out of a Princequillo mare; and Secretariat was by Nasrullah's son Bold Ruler out of a Princequillo mare. The same cross was extemely effective when Princequillo's son Round Table was used on mares by Nasrullah or sons of Nasrullah. At least ten high-class horses, including the champion mare Drumtop, were bred in this way.

Bull explained his liking for this kind of mating in an interview with Charles R. Koch published in *The Blood-Horse* on 1 February 1971:

You like to drill where oil has been found. Nick may be a bad word, but it gives you an outcross in which some things in the stallion compensate for their absence in the mare. The Round Table – Nasrullah cross might be considered a nick. Nasrullah was a very fiery horse; Round Table was rather phlegmatic. Round Table was not too big; Nasrullah mares are big and rangy.

Nicks, real or imaginary, are often presented as transcending all reason. Bull Hancock, the supremely practical breeder, was able to rationalize one of the most effective nicks in thoroughbred history with a logic that not even the most hardened sceptic could deny.

The acquisition of Nasrullah was Bull Hancock's greatest triumph. It gave the impetus to a sustained upward surge in the quality of the American thoroughbred. Nasrullah supplied a fresh source of the fire and brilliance without which the racehorse tends to revert to a norm of mediocrity. And if it was in conjunction with Prince-quillo that he exerted much of his influence on generations beyond the generation of his own progeny, then that fact testifies all the more strongly to the superiority of the judgement of Bull, who detected Princequillo's potential excellence as a stallion when every other studmaster was blind to the horse's merit and inclined to dismiss him as a specialist stayer with an unappealing pedigree. The purchases and exploitation of Nasrullah and Princequillo are the surest proof of Bull's genius – using that ambiguous and much abused term in the sense of a power to make the difficult seem deceptively easy and not in Carlyle's sense of transcendent capacity for taking trouble.

It is impossible to be dogmatic whether Nasrullah fitted Bull's preconceived notion of what is required in a good stallion, or whether his idea of what is required in a good stallion was drawn from the model of Nasrullah. Certainly Nasrullah possessed in highly developed form all the five qualities which Bull stipulated as necessary in a potential stallion when he was interviewed by William Robertson in 1965. They were:

He must have been a better than average two-year-old.
He must have demonstrated ability to stay the American Classic distance of 1¼ miles.

He must be sound.

He must have a masculine appearance.

He must have the right kind of pedigree.

In assessing pedigree Bull relied heavily on the *Family Tables of Racehorses* compiled by Kazimierz Bobinski and first published in 1953. The *Tables* were intended to be both an aid to genealogical research and a basis for the practical study of racehorse breeding. The requirement in both instances, Bobinski stated in the explanatory note introducing the *Tables*, was the extended pedigree together with the records of the achievements on the turf of all successful racing stock. He determined a qualification for eligibility based on success in a maximum of 287 Classic and other important races at any given period, taking all the main racing countries into account. His criteria were necessarily subjective, and would need some revision in the light of the later introduction of the Pattern and Graded races system, but Bobinski's work has stood the test of time as an invaluable and unique means of classifying thoroughbred strains. Bull applied the Bobinski test to every prospective stallion, and rejected members of families with a poor record of producing good stallions. 'I don't like families with not enough stallions,' he told Robertson.

Bull did not place an order of importance on his stallion qualifications, declaring that a stallion should satisfy them all. He recalled that he once accepted a stallion because it satisfied four of the qualifications so strongly that it seemed reasonable to excuse a deficiency in the fifth. 'I made a mistake,' he stated. 'The horse was a disappointment.'

On another occasion, when elaborating his criteria for stallion selection, Bull expounded his belief that a potential stallion should have been capable of a decisive burst of speed at some stage of a race. More specifically, he preferred a horse with the initial speed to dominate a race from the start, or at least to lie up with the leaders the whole way and accelerate when required. It was his ability to force the pace and take his opponents off their legs which attracted Bull to Forli, the winner of the Argentine Quadruple Crown in 1966. Forli's performance in the Argentine 2000 Guineas (Pollo di Potrillos) was brilliant, as he made all the running to outclass his field and win by 12 lengths in record time. He was not headed in any of his other races in Argentina ranging from 5 furlongs to 15 furlongs, which Bull regarded as a sure indication of his exceptional speed and class.

Forli began stud duties at Claiborne in 1968 and, although Bull lived long enough only to see his first two crops reach the race track, he proceeded to justify completely the decision to buy him. His progeny showed top-class form in both North America and Europe and included such celebrities as Forego, Forceten, Intrepid Hero, Thatch, Posse, Formidable and Home Guard.

Although Forli was a grandson of Hyperion and Bull professed a high regard for the male line of Hyperion, it appears that the class and racing style of the Argentinian horse was the more important consideration in Bull's resolve to acquire him. The Hyperion male line was fairly well represented in the United States through the presence of his sons Heliopolis, Alibhai and Khaled, all top-class stallions and all bred in the British Isles. Bull could not find suitable descendants of Hyperion in England and Ireland, and therefore turned to Australia where Hyperion's grandson Star Kingdom was revolutionizing a thoroughbred population previously orientated towards stamina by a powerful infusion of the speed with which he was richly endowed. Bull's choice fell on Star Kingdom's son Sky High, a wonderfully sound and talented horse who had won twenty-nine of his fifty-four races between two and six years of age, showing top-class speed to win two of the principal races, the Champagne Stakes and the Golden Slipper Stakes, as a two-year-old and similar middle-distance ability to win the Victoria Derby the next year. Sky High sired one really good horse, the Jockey Club Gold Cup winner Autobiography, but was overshadowed by another son of Star Kingdom, Noholme, who began his stud career with none of the advantages enjoyed by Sky High at Claiborne. Noholme spent his early stud seasons covering mares of poor quality in Arkansas and forced his way to the top by sheer merit.

Claiborne held a commanding position in the international stallion market since the days of Sir Gallahad as a result of the ability of the Hancocks to call on the practically limitless financial resources of wealthy American owner – breeders for the purpose of completing syndications. This command was never more absolute than in the 1950s and 1960s when Bull was pursuing the means of practising the international outcross with single-minded vigour, and once he set his sights on a potential stallion it usually found its way to Claiborne. Even Bull, however, had to face occasional rebuffs. Without question the most desirable prize for any studmaster seeking a representative of the Hyperion male line during this period was Right Royal. This magnificent brown horse passed with honours each of the tests that Bull habitually applied to a potential stallion. He was the best French two-year-old of 1960. As a three-year-old he won the French 2000 Guineas and the French Derby, and outpaced the previous year's Derby winner St Paddy with an invincible burst of speed in the final stages of the King George VI and Queen Elizabeth Stakes at Ascot. He was flawless in respect of soundness and constitution. He had a masterful character. As for his breeding, he was by Hyperion's only Derby winning son Owen Tudor and came from the same family as the great French Classic stallion Wild Risk.

Right Royal retired from training at the end of his three-year-old campaign and went to the Haras du Mesnil of his owner – breeder Elisabeth Couturié near Le Mans. Bull travelled to Le Mesnil confident of making a deal to buy Right Royal, but was pulled up short when Elisabeth Couturié's response to his request was that the horse was not for sale. The scene in the sitting room, with the bay window overlooking a vista of stately plane trees flanked by neatly railed paddocks, was set for a confrontation – on one hand the brash commercialism pervading the thoroughbred industry of the New World, on the other hand the exaltation of the mystique of the thoroughbred still lingering in the Old World. Bull drew his cheque-book from his pocket and laid it open on the table, placing his fountain pen beside it. 'Please fill in the cheque for whatever amount you think Right Royal is worth. I can promise there will be no dispute about the price,' he told her.

Elisabeth Couturié did not move from her armchair. She extinguished all his hopes with the vehemence of her reply. 'Mr Hancock, I told you he is not for sale. Right Royal will never leave Le Mesnil'

Right Royal indeed spent the rest of his days at Le Mesnil, and his grave there became an object of pilgrimage for lovers of a truly great thoroughbred.

The Hyperion branch was far the most numerous and successful, but did not exhaust Bull's admiration for the Hampton male line from which it sprang. Hampton himself would not have passed the

Claiborne test of a desirable prospective stallion; foaled in 1872, he gained two of his three victories as a two-year-old in selling races, and so little was thought of him that he was bought in for only 150 guineas after the second of them. He developed into a good stayer and won the Goodwood and Doncaster Cups, but never displayed the ability to accelerate and dominate his rivals which Bull made a condition for a potential stallion. Nevertheless, another branch of the line besides the Hyperion, that of Son-in-Law, persisted as a source of high-class performers and in the 1960s the most prominent scion of it was Herbager, who had won all but two of his eight races including the French Derby and the Group 1 Grand Prix de Saint Cloud before going to stud in France. He proved himself as a stallion by siring Grey Dawn, the best French two-year-old of 1964, in his second crop of foals. Bull decided that he was worth having and bought him. Herbager did well at Claiborne, and his progeny included Bull's own horse Dike, the third best colt in the vintage Classic crop of 1969 which was headed by Majestic Prince and Arts and Letters.

Adherenece to the idea of the international outcross dictated an interest in the Tourbillon male line which was one of the mainsprings of Marcel Boussac's dominance of Classic breeding in Europe but had barely a foothold in North America. Bull's first attempt to introduce the line to Claiborne ended in disaster. In 1948 he bought Tourbillon's grandson Djelal, a high-class miler and normally the quietest of travellers. Unpredictably he went berserk in the aeroplane over the Atlantic, smashed his stall to pieces, broke a leg and was dead by the time the plane, having turned back, landed in England. The same year Tourbillon's son Ambiorix was the best two-year-old in France. The next year Ambiorix won the Group 1 Prix Lupin over 10½ furlongs but was outstayed by a grandson of Tourbillon, Good Luck, in the French Derby. Good Luck was on offer as a stallion, but his pedigree did not appeal to Bull as much as that of Ambiorix. Boussac was not keen to retain Ambiorix for stud, and Bull was able to buy him for $250,000 for a syndicate comprising Harry F. Guggenheim, the Phipps family, William Woodward, Mrs John D. Hertz and Claiborne Farm. Bull's judgement was sound. Good Luck had little influence on the breed, but Ambiorix became a top-class stallion at Claiborne, finishing second in 1960 and displacing his stud companion Nasrullah at the top of the list of sires of winners the next year.

Bull Hancock was essentially a stallion man. Although he had steady, enviable and sometimes spectacular success as a breeder of talented performers on the racecourse, it was as the man who gave credibility to the international outcross by assembling stallions of such varied origins as Princequillo, Nasrullah, Herbager, Forli and Ambiorix, and giving them the right conditions for the full expression of their genetic assets that he stood above the large majority of his contemporary breeders. These foreign-bred stallions were ranged alongside many of the best American stallions – horses like Double Jay, Bold Ruler and Buckpasser – in the Claiborne barns. For this reason he deserves to be remembered as one of the most original and innovative breeders of the twentieth century. The emphasis on stallions is nowhere more clearly expressed than in the typically Hancock dictum: 'A good bull is half the herd. A bad bull is the whole herd.'

Bull Hancock never made the mistake of thinking that he could select the mares to be covered by Claiborne stallions, and veto those he did not like on grounds of pedigree or conformation. At Claiborne an approved mare was one that was healthy and fit to breed. 'I pick the people, not the mares, and I'm lucky to have such fine people,' he told William Robertson. The owners boarding mares at Claiborne tended to be knowledgeable as well as wealthy. What the studmaster can do to make the best of a stallion's opportunities is to ensure that the stallion is fit and healthy, and carefully managed so that his number of covers in a season is kept to the minimum. This side of the business was as efficiently controlled at Claiborne as on any stud farm in Kentucky.

The records of Claiborne stallions testify eloquently to their own quality and to the quality of their selection, promotion and management in the Bull Hancock era. From 1954 until his death eighteen years later Claiborne stallions headed the list of sires of winners sixteen times (Nasrullah five times, Bold Ruler seven times, Princequillo twice and Ambiorix and Round Table once each); Claiborne stallions filled the first two places in the list six times, and the first three places once.

Although 300 mares comprising boarders and the farm's own mares were at Claiborne and its satellite farms at the time of Bull's death, Claiborne gave the visitor the impression that it was primarily a stallion operation. Situated close to the little town of Paris in Bourbon County and bisected by a quietly flowing stream, Stoner Creek, the rolling acres of Claiborne seemed to be the domain of the great stallions. The headstones commemorating past champions stood in a small plot of grass near the farm office; stallion barns were within a stone's throw; and beyond the barns lay small paddocks traced out by rows of maples, pin oaks and sycamores in which the stallions spent most of their days at leisure. The first Arthur Hancock and Bull were believers in the virtue of an abundance of trees on stud farms, and gave free rein to their belief in their planting programmes at Claiborne. The stallions could see each other and commune with each other as they liked, and their proximity brought contentment and scope for the development of personality denied to stallions lacking the same freedoms. No stallion responded more fully to the Claiborne environment than the playful Buckpasser, who delighted in plucking twigs from the trees with his teeth and galloping away, flinging them over his shoulder as he went. Buckpasser had been a brilliant performer, winning in the best company over distances ranging from 5½ furlongs to 2 miles; though even on the racetrack he was inclined to tease, running lackadaisically until his supporters were reduced to despair and then sprinting to the front irresistibly. At stud he shone as a sire of fillies and broodmares.

Bull had an absolutely sure touch in all practical matters of stallion selection and management, but his attitudes to some of the theoretical aspects of thoroughbred breeding were apt to be ambiguous, even contradictory. He expressed admiration for 'lines', like the Hampton male line, when the eponymous founder must have been at least five or six generations back and have a negligible influence on any contemporary racehorse; and there was only a remote genetic relationship between the various branches of the line springing from Hampton's grandsons Dark Ronald and Bayardo, and no more than a barely significant relationship between some of the subdivisions of those branches.

At the same time he had favourite female strains, or 'families', like the La Troienne, the Bourtai, the Alcibiades, the Brulette, the

Simon's Shoes – which he called the 'Slipper' family – and the Feola; the two last named being the sources of Rough Shod and Knight's Daughter respectively. Some of those mares were close enough in terms of generations to be significant in contemporary pedigrees, and others were not. As was proper for a student of genetics, he agreed that an individual ancestor made a negligible contribution to a horse's genetic make-up at more than three generations. The first Arthur Bull Hancock had believed that the family was more important than the individual, as he had had some unfortunate experiences with good racemares that had failed at stud. He mistrusted mares that had been hard-raced. Bull had a preference for the sisters and daughters of great racemares, but had no prejudice against great racemares themselves. He agreed with another highly respected Kentucky breeder, Hal Price Headley, that mares who had failed the racecourse test ought to be culled, but unraced mares may have high breeding value.

About artifical insemination, a subject which has vexed the breeding industry for a long time, Bull expressed directly contrary opinions at different times. In *A Treasury of Questions and Answers* he replied to a correspondent:

In my opinion the principal danger of the practice of artificial insemination would be that top stallions, such as Bold Ruler, would become too popular. That is, everyone would want to have his mare impregnated with the semen of Bold Ruler or a few other top stallions, and eventually, after a number of years, there would be a tremendous number of horses from the same family. Thus it would be extremely difficult to find an outcross for future breedings.

In other words, the practice of AI would be on course for a head-on collision with Bull's belief that outcrosses invigorate the thoroughbred. But he took the opposite view in a discussion at a Jockey Club Round Table at Saratoga on 10 August 1969, when he spoke about thoroughbred fertility:

If we get 75 per cent we think we've done pretty well. I think we could do better. I believe we could increase our percentage 10 per cent if we were allowed to artificially inseminate. I know it is dangerous and there is thought against it, but I believe if every farm or every stallion manager was required to send the Jockey Club a list of forty-five or fifty mares, whatever the Jockey Club wants us to limit it to, and then we were allowed to artificially inseminate those mares ourselves, we could do a better job, we could raise better horses in the end and probably step up the number of mares we have to a horse.

Although his advocacy of AI at the Round Table purported to be solely in the interests of stud farm efficiency, if accepted it would have had the result of improving stallion fertility and compounding the improvement by increasing the number of mares covered – thereby producing the very effects which he had formerly condemned. Artificial insemination was one subject on which Bull Hancock was unable to adopt a consistent stance.

Bull Hancock was at Saratoga as usual in 1972, buying yearlings for some of his clients, transacting stallion business, playing golf and enjoying the social life of the leafy spa where the American thoroughbred community congregates for the racing and the yearling sales during the month of August. From Saratoga he went to Scotland for a shooting holiday, but became ill and was flown back to the United States, where he was admitted to hospital in Nashville, Tennessee. An operation revealed cancer, and he died on 14 September.

'Bull' may have been a nickname attached to him in adolescence, but it fitted the man to perfection. Bull was the biggest man, physically speaking, in the thoroughbred industry of his day, and towered above most of his contemporaries in professional ability and the dominance of his personality. He was fiercely competitive in everything he did, in business and in his recreations of cardplaying, shooting and golf. In his youth he had been an ardent football and baseball player.

His achievements in the world of the thoroughbred were on a titanic scale. Apart from his prowess as a promoter of stallions, he was leading American breeder four times, once in nominal partnership with his ailing father and three times on his own. He built up the Claiborne estate by the purchase of new land and farms so that it extended to more than 5700 acres at the time of his death. It included a training centre at Xalapa Farm where the Claiborne yearlings were broken and prepared for racing. During one period the champion two-year-old colt or filly was broken at Xalapa five years in succession.

His abundant energy was not restricted to the pursuit of his own interests but was also harnessed to numerous enterprises designed for the benefit of the thoroughbred industry. He was a director of the Grayson Foundation, a charitable organization financing research into equine diseases at various institutions; and was one of the voting trustees of the Keeneland Association which leased the Keeneland racetrack to an operating company, held the most important yearling and breeding stock sales in the United States and devoted all its nett income to veterinary research. He was one of a group of Kentucky breeders who bought shares in Churchill Downs, the home of the Kentucky Derby, to prevent a takeover bid that would have threatened the future of racing at the track, and became a director of the company. He was simultaneously president of the American Thoroughbred Breeders' Association and the Thoroughbred Club of America, and superintended the amalgamation of those two bodies to form the Thoroughbred Owners' and Breeders' Association; an offshoot of the amalgamation was the American Horse Council, formed to represent the interests of horse owners and lobby Congressmen in Washington. His many unselfish activites brought him well-deserved honours. He was the first professional member of the racing and breeding industry to be elected a member of the Jockey Club; and in 1960 he was the Honoured Guest at the Thoroughbred Club Testimonial Dinner, as his father had been sixteen years earlier.

Essentially Bull Hancock was a direct, plain-spoken, down-to-earth man who scorned magic formulas and shortcuts to success in breeding. His preferred maxim was: 'We just try to do the usual, unusually well.' That scarcely did justice to his inspired practice of the international outcross which transformed the post-Second World War American thoroughbred and prepared the way for the primacy of American breeding on the world racing scene in the last quarter of the twentieth century.

9

Tim Rogers
1922–83

Charles Haughey, then Minister for Agriculture and Fisheries, observed in his address at the first meeting of the Survey Team of the Irish Horse Breeding Industry on 13 January 1965:

Traditionally, the horse has been a part of the Irish way of life. In many parts of the world, the name of Ireland is known only through the reputation of her horses, and the prestige of Ireland is closely linked with the quality of the horses we send out to all parts of the world.

He was referring not only to thoroughbreds but to breeds of horses in general. Indeed, traditionally Ireland was regarded as a source not so much of quality thoroughbreds as of steeplechasers and hunters. Professor Michael MacCormac stated in his *Economic Analysis of the Irish Racing and Bloodstock Industry*, published in 1978, that until the nineteenth century 'the system of horse breeding in Ireland to a large extent was haphazard. The nearest and cheapest stallions were patronized and breeding was not treated with the same degree of careful thought and method as in Britain, where the production of horses was beginning to be looked upon as an industry.'

There was a gradual change during the nineteenth century and some large studs were formed. However, it was not until the last quarter of the century that men like John Gubbins and Sir Henry Greer began to establish top-class stallions on Irish studs. Gubbins, who had Kendal on his stud in County Tipperary, bred the 1897 Triple Crown winner Galtee More; and Greer introduced Gallinule, who sired the 'peerless' Pretty Polly, winner of the 1000 Guineas, the Oaks and the St Leger in 1904.

The growth of the Irish thoroughbred industry, however, was checked by the adverse effects of the First World War, followed by the war of independence and the civil war. Although a few large breeders, like the Aga Khan, founded studs in Ireland during the 1920s, the temporary imposition of a 40 per cent duty by the British government on bloodstock imports from Ireland was another sharp setback. The value of Irish thoroughbred exports fell by half between 1930 and 1932, and Blandford, the greatest Classic stallion of the period between the two world wars, was transferred from Ireland to England. Although there was a slow recovery in the late 1930s, this was damped down by the depressed conditions of the Second World War. Irish thoroughbred production lagged behind British in quantity, but more significantly in quality. In 1946 there were sixty stallions with top-class racing form at stud in Britain, but only twenty-three in Ireland, a ratio of 2.6 to 1 in favour of Britain. The Irish stallions included only one winner of a Classic race outside Ireland, and that was the wartime St Leger winner Turkhan. But the next quarter of a century saw a mighty transformation. In 1983 the number of stallions with top-class racing form in Britain had increased to 106, but the number in Ireland had increased at a much faster rate and multiplied nearly fourfold to eighty-three, leaving a ratio of only 1.3 to 1 in favour of Britain. The Irish stallions included the Derby winners Golden Fleece and Henbit – they would have included Shergar also but for the abduction of the 1981 Derby winner – the St Leger winner Cut Above, the 2000 Guineas winner Tap On Wood and the French 2000 Guineas winner Nishapour.

Good stallions attract good mares, and the conjunction of good stallions and good mares brings the production of quality offspring. The standard of Irish thoroughbreds improved so dramatically that in 1981, twenty-two of the forty-nine Group 1 Pattern races (the championship races) run in the three principal European racing countries Britain, France and Ireland were won by Irish-bred horses; and as eleven of the remaining Group 1 races were won by American-bred horses, it follows that Irish production of top-class racehorses had outstripped, at least as far as that year's racing results were concerned, British and French production combined. Ireland had leapt right into the front rank of world producers of quality horses.

It was not the luck of the Irish that had brought about a transformation for which there is no parallel in thoroughbred history. The emergence of Ireland as a world power in terms of the thoroughbred was due in no small measure to the initiative and example of one man: Captain A. D. D. (Tim) Rogers of the Airlie Stud in County Dublin.

Tim Rogers was born on 28 November 1922 into a distinguished Anglo-Irish racing family. His grandfather J. T. (Jack) Rogers was born an Englishman, and was a leading amateur rider on the flat and over fences about the turn of the century. He began training at the Curragh in Ireland during the First World War, when he was in his fifties. His skill and dedication took him to the top of his profession, and he was the leading trainer in Ireland three years running in the 1930s. His most successful season was in 1935 when he achieved the unique feat of winning all the Irish Classic races – The Triple Crown with Museum, who also travelled to York to win the Ebor Handicap, and the 1000 Guineas and Oaks with Smokeless.

William Barnett, the head of a Belfast firm of grain shippers and importers, was one of his principal owners. J. T. Rogers trained Trigo to win the Phoenix Plate, then the most important two-year-old race in Ireland, at Phoenix Park and the Railway Stakes at the Curragh for Barnett in 1928, but the colt was transferred to Dick Dawson at Whatcombe for the three-year-old campaign which brought victories in the Derby and the St Leger. Rogers won the Irish 1000 Guineas for Barnett in 1936 with Harvest Star. In this way a link was forged between the Barnetts and the Rogers which was to prove decisively beneficial at a critical point in Tim's career. Tim was intensely proud of his grandfather's achievements, and it was to commemorate him that he and his brother Micky initiated sponsorship of the Group 2 Rogers' Gold Cup Ballymoss Stakes at the Curragh in April 1983.

Tim's father, Darby Rogers, was training at Chitterne on Salisbury Plain and Wimborne St Giles in Dorset during Tim's boyhood, but was struggling to make a living for much of the time with only about a dozen horses in his yard. Tim attended Sherborne Preparatory School and then moved on to Sherborne Public School. However, after only half a term in the senior school he broke an ankle badly when one of his father's horses reared up and fell over backwards with him at exercise. He had a long spell in hospital at Bournemouth while his ankle slowly mended. When he was discharged he did not return to Sherborne but went instead to Ireland, where his father had taken over from J. T. Rogers at Crotanstown Lodge on the Curragh. Tim's school days were over, but his lack of academic qualifications had no adverse effect on his career.

Tim joined up in the anti-aircraft artillery as soon as he could in the Second World War. He was posted to Northern Ireland, where he found himself in the same unit as Charlie Smirke, the supremely talented jockey who had already won the Derby on Windsor Lad and Mahmoud and was to win two postwar Derbys on Tulyar and Hard Ridden, the last-named trained by Micky Rogers. Smirke used to get weekend leave to ride over hurdles in the south during the winter of 1940–41, and Tim would travel down with him to go racing and ride out on his father's horses at Crotanstown. Later he transferred to the Armoured Corps, passed through the officers' training unit at Sandhurst and received a temporary commission in the 4th Hussars, the regiment in which Winston Churchill had served as a junior officer and of which he had afterwards been colonel. He joined the regiment, then re-forming in the Egyptian desert after suffering disastrous losses in the Greek campaign, in the summer of 1942.

The fortunes of the imperial forces in the Middle East were at their nadir at that time. Owing to bad generalship, the 8th Army had been defeated by the German and Italian forces west and south of Tobruk during June, and had been chased all the way back to El Alamein, 70 miles west of Alexandria, where the line was stabilized in a series of inconclusive slogging matches in July. It was obvious that the higher command in that theatre of the war was in urgent need of reorganization, and Winston Churchill stopped in Cairo on his way to a conference in Moscow in order to attend to the problem. As a result Auchinleck was relieved of his Middle East and 8th Army commands and was replaced by the team of Alexander and Montgomery which was to achieve decisive victory at El Alamein three months later.

Churchill needed an aide during his week's stay in the desert and Cairo, and it was only natural that the 4th Hussars, who were not in action at the time, should be called on to supply one. The regiment's commanding officer, Bobby Kidd, detailed his most newly joined subaltern, Tim Rogers, for the task and, remarkably in view of the fact that he came from the Irish Republic, the nomination was accepted without any kind of security check. Just as surprisingly, an instant and instinctive rapport sprang up between the two men, easily spanning the seemingly unbridgeable gap between their lives and circumstances – on the one hand, the raw young cavalry officer, not yet twenty years old, with hardly more than an elementary education and little knowledge of any subject outside the Turf; on the other, the sixty-eight-year-old Prime Minister and Minister of Defence, with the responsibility for the conduct of a critical phase of a world war lying heavy on his shoulders, the master of the English language in both its spoken and its written forms. Yet Tim had qualities that fitted him peculiarly for his position; he had a depth and maturity of character unusual in a man of his age; and he had a self-assurance and an independence of spirit which, with his charm and ability to move easily between moods of gravity and humour as the situation demanded, must have endeared him to the Prime Minister. When Churchill, having satisfied himself that the direction of the war in the Middle East was in the right hands, flew out of Cairo he had been so favourably impressed by Tim Rogers that he insisted on having him back as his aide on all his subsequent visits to the army in Africa and Italy.

After the North African campaign had ended with the surrender of the German and Italian armies, Tim was sent on a course at the Armoured Corps' school at Constantine in Algeria. He was attached to the 12th Lancers, an armoured-car reconnaissance regiment, for the Sicily landing, then rejoined his own regiment, mounted in tanks, at Bari in the heel of Italy and fought through the Italian campaign to the end of the war in Europe, being decorated with the Military Cross. Churchill was ousted from the premiership as a result of the Labour Party's landslide victory in the General Election of July 1945, but that did not mean an immediate end to Tim's periodic duties as his aide. Churchill flew out to Italy in the following September for a holiday at his trusted friend Field Marshal Lord Alexander's Villa Rosa on Lake Como. By then Alexander was a man of great eminence in his own right, as he had been appointed Supreme Allied Commander Mediterranean Forces the previous December. The weather and the scenery were idyllic, and the two great men were able to indulge themselves to the full in the leisure activity for which they had a shared predilection, landscape painting in oils. From the privileged position of watching both men at work simultaneously, often painting the same subject, Tim formed the opinion that Alexander was the better artist.

A plane was sent to pick up Churchill at Milan at the end of the holiday. But Churchill, in the spirit of an errant and mischievous schoolboy, made a bolt for it in the direction of the Italian Riviera, taking Tim with him, and went to ground in the Town Major's office at Genoa. There he was overtaken by dispatches from London, inluding a request from Clement Attlee, the Labour Prime Minister, for advice concerning proposals for international control of the atomic bomb and the sharing of atomic secrets. While Churchill stayed in bed to write his reply, he sent Tim ahead in Alexander's yellow armour-plated Mercedes to try and make reservations in the Hôtel de Paris at Monte Carlo, then just reopening after the war. Having succeeded in this mission, Tim returned with the good news to Genoa, where he was promptly sent out again to get Churchill's reply to Attlee typed in readiness for transmission to London. Churchill politely but firmly crushed Attlee's proposal for an 'Act of Faith' in sharing atomic secrets internationally. He wrote:

This will in the existing circumstances raise immediate suspicions in American breasts. Moreover we have a special relationship with them in this matter as defined in my agreement with President Roosevelt. This almost amounts to a military understanding. I should greatly regret it if we seemed not to value this and pressed them to melt our duel agreement down into a general international arrangement consisting I fear of pious empty phrases.

So Churchill spelt out from the Town Major's house in Genoa the concept of a special and exclusive relationship which was to become an ingrained feature of British and American foreign policy.

They moved to Monte Carlo the next day and settled down to a pleasant and leisurely routine in the Hôtel de Paris. Churchill would work at his correspondence in bed until 11.30, when he would get up, have an early lunch, and spend the rest of the day painting. He and Tim would have dinner together, and Churchill would retire to bed early, leaving Tim with the not insoluble problem of amusing himself in Monte Carlo for the rest of the evening. Early in their stay Tim received an urgent message from Clementine Churchill enjoining him at all costs to prevent Churchill gambling in the casino. The subject was not raised until four days before their departure, when Churchill remarked that it would be fun to have a flutter. Tim told him that he had instructions from Clemmie to scotch any such idea. 'Then you shall go and gamble for me,' was Churchill's rejoinder.

Tim played with great circumspection the whole evening and ended up £250 to the good. He returned to the hotel and reported to Churchill, who told him scornfully, 'That's not the way to gamble; I shall have to go down myself tomorrow and show you how to do it.' Churchill had taken the bit between his teeth, and Tim knew that further remonstrance would be useless. The next night Churchill won £3000, but the night after that he lost it all; and on the final night he lost £7000. On the morning they were to leave, Churchill wrote a cheque for £7000 and instructed Tim to hand it to the casino manager with a request that it should not be presented until Churchill sent word, because foreign exchange controls made immediate payment awkward. Tim delivered the cheque and the message. Flourishing the cheque above his head, the manager answered in theatrical tones, 'Pray tell Mr Churchill that this cheque will never be presented.'

Tim hurried back to the hotel and, as he came into the room, Churchill asked anxiously, 'Well, what did he say?' 'He said that the cheque will never be presented.' 'That's much more agreeable,' said Churchill. 'We'll have a bottle of champagne.'

So, over glasses of champagne, the last link in the friendship between these two strangely assorted men was forged – a friendship which, like the family friendship with the Barnetts, was to give a powerful impetus to Tim's career as a breeder years later.

Churchill flew home to England later the same day, and Tim made his way back to his regiment stationed in the north of Italy. Those were halcyon days for the British occupying forces in North Italy and Austria. In contrast to Britain, where rationing became more stringent in the early years of peace, petrol, rations and wine were all abundant. There were also plenty of horses. There were some thoroughbreds, a few bought out of Milan training stables; there were larger numbers of half-breds, mostly hunter types, that had seen service with the 1st British Cavalry Division in Palestine; and there were more still that had been captured from the Germans and covered a wide range of breeds from Hanoverians to near-thoroughbreds. The chief enemy was no longer the Germany army but boredom, and one of the recreations which received official encouragement was horse racing, making use of those of the available horses that had some pretensions to speed. During 1945 and 1946 there were regular meetings, staging mixed programmes of flat races and steeplechases, at Treviso, near Venice, and Aiello, near Udine, in northern Italy, and at Klagenfurt, Graz and Vienna in Austria. The Stewards of the Jockey Club exempted these meetings from the normal penalties applied to unlicensed meetings and the people who took part in them; and James Weatherby, a member of the firm of Turf administrators then serving with the 10th Hussars, produced a regular publication giving local racing results and news in the familiar official *Racing Calendar* format. Numerous army units formed their own amateur racing stables, and the spirit of rivalry between them was extremely keen.

Giving a foretaste of that shrewdness that was to characterize his later dealings in horses, Tim acquired one of the best thoroughbreds, and made sure that he always rode it himself. It was a bold, strong bay horse that he appropriately called Colonel Warden, the codename for Churchill in wartime communications. The Ascot of the military meetings was Vienna where the course used was the Freudenau, the normal headquarters of Austrian thoroughbred racing, as compared with the improvised racetracks used for the other military meetings. The betting market at Vienna was much stronger than it was on the other courses; and it was at the Freudenau in July 1946 that Tim brought off a well-prepared betting coup with Colonel Warden which netted him the equivalent of £2000. The trouble was that the payout was in occupation Austrian schillings, worthless outside the country and subject to strict exchange controls. However, thanks to the good offices of a complaisant member of the allied military government, Tim was able to change his winnings into lire and buy a small villa on the Italian lakes. The whole operation gave clear evidence of an exceptional ability to develop an ingenious plan, keep his own counsel and conceal his thoughts and intentions from even his closest associates when secretiveness would serve his own ends best.

Demobilized from the army and back in Ireland, Tim found no immediate outlet for his talents. His father and his brother Micky were already training at the Curragh, and there was no scope for a third member of the family in their profession. For lack of a better opportunity he took the job of manager of his father's Airlie Stud at a salary of £5 a week. Two second-class stallions, Greek Star (fee £48) and Heron Bridge (fee £36), were stationed there, but otherwise the main purpose of the stud was to look after lame or sick horses from his father's stable. An atmosphere of pleasure-seeking procrastination prevailed in Irish society in the postwar years and Tim attuned himself to it easily. During this period he was untroubled by ambition, content to drift in an undemanding job and go to as many parties as possible.

This period lasted for Tim until the late 1950s, when his attitudes and his way of life suffered a change of Pauline suddenness. The catalyst of his conversion was the victory of Hard Ridden in the 1958 Derby. Years later he explained, 'I had been very close to Micky since I came home from the war. When he won the Derby with Hard Ridden my eyes were opened for the first time to the fact that he had got to the top of his profession, and that I was getting nowhere in mine. From that moment I became determined that I too would excel.'

The first condition for the advancement of his career was control of the breeding operations at Airlie and the independence of action and policy which that would confer. He managed to borrow £7000 and, with William Barnett (nephew of the owner of Trigo and then head of the firm) coming in as partner and supplying the rest of the capital, bought Airlie for £28,000. Later, as his financial position improved, he was able to buy his partner out, and Barnett moved his bloodstock to the Adstock Manor Stud in Buckinghamshire. More immediately, he syndicated his first stallion at the end of 1958 and installed him at Airlie for the next covering season. This was Ommeyad, who on pedigree and performance was a big improvement on the stallions who had stood there previously. Ommeyad was a beautifully bred horse by Hyperion out of Minaret, a member of the talented Lady Juror family. He had won races in France at Deauville and Le Tremblay besides the Irish St Leger, and gave one of his best performances when third to Ballymoss and Fric in the

Coronation Cup at Epsom. The upgrading of the Airlie operation had begun.

Tim's business sense and eye for a thoroughbred bargain had not been wholly dormant during the lotus-eating years. In 1951 the three-year-old filly Discipliner was submitted from Darby Rogers's stable at the Ballsbridge September sales. She was well bred, as she was by the 2000 Guineas winner and top-class stallion Court Martial out of Edvina by the sprinter Figaro. But her racing record was dismal. Her only public appearances had been in two races at Phoenix Park as a two-year-old; on the first occaison she finished fifth of six runners, and on the second she was left and took no part. Her behaviour at the start of both races was appalling, and she actually lay down at the start of her second race. Clearly she was incorrigible as far as racing was concerned. But Tim knew something of which other possible buyers were ignorant: that she was brilliant at home and could make rings round any other horse in the stable. He stepped in and bought her for 1000 guineas.

Discipliner bred eight winners at Airlie. Her first two winning offspring were nothing out of the ordinary. Her third, Martial, won the 2000 Guineas, and her next two offspring Skymaster and El Gallo were high-class sprinters. All three were sold as yearlings at the Newmarket October sales. Their sales were hardly profitable. Martial realized only 2400 guineas, and although Skymaster and El Gallo realized larger sums, Skymaster was sold before Martial had advertised their dam by his Classic victory, and the aggregate price for all three was no more than 14,100 guineas. It is a triusm that what matters for the breeder is not so much the price that a high-class product of his stud may fetch as a foal or yearling, but the effect the product's racing achievements may have in increasing the value of his close relations. The cumulative impact of the racing class shown by Martial, Skymaster and El Gallo on the reputation of Discipliner as broodmare caused the prices realized by her later offspring to soar. Her sons St George and High Marshal, sold in 1962 and 1964 respectively, realized 16,500 guineas each; and in order to set those prices in the perspective of the subsequent runaway inflation of bloodstock values it is necessary to add that the average prices of yearlings at the Newmarket October sales in those two years were 1665 guineas and 2046 guineas. The prices realized by St George and High Marshal were largely instrumental in raising Airlie

Stud to second place in the list of October sales vendors by aggregate and top by average in 1962, and third by both aggregate and average in 1962. Ironically, although both St George and High Marshal showed winning form, neither was in the same class as Martial, Skymaster and El Gallo. The stud career of Discipliner established Airlie as a leading supplier of yearlings to the commercial market, and her prime years coincided with the period when the stud was being upgraded as an important stallion station.

The Rogers family connection with the Barnetts had been an essential factor in giving Tim his start as an independent breeder. His friendship with Winston Churchill played an equally vital part in the evolution of Airlie. Appropriately, in view of their mutual contacts with the Rogers, the Barnett and Churchill interests were briefly united when Sir Winston leased Dark Issue from William Barnett and the filly, trained by Darby Rogers, won the Irish 1000 Guineas in 1955. Sir Winston's participation in racing had begun some years earlier when, at the age of seventy-five, he registered his colours for the first time and bought the grey colt Colonist II as a maiden three-year-old in France. Colonist won thirteen races, and as a high-class stayer showed much of his owner's durability and indomitable spirit. Colonist fired Sir Winston's enthusiasm for racing, and his interest was strongly encouraged by his son-in-law Christopher (later Lord) Soames, who had married his youngest daughter Mary. Sir Winston bought the Newchapel Stud in Surrey during the 1950s and there bred the two good sprinters Welsh Abbot and Tudor Monarch and the high-class middle-distance performers High Hat and Vienna.

High Hat, foaled in 1957, was the last good horse sired by Hyperion. High Hat won the Oxfordshire Stakes at Newbury as a three-year-old and three more races including the Winston Churchill Stakes at Hurst Park the next year. His racing career had its climax when he beat the superbly gifted mare Petite Etoile in the Aly Khan International Memorial Gold Cup over 1½ miles at Kempton.

Vienna was the same age as High Hat, but was by Hyperion's son Aureole. He showed form of Classic standard by finishing third to St Paddy in the St Leger and won two Pattern races, the Group 3 Blue Riband Trial Stakes over 8½ furlongs at Epsom and the Group 2 Prix d'Harcourt over 10½ furlongs at Longchamp. Tim's friendship with Sir Winston was the lever he needed to obtain both horses as stallions for Airlie.

Tim began to negotiate for the purchase of High Hat in the early summer of 1961, when the horse was four. In July terms were agreed by which he should pay a deposit of £8000, with a further payment of £72,000 at the end of the season if the horse passed a veterinary examination as fit for breeding. The deal was duly completed and High Hat was successfully syndicated. High Hat possessed abundant stamina and had won over distances up to 2 miles. Tim was convinced that he needed fast mares, and in order to give him the best chance at the outset of his stud career he selected the eleven-year-old Dryad from the Newmarket December sales catalogue and bought her for 4000 guineas. Dryad was by the great sprinter and sire of sprinters Panorama and was the dam of Victorina, who had won five races as a two-year-old that year. He would surely have had to pay more for Dryad a year later after Victorina had won the Goodwood Stewards' Cup, one of the most hotly contested sprints of the season. Dryad fulfilled her purpose to perfection. Mated with High Hat in his first stud season, she produced the filly Glad Rags, who proved a wonderful advertisement for her sire by winning the 1000 Guineas.

The Churchill connection also brought Vienna to Airlie, though he raced until he was five and therefore arrived there a year later. His presence at Airlie did not have the same happy outcome. By the time his second crop were two-year-olds Tim had doubts about him and was inclined to give an affirmative response to French inquiries to lease him. In August he rang round every trainer who had a Vienna two-year-old and failed to elicit a good word about any of them. Walter Wharton, who trained Vaguely Noble, said that he would win a maiden race but that he did not amount to much. Accordingly Tim agreed to lease Vienna to France for three years, and granted the lessees the right to purchase at a fixed price at the end of the lease. Within a month Vaguely Noble won the Sandwich Stakes at Ascot by 12 lengths, and went on to win the Observer Gold Cup (now the Group 1 William Hill Futurity) by 7 lengths, proving himself the outstanding two-year-old in Europe.

Owing to the death of his owner – breeder Major Lionel Holliday, Vaguely Noble was submitted at the Newmarket December sales the same year. In an attempt to repair the damage of a seemingly disastrous lease, Tim tried to buy him, but he and Vincent O'Brien reached their limit and dropped out of the bidding at 125,000 guineas. Finally Vaguely Noble was knocked down for the world record price for a horse in training of 136,000 guineas. He proved to be worth many times that sum when he won the Prix de l'Arc de Triomphe the following October and then went to the United States and became one of the world's best Classic stallions. However, the lease of Vienna turned out to be not so disastrous after all; Vaguely Noble was unique among his progeny; he never sired another high-class horse and sank progressively lower in the esteem of breeders.

Vienna was quickly banished. High Hat was at Airlie for ten covering seasons and was then exported to Japan, so neither of the Churchill stallions completed his stud career at Airlie. On the other hand, each made a significant contribution to the renown of Airlie as an international stallion station, and helped to lay the foundation for the rapid expansion of the late 1960s and the 1970s.

Habitat and Petingo are the two most successful stallions to have stood at the Airlie group of studs. It is necessary to refer to a group of studs, because the growth of the stallion population soon necessitated the addition of other properties. Indeed, Airlie housed neither Habitat nor Petingo. Habitat stood at Grangewilliam and Petingo stood at Simmonstown, all three studs being located within a few miles of each other near the borders of County Dublin and County Kildare. Although other studs were included in the group for special purposes, Airlie – Grangewilliam – Simmonstown formed the heart of the stallion operation, while the majority of the 100 mares owned wholly or in partnership by Tim Rogers resided at Airlie.

Petingo, foaled in 1965, was the older of the pair by one year. A big, deep-bodied, lengthy dark bay colt, he was a cheap buy at 7600 guineas as a yearling. His trainer, the late Sam Armstrong, bought him for the Greek ship owner Captain Marcos Lemos and was delighted with his acquisition. 'Like Sayajirao and other top-class horses I trained, Petingo stood out from the moment he started to canter, and seemed to know instinctively what to do. He was a sweet horse and never put a foot wrong. By Christmas I was able to tell Captain Lemos that he would win the Gimcrack Stakes,'

Armstrong once recalled. That prediction proved to be accurate. Petingo went on to win the Middle Park Stakes two months later, and as a three-year-old developed into an excellent miler, winning the St James's Palace Stakes at Royal Ascot and the Sussex Stakes at Goodwood, and finishing second to Sir Ivor in the 2000 Guineas.

Petingo had changed hands by the time he ran in the Sussex Stakes, the most important mile race in England for three-year-olds and older horses. Tim had been negotiating to buy him for some time. Finally a price of £200,000 was agreed, on the condition that the money was deposited at Captain Lemos's bank by noon on 31 July, three hours before the race was due to be run. There was a flurry of last-minute activity, and the money arrived just in time thanks to the cooperation of the Bank of Ireland. Tim afterwards syndicated him at £5000 a share.

Petingo was an immediate success as a stallion. His first crop included Satingo, who won the Grand Criterium and was third in the French 2000 Guineas; his second crop included the Irish Sweeps Derby winner English Prince and Pitcairn, the latter bred by Tim Rogers himself, who won three Pattern races and was second in the Irish 2000 Guineas. Later crops included the Oaks and Irish Guinness Oaks winner Fair Salinia and the Derby and Irish Sweeps Derby winner Troy. But by the time Fair Salinia and Troy gained their Classic victories Petingo was dead. At the age of only eleven he had a heart attack in the act of covering a mare, and was dead by the time he hit the ground. His premature death was a grievous loss not only to Tim Rogers but to thoroughbred breeding as a whole, as he gave every sign of being not only an outstanding sire of winners but also an exceptional sire of sires.

Habitat was slower than Petingo to make his mark on the race-course. Trained by Fulke Johnson Houghton, he bruised a foot so badly when he trod on a stone on the Berkshire Downs in mid-summer that he could not run at all as a two-year-old, and was beaten in his first two races as a three-year-old. From then on he began to assert himself, and victories in the Lockinge Stakes at Newbury, the Prix Quincey at Deauville and the Wills Mile at Goodwood stamped him as a miler of great merit. Whether he could fairly be called the champion miler of Europe hinged on his performance in the Prix du Moulin, run at Longchamp on the first Sunday of October, the day of the Prix de l'Arc de Triomphe. Tim had his eye on him as a potential stallion from the day he won the Lockinge Stakes, but made no formal offer until he met David McCall, the racing manager for Habitat's owner Charles Engelhard, the American precious-metals magnate, in the Celtic Hotel in Paris on the eve of the Prix du Moulin. Tim then made a firm offer to buy Habitat for $1 million on condition that the horse won the next day. Neither man had any writing paper to hand, so McCall tore open an empty cigarette packet and Tim jotted down the details of the offer on the inside. In the morning McCall went round to see Engelhard and told him about the offer.

'What sort of contract have you got?' asked the American. 'Well, I don't know about a contract, but I've got some figures which Tim wrote down on this cigarette packet,' answered McCall. Engelhard inspected the 'document' and commented dubiously, 'I don't know what my lawyers are going to make of this.'

However, he admitted later that this was one of the quickest and easiest deals he ever made. Habitat set the seal on the transaction by winning the Prix du Moulin decisively that afternoon, and the financial details of the transaction were completed without a hitch.

The purchase price was the equivalent of about £400,000 at the current rate of exchange, and Tim immediately stated his intention of syndicating him in forty shares of £10,000 each. He flew to London the next day with William Hill, the bookmaker who had become one of the leading breeders in England. 'I can't see anyone paying that sort of money,' said Hill when Tim told him about the syndication. Nevertheless, Hill changed his mind a few days later and bought five shares for his Whitsbury Manor Stud, and the syndication was completed successfully. Owing to the currency exchange Tim lost £23 on the syndication.

None of the original shareholders in Habitat ever regretted their investment. From the time that his first runners took him to the top not only of the list of first-season sires but of the list of all sires of two-year-olds, it was clear that he was to become a great stallion, and the value of his shares and nominations escalated until, twelve years after he had gone to stud, nominations were changing hands for a split fee of £30,000 and £30,000 the first being a down payment and the second payable if the mare got in foal. He became the world's leading sire of specialist speedy performers as crop after crop included several individuals of true class and his progeny won

Pattern races by the dozen. He sired numerous fillies of undoubted brilliance like Sigy, Marwell, Habibti and Flying Water, of whom the last-named stayed well enough to win the 1000 Guineas and the Champion Stakes. Others of his daughters, like Roussalka and Rose Bowl, won over 1¼ miles in the best company, but that distance generally represented the limit of the stamina of all his progeny. He also sired many top-class colts like Habat, Habitony, Steel Heart, Hot Spark, Hittite Glory and Double Form. A big, powerfully built bay with black points, he was also a thinskinned horse and hated cold weather. He was a poor coverer in the early part of the season and seldom got many mares in foal in the months of February and March. He was exceptionally fertile when the weather warmed up, and achieved a fertility as high as 97.82 per cent in one season.

Many tempting offers to buy Habitat were received from the United States, but Tim resisted them all. He was adamant that Habitat should spend all his stud life at Grangewilliam, and declared that he would never have let Petingo go. Otherwise he was content to bow to market forces in respect of his stallions, assessing every offer in the light of his own valuation of the horse concerned. One of the most powerful factors in his success in promoting stallions was his uncannily accurate judgement of what the market would stand. If the asking price for a prospective stallion was above the price at which, in his estimation, it could be readily syndicated or financed as a partnership, he was not a buyer whatever its other attractions might be.

His principle with the Airlie – Grangewilliam – Simmonstown stallions was to take stock of them when they had their second crop of two-year-old runners, as he did in the case of Vienna. If his own assessment of a particular stallion's progeny at that stage, backed by a canvass of trainers' opinions, was unfavourable then the stallion was on the market. Although this principle involved the risk of premature disposal of a stallion of genuine merit who might be a slow starter at stud, it avoided the graver risk of being cumbered with failed stallions of rapidly declining value.

In later years Tim became owner or part owner of an increasing number of top-class horses in training. These were mostly horses who could, if their form justified it and circumstances were favourable, retire to one of his studs as stallions. These horses included Ela-Mana-Mou, Northern Baby, Le Marmot and Nadjar, and Malacate, who was installed at Airlie after winning the Irish Sweeps Derby in 1976, but was sent back into training after showing poor fertility in his first stud season and won the Group 3 Prix Foy at Longchamp.

Tim was part owner of Ela-Mana-Mou during the four-year-old campaign of 1980 which brought Group 1 victories in the Coral Eclipse Stakes and the King George VI and Queen Elizabeth Diamond Stakes, and third place in the Prix de l'Arc de Triomphe. Ela-Mana-Mou was a particularly favoured new arrival at Simmonstown at the end of that year because he was a son of Pitcairn, who was bred at Airlie, and a grandson of Petingo. Ela-Mana-Mou was heir to the place of honour in Petingo's old box.

In 1970 each of Tim's three main studs held two top-class stallions. Astec, winner of the French Derby, and High Hat were at Airlie; Habitat and Sea Hawk II, winner of the Group 1 Grand Prix de Saint Cloud, were at Grangewilliam; and Petingo and the French 2000 Guineas winner Don II were at Simmonstown. As Tim remarked, 'Ireland has always been recognized as a great country for breeding good sprinters like Panorama. What I believe I had helped to do was to raise its international status as a country with the stallion resources also to produce top-class middle-distance horses.'

Tim had shown the way and created a worldwide climate of opinion favourable to the expansion of quality breeding in Ireland. Before long others began to follow his example. In 1970 the Coolmore Stud in County Tipperary had two stallions, Gala Performance and King Emperor, American horses with less than inspiring credentials. By 1983 the Airlie repertoire of stallions had increased to eleven. They were headed by Habitat, the Derby winner Henbit, the St Leger winner Cut Above, Ela-Mana-Mou and the Sussex and Eclipse Stakes winner Artaius. But the growth rate at Coolmore, where even greater financial resources became progressively available, was much faster. By 1983 the Coolmore Stud had become the Coolmore – Castle Hyde group of seven studs containing sixteen high-class stallions also headed by a Derby winner, Golden Fleece. Tim's example had proved as effective as his actions in raising the standards of Irish thoroughbred breeding.

Tim's acumen in seizing on and exploiting a fiscal advantage enjoyed by Irish breeders had provided the motive power for his rapid progress in high-class stallion promotion in the 1960s. This advantage had been incorporated in the Finance Act of 1939, under which earnings from stallions standing on a farm were regarded as included in the Schedule B assessment on the land, thus effectively exempting profits derived from stallion fees and other trading in thoroughbreds from income tax. It enabled him to build up the sums necessary for expansion.

The Survey Team of 1965 recommended that sales of stallion nominations and shares should be exempt from tax. This recommendation was incorporated in the Finance Act of 1969 to the exclusion of the former concession, and provided a strong incentive to investment in high-class stallions which fuelled the more broadly based growth of the following decade.

Tim's policy, while making use of these tax advantages to expand his own business, had been to plough back all the profits into horses and stud land and eschew investment in stocks and shares. Consequently, he was able to represent himself to the Irish government as a full-time professional putting money into the industry. It was as a stallion promoter that he was a pathfinder and pioneer. But his involvement with mares, as owner and part owner, also was enormous, and he was a regular supplier to the yearling markets at Newmarket and at Kill, the shop window of the Irish thoroughbred, where he invested heavily in the operating company Goff's Bloodstock Sales Ltd.

Many high-class horses were bred at the Airlie studs after the days of Martial and Glad Rags. They included Pitcairn, Lorenzaccio, the sensational conqueror of Nijinsky in the Champion Stakes, the Irish 2000 Guineas winner Northern Treasure, Mark Anthony, Sorbus and that admirable filly on the international scene, Sangue. Tim also made a notable contribution to National Hunt racing by breeding Midnight Court, winner of the Cheltenham Gold Cup in 1978.

More than 400 new boxes, including a block with a covered interior exercise yard for mares and foals at Grangewilliam, were built on the Airlie studs. Grangewilliam was also the site of a modern laboratory equipped to look after the veterinary needs of the whole group. The laboratory was able to handle the culturing of CEM (Contagious Equine Metritis, a venereal disease first identified in 1977) swabs, had sophisticated microscopes for identifying bacterial infections and the world's first blood gas analysis machine adapted for equine use. Rigorous measures for disease control were seen as essential at an international stallion station.

Tim adopted the same policy of being seen to be a putter-in rather than a taker-out in his breeding operations in New Zealand. The country appealed to him as an ideal environment for the thoroughbred, and he was impressed by its consistent record of producing good racehorses from low investment in bloodstock. He was one of a very small number of foreigners who have been permitted to buy land in New Zealand, and his application in the late 1970s was granted at prime ministerial level in return for definite assurances of his intentions to be a nett investor in the breeding industry.

He renamed the 300-acre stud he purchased near Wanganui in the North Island Grangewilliam. There he assembled a dozen high-class mares, and installed the stallion Standaan. Standaan, an extremely fast winner of the Goodwood Stewards' Cup, was calculated to improve the speed of the New Zealand thoroughbred in line with the requirements of Australian racing, the principal market for New Zealand horses. He sent Pevero, who had been fourth in the Prix de l'Arc de Triomphe besides winning the Prix Foy, to the nearby Cranleigh International Stud; and the high-class sprinter Three Legs to the Okawa Stud in the Hawkes Bay region. His commitment to invest in New Zealand breeding and help to improve the New Zealand thoroughbred was manifestly being honoured.

Nearer home, he took a close interest in such important enterprises as the Irish National Stud and the Irish Equine Centre. He was a director of the Irish National Stud for a number of years, and in the late 1970s was called in, together with the eminent veterinary surgeon Maxie Cosgrove, by the then Minister of Finance Charles Haughey to report on the state of the stud. They commissioned a professional study, and their final report recommended sweeping changes in line with its recommendations. Consequently, another veterinary surgeon, the dynamic Michael Osborne, was appointed manager and initiated a general reorganization which made the National Stud a showpiece of Irish breeding while meeting its statutory obligation 'to locate high-class stallions at reduced prices' for the benefit of Irish breeders. During Osborne's term of office, which lasted throughout the decade, some of the most successful middle-range stallions in Ireland, including Sallust, Lord Gayle, African Sky and Tudor Music, were stationed at the stud.

Tim suffered from recurrent bouts of breathlessness during 1977, and was admitted to hospital in December for examination. Blood tests revealed that he had leukaemia, and the doctors informed him frankly that he probably had only a few months, and at most two years, to live.

There is no surer measure of the moral courage and the strength of character of the man than his instant decision, steadfastly upheld, not merely to preserve his breeding empire intact and retain control of it in his own hands, but to proceed with the consolidation of its status as a focal point in world breeding. For six years, until his death on New Year's Day, 1984, he continued in charge, constantly planning for the future. It is true that he had the benefit of the best specialist treatment and the newest techniques for the control of the disease in Ireland, France and England. It is true that he had the devoted and protective care of his beautiful and intelligent wife, the former Sonia Pilkington, whom he married in 1966. But it must also be true that his survival far beyond the limits of the original prognosis represented, to a large extent, a triumph of the will, of sheer force of personality in the patient.

Tim, in principle, took things more easily after his illness was diagnosed. At home he tended to lapse into lethargy, but away from home he often tapped new sources of energy within himself and began to develop fresh sets of ambitious plans. His travels around Europe were facilitated by his own two-engined plane. A typical expedition might comprise a Sunday flight to Paris to see one of his horses or a prospective stallion run; then to Germany to inspect a mare of attractive pedigree that might be for sale; to Newmarket for a day or two at the sales; and finally the flight home to Dublin. He made annual winter trips to visit his stud and the national yearling sales in New Zealand. His restless brain was always aware of the fluctuations of the bloodstock market, of the availability of valuable stallions and of significant moves within the international racing community.

In later years he tended to delegate more authority within the Airlie group of studs. He became conscious that this had involved some relaxation of his formerly tight control, and that some loss of efficiency was inevitable. At times he found himself forced onto the defensive, suspecting that rivals were trying to take advantage of his relative weakness. But he was never acquiescent. Under pressure he struck a defiant note: 'They'll find that the old tiger's still got some fangs left.'

For all that his formal education was cut short, Tim had a breadth of interest within and without the world of the thoroughbred which is untypical of professional breeders. Few of his kind have the sense of history or the feeling for the subtleties of the evolution of the breed that led him to build a library at the Irish Grangewilliam and fill it with probably the finest collection of international stud books in private hands. The place was a researcher's dream come true.

The mainsprings of his advancement in the intensely competitive stallion market may have been his acute business sense, his independence of judgement and the self-reliance of which he gave early warning in the coup with Colonel Warden in the far-off days at the Freudenau. But a complementary aspect of his character as a breeder was his instinctive affinity for animals. It is no coincidence that he was an extensive and discriminating collector of Meissen animals and birds. In direct contacts his closest fellowships were with dogs and horses. It was necessary only to see him at leisure with his miniature dogs or in communion with a favourite stallion like Ela-Mana-Mou to appreciate the depth of their mutual understanding.

His twin preferences among animals were reflected in his collection of pictures. Canine subjects by Marshall and Landseer vied for pride of place with equine subjects by Herring, Alken and Ferneley and the portraits of many famous horses with which he had been associated.

Tim Rogers was not a man to dwell on past reverses. Nevertheless, even he could not help recalling from time to time, a little wistfully, how he bid $6.4 million for Secretariat before his victories in the American Triple Crown races and lost him, and how he sold Lyphard to Alec Head privately for £15,000 after he had failed to reach his reserve at the Newmarket Houghton yearling sales, only to see him become champion sire in France twice and command a covering fee of $150,000 for the 1983 season at Gainesway Farm in

Kentucky. But who else, he could ask himself, has revolutionized his country's standing in the world of the thoroughbred or promoted a stallion as great as Habitat; or more completely fulfilled his ambition to excel?

Index

Horseraces are listed under their individual names,
e.g. Derby, Middle Park Stakes